Theory Test for Car Drivers, Guide to Passing the Driving Test, and Handbook

3 IN 1 COMBINED EDITION

D1610593

MALCOLM GREEN

WITHDRAWN

THE CHOIR PRESS

First published in the United Kingdom in 2019 by The Choir Press

ISBN 978-1-78963-045-9

DVSA Theory disclaimer

Crown Copyright material has been reproduced under licence from the Driver and Vehicle Standards Agency (DVSA) which does not accept any responsibility for the accuracy of the reproduction.

The author fully acknowledges the Crown Copyrighted Official Highway Code as being the source of road signs and symbols used in this publication. The recreation of all signs and symbols has been undertaken to the highest standard.

Highway Code

This representation of the Highway Code contains Public Sector Information. It has been reproduced in accordance with the terms and conditions of the "Open Government Licence". The information source being www.highwaycodeuk.co.uk /Date taken 10.06.2018. The referenced information is found on pages 237–253.

"Show me, Tell me" & using your own car for your test.

The representation of the above contains Public Sector Information. It has been reproduced in accordance with the terms and conditions of the "Open Government Licence". The information sources being www.gov.uk 'show me, tell me' questions: car driving test & www.gov.uk/drivingtest/using-your-own-car/Date taken 10.06.2018. This referenced information is found on pages 188–191/183–187.

Contents

Preface

Written under full 2018 compliant DVSA licence

This book contains the entire 15 theory test revision question and answer sections as well as in-depth comprehensive advice and guidance for passing the practical driving test. For on going support, there is also an invaluable additional extra 14 chapter 'How to' follow on handbook.

It is written in collaboration with both an experienced driving instructor and examiner. The combination of their knowledge with added user friendly guides provides everything necessary for success in advancing from L plates to a pass certificate, ultimately progressing with a confident freedom, to the open road.

Introduction

Theory and Hazard Awareness Tests

Arriving at the Test Centre

You must make sure that when you arrive at the test centre you have all the relevant documents with you. If you don't have them, your test will be terminated and you'll lose your fee.

* You'll need your signed photo card licence, or your signed old-style paper driving licence

* Valid passport (your passport doesn't have to be British)

* All documents must be original. Photocopies will not be accepted!

Multiple Choice Questions

- The theory test is one test made up from two parts. The first is the multiple choice part consisting of fifty questions. You select your answers for this part of the test by using a mouse on a computer.

- Before you start, you'll be given the chance to work through a practice session for up to 15 minutes to get used to the system. Staff at the test centre will be available to help you if you have any difficulties.

- The questions will cover a variety of topics relating to road safety, the environment and documents. Only one question will appear on the screen at a time, and you'll be asked to mark one correct answer.

- Take your time and read the questions carefully. You're given 57 minutes for this part of the test, so relax and don't rush. Some questions will take longer to answer than others, but there are no trick questions. The time remaining is displayed on screen.

- You may be allowed extra time to complete the test if you have special educational needs (e.g. dyslexia) and you let the test centre know when booking.

- You'll be able to move backwards and forwards through the questions and you can also 'flag' questions that you'd like to revisit again. It's easy and you're allowed to change your answers until the end of the time limit if you wish.

- Try to answer all the questions. If you're well prepared, you shouldn't find them difficult.

- Before you finish this part of the test, if you still have time, you can use the 'review' feature to check your answers. If you want to finish your test before the full time then click the 'review' button and finally the 'end' button on the review screen.

Hazard Perception

- The second part of the test consists of a series of computer-generated video clips, shown from a driver's point of view. You'll be using a mouse for this part of the theory test which is designed to judge your skill at hazard perception.

- Before you start this part of the test you'll be shown a short CGI video that explains how the test works and gives you a chance to see a sample clip. This will help you to understand what you need to do. You can play this video clip again if you wish.

- During the test, you'll be shown 14 CGI video clips. Each clip contains one or more developing hazards. You should press the mouse button as soon as you see a hazard developing that may need you, the driver, to take some action like changing speed or direction. The earlier you notice a developing hazard and make a response, the higher your score. There are one or more hazards per clip for which you can score points.

- Your response won't change what happens in the scene in any way. However, a red flag will appear on the bottom of the screen to show that your response has been noted.

- Before each clip starts, there'll be a 10-second pause to allow you to see the new road situation.

- The hazard perception part of the test lasts about 20 minutes. For this part of the test no extra time is available, and you can't repeat any of the clips. You don't get a second chance to see a hazard when you're driving on the road and so no answer changes are allowed.

- You have to pass both parts of the theory test before going forward to doing the practical driving test.

- As the theory test is one test made up of two parts, you're required to pass both parts to pass. These parts are made up of multiple choice questions and hazard perception clips and can be taken at different times.

What is the Pass Mark?

- To pass the multiple choice part of the theory test, you must answer at least 43 out of 50 questions correctly.

- To pass the hazard perception part of the test, you must reach the required pass mark of 44 out of a possible 75.

If I Don't Pass, When Can I Take the Test Again?

- If you fail your test, you've shown that you're not fully prepared. You'll have to wait at least three clear working days before you take the theory test again.

- Good preparation will save you time and money.

Useful Information:

Booking

Visit www.gov.uk/ (For Northern Ireland use;nidirect.gov.uk/motoring)

If you have any special needs for the theory test, call 0300 200 1122(0845 600 6700 for Northern Ireland).If you're a Welsh speaker, call 0300 200 1133

If you have hearing or speech difficulties and use a minicom machine, call 0300 200 1166

- Mock tests: you can take a mock test for the multiple choice part of the theory test on line at: safedrivingforlife.info/practicetheorytest.

- Test revision reading: The Official Highway Code/Know Your Traffic Signs.

- Residency requirements: You are not allowed to take a test or apply for a full licence unless you're normally a resident in the United Kingdom. Normal residency means the place where, because of personal or occupational (work) ties, you reside. However, if you've moved to the UK having recently been permanently resident in another state of the EC/EEA (European Economic Area), you must have been normally residing in the UK for 185 days in the 12 months before you apply for a driving test or full driving licence.

- Provisions for special needs: state your needs when you book your test.

- Reading difficulties. There's an English language voice over on a headset to help you if you have reading difficulties or dyslexia. You can ask for up to twice the normal time to take the multiple choice part of the test. You will be asked to provide a letter from a suitable independent person who knows about your reading disability, such as a teacher or employer. Please check with the Special Needs section (call on the normal booking number).

- If you're deaf or have other hearing difficulties, the multiple choice part and the introduction to the hazard perception part of the test can be delivered in British Sign Language (BSL) by an on screen signer. A BSL interpreter/signer can be provided if requested at the time of booking. If you have any other requirements, please call the Special Needs section on the normal test booking number.

- Physical Disabilities. If you have a physical disability that would make it difficult for you to use a mouse button in the theory test, the centre may be able to make special arrangements for you to use a different method if you let them know when you book your test.

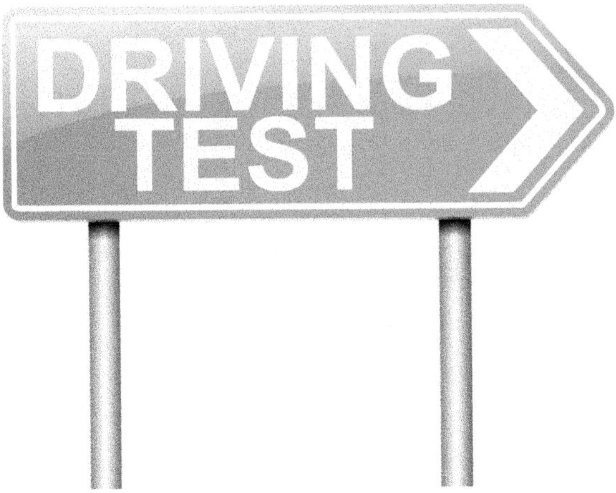
DRIVING
TEST

Part 1
Questions and Answers

Section 1 Alertness

1.1 What should you do before making a U-turn?

☐ Give an arm signal as well as using your indicators

☐ Check signs to see that U-turns are permitted

☐ Look over your shoulder for a final check

☐ Select a higher gear than normal

If you have to make a U-turn, slow down and ensure that the road is clear in both directions. Make sure that the road is wide enough for you to carry out the manoeuvre safely.

1.2 What should you do as you approach this bridge?

☐ Move to the right

☐ Slow down

☐ Change gear

☐ Keep to 30 mph

You should slow down and be cautious. The bridge is narrow and there may not be enough room for you to pass an oncoming vehicle at this point. Also, there's no footpath, so be aware of pedestrians in the road.

1.3 In which of these situations should you avoid overtaking?

☐ Just after a bend

☐ In a one-way street

☐ On a 30 mph road

☐ Approaching a dip in the road

As you begin to think about overtaking, ask yourself whether it's really necessary. If you can't see well ahead, stay back and wait for a safer place to pull out.

1.4 What does the curved arrow on the road mean?

☐ Heavy vehicles should take the next road on the left to avoid a weight limit

☐ The road ahead bends to the left

☐ Overtaking traffic should move back to the left

☐ The road ahead has a camber to the left

In this picture, the road marking shows that overtaking drivers or riders need to return to the left. These markings show the direction drivers must pass hatch markings or solid double white lines. They are also used to show the route that high vehicles should take under low arched bridge.

1.5 Your mobile phone rings while you're travelling. What should you do?

☐ Stop immediately

☐ Answer it immediately

☐ Ignore it

☐ Pull up at the nearest kerb

It's illegal to use a hand-held mobile or similar device when driving or riding, except in a genuine emergency. The safest option is to switch off your mobile phone before you set off, and use a message service. If you've forgotten to switch your phone off and it rings, you should ignore it. When you've stopped in a safe place, you can see who called and return the call if necessary.

1.6 Why are these yellow lines painted across the road?

- ☐ To help you choose the correct lane
- ☐ To help you keep the correct separation distance
- ☐ To make you aware of your speed
- ☐ To tell you the distance to the roundabout

These lines are often found on the approach to a roundabout or a dangerous junction. They give you extra warning to adjust your speed. Look well ahead and do this in good time.

1.7 What should you do when you're approaching traffic lights that have been on green for some time?

- ☐ Accelerate hard
- ☐ Maintain your speed
- ☐ Be ready to stop
- ☐ Brake hard

The longer traffic lights have been on green, the sooner they'll change. Allow for this as you approach traffic lights that you know have been on green for a while. They're likely to change soon, so you should be prepared to stop.

1.8 What should you do before stopping?

- ☐ Sound the horn
- ☐ Use the mirrors
- ☐ Select a higher gear
- ☐ Flash the headlights

Before pulling up, check the mirrors to see what's happening behind you. Also assess what's ahead and make sure you give the correct signal if it will help other road users.

1.9 You're following a large vehicle. Why should you stay a safe distance behind it?

- ☐ You'll be able to corner more quickly
- ☐ You'll help the large vehicle to stop more easily
- ☐ You'll allow the driver to see you in their mirrors
- ☐ You'll keep out of the wind better

If you're following a large vehicle but are so close to it that you can't see its exterior mirrors, the driver won't be able to see you. Keeping well back will also allow you to see the road ahead by looking past on either side of the large vehicle.

1.10 When you see a hazard ahead, you should use the mirrors. Why is this?

- ☐ Because you'll need to accelerate out of danger
- ☐ To assess how your actions will affect following traffic
- ☐ Because you'll need to brake sharply to a stop
- ☐ To check what's happening on the road ahead

You should be constantly scanning the road for clues about what's going to happen next. Check your mirrors regularly, particularly as soon as you spot a hazard. What's happening behind may affect your response to hazards ahead.

1.11 You're waiting to turn right at the end of a road. Your view is obstructed by parked vehicles. What should you do?

☐ Stop and then move forward slowly and carefully for a clear view

☐ Move quickly to where you can see so you only block traffic from one direction

☐ Wait for a pedestrian to let you know when it's safe for you to emerge

☐ Turn your vehicle around immediately and find another junction to use

At junctions, your view is often restricted by buildings, trees or parked cars. You need to be able to see in order to judge a safe gap. Edge forward slowly and keep looking all the time. Don't cause other road users to change speed or direction as you emerge.

1.12 What may happen if you hang objects from your interior mirror?

☐ Your view could be obstructed

☐ Your sun visor might get tangled

☐ Your radio reception might be affected

☐ Your windscreen would mist up

Ensure that you can see clearly through the windscreen of your vehicle. Stickers or hanging objects could obstruct your view or draw your attention away from the road.

1.13 You're on a long motorway journey. What should you do if you start to feel sleepy?

☐ Play some loud music

☐ Stop on the hard shoulder for a rest

☐ Drive faster to complete your journey sooner

☐ Leave the motorway and stop in a safe place

If you feel sleepy, you should leave the motorway at a service area or at the next exit and stop in a safe place to rest. A supply of fresh air can help to keep you alert before you reach the exit, but it isn't a substitute for stopping and resting.

1.14 Why should you switch your lights on when it first starts to get dark?

☐ To make your dials easier to see

☐ So others can see you more easily

☐ So that you blend in with other drivers

☐ Because the street lights are lit

Your headlights and tail lights help others on the road to see you. It may be necessary to turn on your lights during the day if visibility is reduced; for example, due to heavy rain. In these conditions, the light might fade before the street lights are timed to switch on. Be seen to be safe.

1.15 What's most likely to distract you while you're driving?

☐ Using a mobile phone

☐ Using the windscreen wipers

☐ Using the demisters

☐ Checking the mirrors

It's easy to be distracted. Planning your journey before you set off is important. A few sensible precautions are to tune your radio to stations in your area of travel, take planned breaks, and plan your route. Except for emergencies, it's illegal to use a hand-held mobile phone while driving. Even using a hands-free kit can severely distract your attention.

1.16 When may you use a hand-held mobile phone in your car?

☐ When receiving a call

☐ When suitably parked

☐ When driving at less than 30 mph

☐ When driving an automatic vehicle

It's illegal to use a hand-held mobile phone while driving, except in a genuine emergency. Even using a hands-free kit can distract your attention. Park in a safe and convenient place before receiving or making a call or using text messaging. Then you'll also be free to take notes or refer to papers.

1.17 You're driving on a wet road. You have to stop your vehicle in an emergency. What should you do?

☐ Apply the handbrake and footbrake together

☐ Keep both hands on the steering wheel

☐ Select reverse gear

☐ Give an arm signal

As you drive, look well ahead and all around so that you're ready for any hazards that might develop. If you have to stop in an emergency, react as soon as you can while keeping control of the vehicle. Keep both hands on the steering wheel so you can control the vehicle's direction of travel.

1.18 What should you do when moving off from behind a parked car?

☐ Give a signal after moving off

☐ Check both interior and exterior mirrors

☐ Look around after moving off

☐ Use the exterior mirrors only

Before moving off, you should use both the interior and exterior mirrors to check that the road is clear. Look around to check the blind spots and, if necessary, give a signal to warn other road users of your intentions.

1.19 You're travelling along this narrow country road. How should you pass the cyclist?

☐ Sound your horn as you pass

☐ Keep close to them as you pass

☐ Leave them plenty of room as you pass

☐ Change down one gear before you pass

Allow the cyclist plenty of room in case they wobble or swerve around a pothole or raised drain. Look well ahead before you start to overtake, because you'll need to use all of the road. Look for entrances to fields where tractors or other farm machinery could be waiting to pull out.

1.20 Your vehicle is fitted with a hand-held telephone. What should you do to use the phone?

☐ Reduce your speed

☐ Find a safe place to stop

☐ Steer the vehicle with one hand

☐ Be particularly careful at junctions

Never attempt to use a hand-held phone while you're driving, except in a genuine emergency. It's illegal and will take your attention away from driving, putting you at greater risk of causing a collision.

1.21 You lose your way on a busy road. What's the best action to take?

☐ Stop at traffic lights and ask pedestrians

☐ Shout to other drivers to ask them the way

☐ Turn into a side road, stop and check a map

☐ Check a map, and keep going with the traffic flow

It's easy to lose your way in an unfamiliar area. If you need to check a map or ask for directions, first find a safe place to stop.

1.22 When do windscreen pillars cause a serious obstruction to your view?

☐ When you're driving on a motorway

☐ When you're driving on a dual carriageway

☐ When you're approaching a one-way street

☐ When you're approaching bends and junctions

Windscreen pillars can obstruct your view, particularly at bends and junctions. Look out for other road users – especially cyclists, motorcyclists and pedestrians – as they can easily be hidden by this obstruction.

1.23 You can't see clearly behind when reversing. What should you do?

☐ Open the window to look behind

☐ Open the door to look behind

☐ Look in the nearside mirror

☐ Ask someone to guide you

If you want to turn your car around, try to find a place where you have good all-round vision. If this isn't possible, and you're unable to see clearly, then get someone to guide you.

1.24 What does the term 'blind spot' mean?

☐ An area covered by your right-hand mirror

☐ An area not covered by your headlights

☐ An area covered by your left-hand mirror

☐ An area not visible to the driver

Modern vehicles provide the driver with a good view of both the road ahead and behind using well-positioned mirrors. However, the mirrors can't see every angle of the scene behind and to the sides of the vehicle. This is why it's essential that you know when and how to check your blind spots, so that you're aware of any hidden hazards.

1.25 What's likely to happen if you use a hands-free phone while you're driving?

☐ It will improve your safety

☐ It will increase your concentration

☐ It will reduce your view

☐ It will divert your attention

Talking to someone while you're driving can distract you and, unlike someone in the car with you, the person on the other end of a mobile phone is unable to see the traffic situations you're dealing with. They won't stop speaking to you even if you're approaching a hazardous situation. You need to concentrate on your driving all of the time, but especially so when dealing with a hazard.

1.26 You're turning right onto a dual carriageway. What should you do before emerging?

☐ Stop, apply the handbrake and then select a low gear

☐ Position your vehicle well to the left of the side road

☐ Check that the central reservation is wide enough for your vehicle

☐ Make sure that you leave enough room for a vehicle behind

Before emerging right onto a dual carriageway, make sure that the central reservation is deep enough to protect your vehicle. If it isn't, you should treat the dual carriageway as one road and check that it's clear in both directions before pulling out. Neglecting to do this could place part or all of your vehicle in the path of approaching traffic and cause a collision.

1.27 You're waiting to emerge from a junction. The windscreen pillar is restricting your view. What should you be particularly aware of?

☐ Lorries

☐ Buses

☐ Motorcyclists

☐ Coaches

Windscreen pillars can completely block your view of pedestrians, motorcyclists and cyclists. You should make a particular effort to look for these road users; don't just rely on a quick glance.

1.28   How should you use a satellite navigation system so that it doesn't distract you when you're driving?

☐ Turn it off while driving in built-up areas

☐ Choose a voice that you find calming

☐ Only set the destination when you're lost

☐ Stop in a safe place before programming the system

Vehicle navigation systems can be useful when driving on unfamiliar routes. However, they can also distract you and cause you to lose control if you look at or adjust them while driving. Pull up in a convenient and safe place before adjusting them.

Section 2 Attitude

2.1 At a pelican crossing, what must you do when the amber light is flashing?

☐ Stop and wait for the green light

☐ Stop and wait for the red light

☐ Give way to pedestrians waiting to cross

☐ Give way to pedestrians already on the crossing

Pelican crossings are signal-controlled crossings operated by pedestrians. Push-button controls change the signals. Pelican crossings have no red-and-amber stage before green; instead, they have a flashing amber light. This means you must give way to pedestrians who are already on the crossing. If the crossing is clear, however, you can continue.

2.2 Why should you never wave people across at pedestrian crossings?

☐ Another vehicle may be coming

☐ They may not be looking

☐ It's safer for you to carry on

☐ They may not be ready to cross

If people are waiting to use a pedestrian crossing, slow down and be prepared to stop. Don't wave them across the road, because another driver may not have seen them, may not have seen your signal, and may not be able to stop safely.

2.3 What does 'tailgating' mean?

☐ Using the rear door of a hatchback car

☐ Reversing into a parking space

☐ Following another vehicle too closely

☐ Driving with rear fog lights on

'Tailgating' is the term used when a driver or rider follows the vehicle in front too closely. It's dangerous because it restricts their view of the road ahead and leaves no safety margin if the vehicle in front needs to slow down or stop suddenly. Tailgating is often the underlying cause of rear-end collisions or multiple pile-ups.

2.4 Why is it unwise to follow this vehicle too closely?

☐ Your brakes will overheat

☐ Your view ahead will be increased

☐ Your engine will overheat

☐ Your view ahead will be reduced

Staying back will increase your view of the road ahead. This will help you to see any hazards that might occur and give you more time to react.

2.5 What's the minimum time gap you should leave when following a vehicle on a wet road?

☐ One second

☐ Two seconds

☐ Three seconds

☐ Four seconds

Water will reduce your tyres' grip on the road. The safe separation gap of at least two seconds in dry conditions should be doubled, to at least four seconds, in wet weather.

2.6   A long, heavily laden lorry is taking a long time to overtake you. What should you do?

☐ Speed up

☐ Slow down

☐ Hold your speed

☐ Change direction

A long lorry with a heavy load will need more time to pass you than a car, especially on an uphill stretch of road. Slow down and allow the lorry to pass.

2.7   Which vehicle will use a blue flashing beacon?

☐ Motorway maintenance

☐ Bomb disposal

☐ Snow plough

☐ Breakdown recovery

Emergency vehicles use blue flashing lights. If you see or hear one, move out of its way as soon as it's safe and legal to do so.

2.8   You're being followed by an ambulance showing flashing blue lights. What should you do?

☐ Pull over as soon as it's safe to do so

☐ Accelerate hard to get away from it

☐ Maintain your speed and course

☐ Brake harshly and stop well out into the road

Pull over in a place where the ambulance can pass safely. Check that there are no bollards or obstructions in the road that will prevent it from passing.

2.9   What type of emergency vehicle is fitted with a green flashing beacon?

☐ Fire engine

☐ Road gritter

☐ Ambulance

☐ Doctor's car

A green flashing beacon on a vehicle means the driver or passenger is a doctor on an emergency call. Give way to them if it's safe to do so. Be aware that the vehicle may be travelling quickly or may stop in a hurry.

2.10   Who should obey diamond-shaped traffic signs?

☐ Tram drivers   ☐ Bus drivers

☐ Lorry drivers   ☐ Taxi drivers

These signs apply only to tram drivers, but you should know their meaning so that you're aware of the priorities and are able to anticipate the actions of the driver.

2.11   On a road where trams operate, which of these vehicles will be most at risk from the tram rails?

☐ Cars   ☐ Cycles   ☐ Buses   ☐ Lorries

The narrow wheels of a bicycle can become stuck in the tram rails, causing the cyclist to stop suddenly, wobble or even lose balance altogether. The tram lines are also slippery, which could cause a cyclist to slide or fall off.

2.12 What should you use your horn for?

☐ To alert others to your presence

☐ To allow you right of way

☐ To greet other road users

☐ To signal your annoyance

Your horn mustn't be used between 11.30 pm and 7 am in a built-up area or when you're stationary, unless a moving vehicle poses a danger. Its function is to alert other road users to your presence.

2.13 You're in a one-way street and want to turn right. There are two lanes. Where should you position your vehicle?

☐ In the right-hand lane

☐ In the left-hand lane

☐ In either lane, depending on the traffic

☐ Just left of the centre line

When you're in a one-way street and want to turn right, you should take up a position in the right-hand lane. This will allow other road users, not wishing to turn, to pass on the left. Indicate your intention and take up the correct position in good time.

2.14 You wish to turn right ahead. Why should you take up the correct position in good time?

☐ To allow other drivers to pull out in front of you

☐ To give a better view into the road that you're joining

☐ To help other road users know what you intend to do

☐ To allow drivers to pass you on the right

If you wish to turn right into a side road, take up your position in good time. Move to the centre of the road when it's safe to do so. This will allow vehicles to pass you on the left. Early planning will show other traffic what you intend to do.

2.15 At which type of crossing are cyclists allowed to ride across with pedestrians?

☐ Toucan ☐ Puffin ☐ Pelican ☐ Zebra

A toucan crossing is designed to allow pedestrians and cyclists to cross at the same time. Look out for cyclists approaching the crossing at speed.

2.16 You're driving at the legal speed limit. A vehicle comes up quickly behind you, flashing its headlights. What should you do?

☐ Accelerate to make a gap behind you

☐ Touch the brakes sharply to show your brake lights

☐ Maintain your speed to prevent the vehicle from overtaking

☐ Allow the vehicle to overtake

Don't enforce the speed limit by blocking another vehicle's progress. This will only lead to the other driver becoming more frustrated. Allow the other vehicle to pass when you can do so safely.

2.17 When should you flash your headlights at other road users?

☐ When showing that you're giving way

☐ When showing that you're about to turn

☐ When telling them that you have right of way

☐ When letting them know that you're there

You should only flash your headlights to warn others of your presence. Don't use them to greet others, show impatience or give priority to other road users, because they could misunderstand your signal.

2.18 You're approaching an unmarked crossroads. How should you deal with this type of junction?

☐ Accelerate and keep to the middle

☐ Slow down and keep to the right

☐ Accelerate and look to the left

☐ Slow down and look both ways

Be cautious, especially when your view is restricted by hedges, bushes, walls, large vehicles, etc. In the summer months, these junctions can become more difficult to deal with, because growing foliage may further obscure your view.

2.19 The conditions are good and dry. When should you use the 'two-second rule'?

☐ Before restarting the engine after it has stalled

☐ When checking your gap from the vehicle in front

☐ Before using the 'Mirrors – Signal – Manoeuvre' routine

☐ When traffic lights change to green

In good conditions, the 'two-second rule' can be used to check the distance between your vehicle and the one in front. This technique works on roads carrying faster traffic. Choose a fixed object, such as a bridge, sign or tree. When the vehicle ahead passes this object, say to yourself 'Only a fool breaks the two-second rule.' If you reach the object before you finish saying this, you're too close.

2.20 At a puffin crossing, which colour follows the green signal?

☐ Steady red

☐ Flashing amber

☐ Steady amber

☐ Flashing green

Puffin crossings have infra-red sensors that detect when pedestrians are crossing and hold the red traffic signal until the crossing is clear. The use of a sensor means there's no flashing amber phase as there is with a pelican crossing.

2.21 You're in a line of traffic. The driver behind you is following very closely. What action should you take?

☐ Ignore the following driver and continue to travel within the speed limit

☐ Slow down, gradually increasing the gap between you and the vehicle in front

☐ Signal left and wave the following driver past

☐ Move over to a position just left of the centre line of the road

If the driver behind is following too closely, there's a danger they'll collide with the back of your vehicle if you stop suddenly. You can reduce this risk by slowing down and increasing the safety margin in front of you. This reduces the chance that you'll have to stop suddenly and allows you to spread your braking over a greater distance. This is an example of defensive driving.

2.22 You're driving on a clear night. There's a steady stream of oncoming traffic. The national speed limit applies. Which lights should you use?

☐ Full-beam headlights

☐ Sidelights

☐ Dipped headlights

☐ Fog lights

Use the full-beam headlights only when you can be sure that you won't dazzle other road users.

2.23 You're driving behind a large goods vehicle. What should you do if it signals left but steers to the right?

☐ Slow down and let the vehicle turn

☐ Drive on, keeping to the left

☐ Overtake on the right of it

☐ Hold your speed and sound your horn

Large, long vehicles need extra room when making turns at junctions. They may move out to the right in order to make a left turn. Keep well back and don't attempt to pass them on their left.

2.24 You're driving along this road. The red van cuts in close in front of you. What should you do?

□ Accelerate to get closer to the red van

□ Give a long blast on the horn

□ Drop back to leave the correct separation distance

□ Flash your headlights several times

There are times when other drivers make incorrect or ill-judged decisions. Be tolerant and try not to retaliate or react aggressively. Always consider the safety of other road users, your passengers and yourself.

2.25 You're waiting in a traffic queue at night. How can you avoid dazzling drivers behind you?

□ Use the parking brake only

□ Use the footbrake only

□ Use the clutch with the accelerator

□ Use the parking brake with the footbrake

In queuing traffic, your brake lights can dazzle drivers behind you. If you apply your parking brake, you can take your foot off the footbrake. This will deactivate the brake lights.

2.26 You're driving in traffic at the speed limit for the road. What should you do if the driver behind is trying to overtake?

□ Move closer to the car ahead, so the driver behind has no room to overtake

□ Wave the driver behind to overtake when it's safe

□ Keep a steady course and allow the driver behind to overtake

□ Accelerate to get away from the driver behind

Keep a steady course to give the driver behind an opportunity to overtake safely. If necessary, slow down. Reacting incorrectly to another driver's impatience can lead to danger.

2.27 There's a bus lane on your left. The signs show no times of operation. What does this mean?

□ The lane isn't in operation

□ The lane is only in operation at peak times

□ The lane is in operation 24 hours a day

□ The lane is only in operation in daylight hours

Bus-lane signs show the vehicles allowed to use the lane and also its times of operation. Where no times are shown, the bus lane is in operation 24 hours a day.

2.28 What should you do when a person herding sheep asks you to stop?

□ Ignore them as they have no authority

□ Stop and switch off your engine

□ Continue on but drive slowly

□ Try to get past quickly

If someone in charge of animals asks you to stop, you should do so and switch off your engine. Animals are unpredictable and startle easily; they could turn and run into your path or into the path of another moving vehicle.

2.29   What should you do when you're overtaking a horse and rider?

□ Sound your horn as a warning

□ Go past as quickly as possible

□ Flash your headlights as a warning

□ Go past slowly and carefully

Horses can be startled by the sound of a car engine or the rush of air caused by a vehicle passing too closely. Keep well back and only pass when it's safe. Leave them plenty of room; you may have to use the other side of the road to go past safely.

2.30   You're approaching a zebra crossing. Pedestrians are waiting to cross. What should you do?

□ Give way to the elderly and infirm only

□ Slow down and prepare to stop

□ Use your headlights to indicate they can cross

□ Wave at them to cross the road

As you approach a zebra crossing, look for pedestrians waiting to cross. Where you can see them, slow down and prepare to stop. Be especially careful of children and older people, who may have difficulty judging when it's safe to cross.

2.31   A vehicle pulls out in front of you at a junction. What should you do?

□ Swerve past it and sound your horn

□ Flash your headlights and drive up close behind

□ Slow down and be ready to stop

□ Accelerate past it immediately

Try to be ready for the unexpected. Plan ahead and learn to anticipate hazards. You'll then give yourself more time to react to any problems that might occur.

Be tolerant of other road users who don't behave correctly.

2.32   You're approaching a red light at a puffin crossing. Pedestrians are on the crossing. When will the red light change?

□ When you start to edge forward onto the crossing

□ When the pedestrians have cleared the crossing

□ When the pedestrians push the button on the far side of the crossing

□ When a driver from the opposite direction reaches the crossing

A sensor will automatically detect that the pedestrians have reached a safe position. Don't drive on until the green light shows and it's safe for you to do so.

2.33   Which instrument-panel warning light would show that headlights are on full beam?

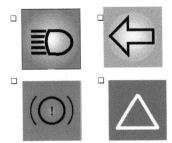

You should be aware of all the warning lights and visual aids on the vehicle you're driving. If you're driving a vehicle for the first time, you should familiarise yourself with all the controls, warning lights and visual aids before you set off.

2.34   In which conditions should you leave at least a two-second gap between your vehicle and the one in front?

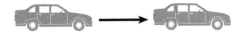

□ Wet □ Dry □ Damp □ Foggy

In good, dry conditions, a driver needs to keep a distance of at least two seconds from the car in front. This should allow enough space for you to stop if the driver in front has to stop suddenly.

2.35 You're driving at night on an unlit road, following another vehicle. What should you do?

☐ Flash your headlights

☐ Use dipped headlights

☐ Switch off your headlights

☐ Use full-beam headlights

If you follow another vehicle with your headlights on full beam, they could dazzle the driver. Leave a safe distance and make sure that the light from your dipped beam falls short of the vehicle in front.

2.36 You're driving a slow-moving vehicle on a narrow, winding road. What should you do?

☐ Keep well out to stop vehicles overtaking dangerously

☐ Wave following vehicles past you if you think they can overtake quickly

☐ Pull in when you can, to let following vehicles overtake

☐ Give a left signal when it's safe for vehicles to overtake you

If you're driving a slow-moving vehicle along a narrow road, try not to hold up faster traffic. If you see vehicles following behind, pull over in a safe place and let the traffic pass before continuing. Don't wave other traffic past – this could be dangerous if you or they haven't seen any hazard that's hidden from view.

2.37 What can a loose filler cap on your diesel fuel tank cause?

☐ It can make the engine difficult to start

☐ It can make the roads slippery for other road users

☐ It can improve your vehicle's fuel consumption

☐ It can increase the level of exhaust emissions

Diesel fuel can spill out if your filler cap isn't secured properly. This is most likely to occur on bends, junctions and roundabouts, where it will make the road slippery, especially if it's wet. At the end of a dry spell of weather, the road surfaces may have a high level of diesel spillage that hasn't been washed away by rain.

2.38 After refuelling your vehicle, what should you do to avoid spillage?

☐ Check that your tank is only three-quarters full

☐ Check that you've used a locking filler cap

☐ Check that your fuel gauge is working

☐ Check that your filler cap is securely fastened

When learning to drive, it's a good idea to practise filling your car with fuel. Ask your instructor if you can use a petrol station and fill the fuel tank yourself. You need to know where the filler cap is on the car you're driving, so you know which side of the pump to park at. Take care not to overfill the tank and make sure you secure the filler cap correctly, so that no fuel leaks onto the road while you're driving.

2.39 What style of driving causes increased risk to everyone?

☐ Considerate

☐ Defensive

☐ Competitive

☐ Responsible

Competitive driving increases the risks to everyone and is the opposite of responsible, considerate and defensive driving. Defensive driving is about questioning the actions of other road users and being prepared for the unexpected. Don't be taken by surprise.

Section 3 Safety and Your Vehicle

3.1 What's badly affected if the tyres are under-inflated?

☐ Braking   ☐ Indicating

☐ Changing gear ☐ Parking

Your tyres are your only contact with the road. To prevent problems with braking and steering, keep your tyres free from defects; they must have sufficient tread depth and be correctly inflated. Correct tyre pressures help reduce the risk of skidding and provide a safer and more comfortable drive or ride.

3.2 When mustn't you sound your vehicle's horn?

☐ Between 10.00 pm and 6.00 am in a built-up area

☐ At any time in a built-up area

☐ Between 11.30 pm and 7.00 am in a built-up area

☐ Between 11.30 pm and 6.00 am on any road

Every effort must be made to prevent excessive noise, especially in built-up areas at night. Don't rev your engine or sound the horn unnecessarily. It's illegal to sound your horn in a built-up area between 11.30 pm and 7.00 am, except when another road user poses a danger.

3.3 What makes the vehicle in the picture 'environmentally friendly'?

☐ It's powered by gravity

☐ It's powered by diesel

☐ It's powered by electricity

☐ It's powered by unleaded petrol

Trams are powered by electricity and therefore don't emit exhaust fumes. They ease traffic congestion by offering drivers an alternative to using their car, particularly in busy cities and towns.

3.4 Why have 'red routes' been introduced in major cities?

☐ To raise the speed limits

☐ To help the traffic flow

☐ To provide better parking

☐ To allow lorries to load more freely

Inconsiderate parking can obstruct the flow of traffic and so make traffic congestion worse. Red routes are designed to prevent this by enforcing strict parking restrictions. Driving slowly in traffic increases fuel consumption and causes a build-up of exhaust fumes.

3.5 What's the purpose of road humps, chicanes and narrowings?

☐ To separate lanes of traffic

☐ To increase traffic speed

☐ To allow pedestrians to cross

☐ To reduce traffic speed

Traffic-calming measures help to keep vehicle speeds low in congested areas where there are pedestrians and children. A pedestrian is much more likely to survive a collision with a vehicle travelling at 20 mph than they are with a vehicle travelling at 40 mph.

3.6 What's the purpose of a catalytic converter?

☐ To reduce fuel consumption

☐ To reduce the risk of fire

☐ To reduce harmful exhaust gases

☐ To reduce engine wear

Catalytic converters reduce a large percentage of harmful exhaust emissions. They work more efficiently when the engine has reached its normal working temperature.

3.7 It's essential that tyre pressures are checked regularly. When should this be done?

☐ After any lengthy journey

☐ After travelling at high speed

☐ When tyres are hot

☐ When tyres are cold

Check the tyre pressures when the tyres are cold. This will give you a more accurate reading. The heat generated on a long journey will raise the pressure inside the tyre.

3.8 When will your vehicle use more fuel?

☐ When its tyres are under-inflated

☐ When its tyres are of different makes

☐ When its tyres are over-inflated

☐ When its tyres are new

Check your tyre pressures frequently – normally once a week. If they're lower than those recommended by the manufacturer, there will be more 'rolling resistance'. The engine will have to work harder to overcome this, leading to increased fuel consumption.

3.9 How should you dispose of a used vehicle battery?

☐ Bury it in your garden

☐ Put it in the dustbin

☐ Take it to a local-authority site

☐ Leave it on waste land

Batteries contain acid, which is hazardous, and they must be disposed of safely. This means taking them to an appropriate disposal site.

3.10 What's most likely to cause high fuel consumption?

☐ Poor steering control

☐ Accelerating around bends

☐ Staying in high gears

☐ Harsh braking and accelerating

Accelerating and braking gently and smoothly will help to save fuel and reduce wear on your vehicle. This makes it better for the environment too.

3.11 The fluid level in your battery is low. What should you top it up with?

☐ Battery acid

☐ Distilled water

☐ Engine oil

☐ Engine coolant

Some modern batteries are maintenance-free. Check your vehicle handbook and, if necessary, make sure that the plates in each battery cell are covered with fluid.

3.12   You're parked on the road at night. Where must you use parking lights?

□ Where there are continuous white lines in the middle of the road

□ Where the speed limit exceeds 30 mph

□ Where you're facing oncoming traffic

□ Where you're near a bus stop

When parking at night, park in the direction of the traffic. This will enable other road users to see the reflectors on the rear of your vehicle. Use your parking lights if the speed limit is over 30 mph.

3.13   How can you reduce the environmental harm caused by your motor vehicle?

□ Only use it for short journeys

□ Don't service it

□ Drive faster than normal

□ Keep engine revs low

Engines that burn fossil fuels produce exhaust emissions that are harmful to health. The harder you make the engine work, the more emissions it will produce. Engines also use more fuel and produce higher levels of emissions when they're cold. Anything you can do to reduce your use of fossil fuels will help the environment.

3.14   What can cause excessive or uneven tyre wear?

□ A faulty gearbox

□ A faulty braking system

□ A faulty electrical system

□ A faulty exhaust system

If you see that parts of the tread on your tyres are wearing before others, it may indicate a brake, steering or suspension fault. Regular servicing will help to detect faults at an early stage and this will avoid the risk of minor faults becoming serious or even dangerous.

3.15   You need to top up your battery. What level should you fill it to?

□ The top of the battery

□ Halfway up the battery

□ Just below the cell plates

□ Just above the cell plates

Top up the battery with distilled water and make sure each cell plate is covered.

3.16   Before starting a journey, it's wise to plan your route. How can you do this?

□ Look at a map

□ Contact your local garage

□ Look in your vehicle handbook

□ Check your vehicle registration document

Planning your journey before you set out can help to make it much easier and more pleasant, and may help to ease traffic congestion. Look at a map to help you do this. You may need maps of different scales, depending on where and how far you're going. Printing or writing out the route can also help.

3.17   Why is it a good idea to plan your journey to avoid busy times?

□ You'll have an easier journey

□ You'll have a more stressful journey

□ Your journey time will be longer

□ It will cause more traffic congestion

No-one likes to spend time in traffic queues. Try to avoid busy times related to school or work travel.

3.18   You avoid busy times when travelling. How will this affect your journey?

☐ You're more likely to be held up

☐ Your journey time will be longer

☐ You'll travel a much shorter distance

☐ You're less likely to be delayed

If possible, avoid the early morning, late afternoon and early evening 'rush hour'. Doing this should allow you to travel in a more relaxed frame of mind, concentrate solely on what you're doing and arrive at your destination feeling less stressed.

3.19   It can be helpful to plan your route before starting a journey. Why should you also plan an alternative route?

☐ Your original route may be blocked

☐ Your maps may have different scales

☐ You may find you have to pay a congestion charge

☐ You may get held up by a tractor

It can be frustrating and worrying to find your planned route is blocked by roadworks or diversions. If you've planned an alternative, you'll feel less stressed and more able to concentrate fully on your driving or riding. If your original route is mostly on motorways, it's a good idea to plan an alternative using non-motorway roads. Always carry a map with you just in case you need to refer to it.

3.20   You're making an appointment and will have to travel a long distance. How should you plan for the journey?

☐ Allow plenty of time for the trip

☐ Plan to travel at busy times

☐ Avoid roads with the national speed limit

☐ Prevent other drivers from overtaking

Always allow plenty of time for your journey in case of unforeseen problems. Anything can happen; for example, punctures, breakdowns, road closures, diversions and delays. You'll feel less stressed and less inclined to take risks if you aren't 'pushed for time'.

3.21   What can rapid acceleration and heavy braking lead to?

☐ Reduced pollution

☐ Increased fuel consumption

☐ Reduced exhaust emissions

☐ Increased road safety

Using the controls smoothly can reduce fuel consumption by about 15%, as well as reducing wear and tear on your vehicle. Plan ahead and anticipate changes of speed well in advance. This will reduce the need to accelerate rapidly or brake sharply.

3.22   Which of these, if allowed to get low, could cause you to crash?

☐ Anti-freeze level

☐ Brake fluid level

☐ Battery water level

☐ Radiator coolant level

You should carry out frequent checks on all fluid levels but particularly brake fluid. As the brake pads or shoes wear down, the brake fluid level will drop. If it drops below the minimum mark on the fluid reservoir, air could enter the hydraulic system and lead to a loss of braking efficiency or even complete brake failure.

3.23   What can cause excessive or uneven tyre wear?

☐ Faults in the gearbox

☐ Faults in the engine

☐ Faults in the suspension

☐ Faults in the exhaust system

Uneven wear on your tyres can be caused by the condition of your vehicle. Having the vehicle serviced regularly will ensure that the brakes, steering, suspension and wheel alignment are maintained in good order.

3.24   What's the main cause of brake fade?

☐ The brakes overheating

☐ Air in the brake fluid

☐ Oil on the brakes

☐ The brakes out of adjustment

Brakes can overheat and lose efficiency when they're used continually, such as on a long, steep, downhill stretch of road. Using a lower gear when you drive downhill can help prevent the vehicle from gaining speed.

3.25   What should you do if your anti-lock brakes (ABS) warning light stays on?

☐ Check the brake-fluid level

☐ Check the footbrake free play

☐ Check that the handbrake is released

☐ Have the brakes checked immediately

Consult the vehicle handbook or a garage before driving the vehicle any further. Only drive to a garage if it's safe to do so. If you aren't sure, get expert help.

3.26   What does it mean if this light comes on while you're driving?

☐ A fault in the braking system

☐ The engine oil is low

☐ A rear light has failed

☐ Your seat belt isn't fastened

If this light comes on, you should have the brake system checked immediately. A faulty braking system could have dangerous consequences.

3.27   It's important to wear suitable shoes when you're driving. Why is this?

☐ To prevent wear on the pedals

☐ To maintain control of the pedals

☐ To enable you to adjust your seat

☐ To enable you to walk for assistance if you break down

When you're going to drive, make sure that you're wearing suitable clothing.

Comfortable shoes will ensure that you have proper control of the foot pedals.

3.28   What will reduce the risk of neck injury resulting from a collision?

☐ An air-sprung seat

☐ Anti-lock brakes

☐ A collapsible steering wheel

☐ A properly adjusted head restraint

If you're involved in a collision, head restraints will reduce the risk of neck injury. They must be properly adjusted. Make sure they aren't positioned too low: in a crash, this could cause damage to the neck.

3.29   You're testing your suspension. You notice that your vehicle keeps bouncing when you press down on the front wing. What does this mean?

☐ Worn tyres

☐ Tyres under-inflated

☐ Steering wheel not located centrally

☐ Worn shock absorbers

If you find that your vehicle bounces as you drive around a corner or bend in the road, the shock absorbers might be worn. Press down on the front wing and, if the vehicle continues to bounce, take it to be checked by a qualified mechanic.

3.30 How will a roof rack affect your car's performance?

☐ There will be less wind noise

☐ The engine will use more oil

☐ The car will accelerate faster

☐ Fuel consumption will increase

A roof rack increases your car's wind resistance. This will cause an increase in fuel consumption, so you should remove it when it isn't being used. An aerodynamically designed roof rack or box will help reduce wind resistance to a minimum, but the rack or box should still be removed when it isn't in use.

3.31 Which of these makes your tyres illegal?

☐ They were bought second-hand

☐ They have a large, deep cut in the side wall

☐ They're of different makes

☐ They have different tread patterns

Your tyres may be of different treads and makes. They can even be second-hand, as long as they're in good condition. They must, however, be intact, without cuts or tears. When checking the side walls for cuts and bulges, don't forget to check the side of the tyre that's hidden from view, under the car.

3.32 What's the legal minimum depth of tread for car tyres?

☐ 1 mm   ☐ 1.6 mm   ☐ 2.5 mm   ☐ 4 mm

Car tyres must have sufficient depth of tread to give them a good grip on the road surface. The legal minimum for cars is 1.6 mm. This depth should be across the central three-quarters of the breadth of the tyre and around the entire circumference.

3.33 You're carrying two 13-year-old children and their parents in your car. Who's responsible for seeing that the children wear seat belts?

☐ The children's parents

☐ You, the driver

☐ The front-seat passenger

☐ The children

Seat belts save lives and reduce the risk of injury. If you're carrying passengers under 14 years old, it's your responsibility as the driver to ensure that their seat belts are fastened or they're seated in an approved child restraint.

3.34 How can drivers help the environment?

☐ By accelerating harshly

☐ By accelerating gently

☐ By using leaded fuel

☐ By driving faster

Rapid acceleration and heavy braking lead to increased

• fuel consumption

• wear on your vehicle.

Having your vehicle serviced regularly will maintain its efficiency, produce cleaner emissions and reduce the risk of a breakdown.

3.35 How can you avoid wasting fuel?

☐ By having your vehicle serviced regularly

☐ By revving the engine in the lower gears

☐ By keeping an empty roof rack on your vehicle

☐ By driving at higher speeds where possible

If you don't have your vehicle serviced regularly, the engine will gradually become less efficient. This will cause increased fuel consumption and, in turn, an increase in the amount of harmful emissions it produces.

3.36 What could you do to reduce the volume of traffic on the roads?

☐ Drive in a bus lane

☐ Use a car with a smaller engine

☐ Walk or cycle on short journeys

☐ Travel by car at all times

Try not to use your car as a matter of routine. For shorter journeys, consider walking or cycling instead – this is much better for both you and the environment.

3.37 What's most likely to waste fuel?

☐ Reducing your speed

☐ Driving on motorways

☐ Using different brands of fuel

☐ Under-inflated tyres

Wasting fuel costs you money and also causes unnecessary pollution. Ensuring your tyres are correctly inflated, avoiding carrying unnecessary weight and removing a roof rack that's not in use will all help to reduce your fuel consumption.

3.38 What does the law require you to keep in good condition?

☐ Gears

☐ Transmission

☐ Door locks

☐ Seat belts

Unless exempt, you and your passengers must wear a seat belt (or suitable child restraint). The seat belts in your car must be in good condition and working properly; they'll be checked during its MOT test.

3.39 Up to how much more fuel will you use by driving at 70 mph, compared with driving at 50 mph?

☐ 10%   ☐ 30%   ☐ 75%   ☐ 100%

Your vehicle will use less fuel if you avoid heavy acceleration. The higher the engine revs, the more fuel you'll use. Using the same gear, and covering the same distance, a vehicle travelling at 70 mph will use up to 30% more fuel than it would at 50 mph. However, don't travel so slowly that you inconvenience or endanger other road users.

3.40 When you use the brakes, your vehicle pulls to one side. What should you do?

☐ Increase the pressure in your tyres

☐ Have the brakes checked as soon as possible

☐ Change gear and pump the brake pedal

☐ Use your parking brake at the same time

The brakes on your vehicle must be effective and properly adjusted. If your vehicle pulls to one side when braking, take it to be checked by a qualified mechanic as soon as you can.

3.41 What will happen if your car's wheels are unbalanced?

☐ The steering will pull to one side

☐ The steering will vibrate

☐ The brakes will fail

☐ The tyres will deflate

If your wheels are out of balance, it will cause the steering to vibrate at certain speeds. This isn't a fault that will put itself right, so take your vehicle to a garage or tyre fitter to have the wheels rebalanced.

3.42 Turning the steering wheel while stationary can cause damage to which part of your car?

☐ Gearbox   ☐ Engine   ☐ Brakes   ☐ Tyres

Turning the steering wheel when the car isn't moving is known as dry steering. It can cause unnecessary wear to the tyres and steering mechanism.

3.43   You have to leave valuables in your car. What's the safest thing to do?

☐ Put them in a carrier bag

☐ Park near a school entrance

☐ Lock them out of sight

☐ Park near a bus stop

If you have to leave valuables in your car, lock them out of sight. This is the best way to deter an opportunist thief.

3.44   Which of the following may help to deter a thief from stealing your car?

☐ Always keeping the headlights on

☐ Fitting reflective glass windows

☐ Always keeping the interior light on

☐ Etching the registration number on the windows

Having your car registration number etched on all your windows is a cheap and effective way to deter professional car thieves.

3.45   Which of the following shouldn't be kept in your vehicle?

☐ The car dealer's details

☐ The owner's manual

☐ The service record

☐ The vehicle registration document

Never leave the vehicle registration document inside your car. This document would help a thief to dispose of your car more easily.

3.46   What should you do when leaving your vehicle parked and unattended?

☐ Park near a busy junction

☐ Park in a housing estate

☐ Lock it and remove the key

☐ Leave the left indicator on

An unlocked car is an open invitation to thieves. Leaving the keys in the ignition not only makes your car easy to steal but could also invalidate your insurance.

3.47   What will improve fuel consumption?

☐ Reducing your speed

☐ Rapid acceleration

☐ Late and harsh braking

☐ Driving in lower gears

Harsh braking, frequent gear changes and harsh acceleration increase fuel consumption. An engine uses less fuel when travelling at a constant low speed.

You need to look well ahead so you're able to anticipate hazards early. Easing off the accelerator and timing your approach at junctions, for example, can reduce the fuel consumption of your vehicle.

3.48   You service your own vehicle. How should you get rid of the old engine oil?

☐ Take it to a local-authority site

☐ Pour it down a drain

☐ Tip it into a hole in the ground

☐ Put it in your dustbin

It's illegal to pour engine oil down any drain. Oil is a pollutant and harmful to wildlife. Dispose of it safely at an authorised site.

3.49   Why do MOT tests include a strict exhaust emission test?

☐ To recover the cost of expensive garage equipment

☐ To help protect the environment against pollution

☐ To discover which fuel supplier is used the most

☐ To make sure diesel and petrol engines emit the same fumes

Emission tests are carried out to make sure your vehicle's engine is operating efficiently. This ensures the pollution produced by the engine is kept to a minimum. If your vehicle isn't serviced regularly, it may fail the annual MOT test.

3.50 How can you reduce the damage your vehicle causes to the environment?

□ Use narrow side streets

□ Brake heavily

□ Use busy routes

□ Anticipate well ahead

By looking well ahead and recognising hazards in good time, you can avoid late and heavy braking. Watch the traffic flow and look well ahead for potential hazards so you can control your speed in good time. Avoid over-revving the engine and accelerating harshly, as this increases wear to the engine and uses more fuel.

3.51 What will be the result of having your vehicle properly serviced?

□ Reduced insurance premiums

□ Lower vehicle tax

□ Better fuel economy

□ Slower journey times

All vehicles need to be serviced to keep working efficiently. An efficient engine uses less fuel and produces fewer harmful emissions than an engine that's running inefficiently. Keeping the vehicle serviced to the manufacturer's schedule should also make it more reliable and reduce the chance of it breaking down.

3.52 You enter a road where there are road humps. What should you do?

□ Maintain a reduced speed throughout

□ Accelerate quickly between each one

□ Always keep to the maximum legal speed

□ Drive slowly at school times only

The humps are there for a reason – to protect vulnerable road users by reducing the speed of traffic. Don't accelerate harshly between the humps. Put the safety of others first and maintain a reduced speed throughout the zone.

3.53 When should you especially check the engine oil level?

□ Before a long journey

□ When the engine is hot

□ Early in the morning

□ Every 6000 miles

An engine can use more oil during long journeys than on shorter trips. Insufficient engine oil is potentially dangerous: it can lead to excessive wear, mechanical breakdown and expensive repairs.

Most cars have a dipstick to allow the oil level to be checked. If not, you should refer to the vehicle handbook.

3.54 You're having difficulty finding a parking space in a busy town. You can see there's space on the zigzag lines of a zebra crossing. Can you park there?

□ No, not unless you stay with your car

□ Yes, in order to drop off a passenger

□ Yes, if you don't block people from crossing

□ No, not under any circumstances

It's an offence to park on the zigzag lines of a zebra crossing. You'll be causing an obstruction by obscuring the view of both pedestrians and drivers.

3.55 What should you do when you leave your car unattended for a few minutes?

□ Leave the engine running

□ Switch the engine off but leave the key in

□ Lock it and remove the key

□ Park near a traffic warden

Always switch off the engine, remove the key and lock your car, even if you're only leaving it for a few minutes.

3.56   When leaving your vehicle, where should you try to park?

☐ Opposite a traffic island

☐ In a secure car park

☐ On a bend

☐ At or near a taxi rank

Whenever possible, leave your car in a secure car park. This will help deter thieves.

3.57   Where would parking your vehicle cause an obstruction?

☐ Alongside a parking meter

☐ In front of a property entrance

☐ On your driveway

☐ In a marked parking space

Don't park your vehicle where it may obstruct access to a business or property. Think carefully before you slow down and stop. Look at road markings and signs to ensure that you aren't parking illegally.

3.58   What's the most important reason for having a properly adjusted head restraint?

☐ To make you more comfortable

☐ To help you avoid neck injury

☐ To help you relax

☐ To help you maintain your driving position

In a collision, rapid deceleration will violently throw vehicle occupants forward and then backwards as the vehicle stops. Seat belts and airbags protect occupants against the forward movement. Head restraints should be adjusted so they give maximum protection to the head and neck during the backward movement.

3.59   What causes the most damage to the environment?

☐ Choosing a fuel-efficient vehicle

☐ Having your vehicle serviced regularly

☐ Driving in as high a gear as possible

☐ Making a lot of short journeys

Avoid using your car for short journeys. On a short journey, the engine is unlikely to warm up fully and will therefore be running less efficiently. This will result in the car using more fuel and producing higher levels of harmful emissions.

3.60   What can people who live or work in towns and cities do to help reduce urban pollution levels?

☐ Drive more quickly

☐ Over-rev in a low gear

☐ Walk or cycle

☐ Drive short journeys

Using a vehicle for short journeys means the engine doesn't have time to reach its normal operating temperature. When an engine is running below its normal operating temperature, it produces increased amounts of pollution. Walking and cycling don't create pollution and have health benefits as well.

3.61   How can you reduce the chances of your car being broken into when leaving it unattended?

☐ Take all valuables with you

☐ Park near a taxi rank

☐ Place any valuables on the floor

☐ Park near a fire station

When leaving your car, take all valuables with you if you can. Otherwise, lock them out of sight.

3.62   How can you help to prevent your car radio being stolen?

☐ Park in an unlit area

☐ Leave the radio turned on

☐ Park near a busy junction

☐ Install a security-coded radio

A security-coded radio can deter thieves, as it's likely to be of little use when removed from the vehicle.

3.63 How can you lessen the risk of your vehicle being broken into at night?

☐ Leave it in a well-lit area

☐ Park in a quiet side road

☐ Don't engage the steering lock

☐ Park in a poorly-lit area

Having your vehicle broken into or stolen can be very distressing and inconvenient. Avoid leaving your vehicle unattended in poorly-lit areas.

3.64 Which of these will help you to keep your car secure?

☐ Vehicle breakdown organisation

☐ Vehicle watch scheme

☐ Advanced driver's scheme

☐ Car maintenance class

The vehicle watch scheme helps to reduce the risk of your car being stolen. By displaying high-visibility vehicle watch stickers in your car, you're inviting the police to stop your vehicle if it's seen in use between midnight and 5 am.

3.65 On a vehicle, where would you find a catalytic converter?

☐ In the fuel tank

☐ In the air filter

☐ On the cooling system

☐ On the exhaust system

Although carbon dioxide is still produced, a catalytic converter fitted to the exhaust system reduces the toxic and polluting gases by up to 90%.

3.66 What can driving smoothly achieve?

☐ Reduction in journey times by about 15%

☐ Increase in fuel consumption by about 15%

☐ Reduction in fuel consumption by about 15%

☐ Increase in journey times by about 15%

By driving smoothly, you'll not only save about 15% of your fuel but will also reduce the amount of wear and tear on your vehicle and the level of pollution it produces. You're also likely to feel more relaxed and have a more pleasant journey.

3.67 Which driving technique can help you save fuel?

☐ Using lower gears as often as possible

☐ Accelerating sharply in each gear

☐ Using each gear in turn

☐ Missing out some gears

Missing out intermediate gears, when appropriate, helps to reduce the amount of time spent accelerating and decelerating – the times when your vehicle uses the most fuel.

3.68 How can driving in an ecosafe manner help protect the environment?

☐ Through the legal enforcement of speed regulations

☐ By increasing the number of cars on the road

☐ Through increased fuel bills

☐ By reducing exhaust emissions

Ecosafe driving is all about becoming a more environmentally friendly driver. This will make your journeys more comfortable, as well as considerably reducing your fuel bills and reducing emissions that can damage the environment.

3.69 What does ecosafe driving achieve?

☐ Increased fuel consumption

☐ Improved road safety

☐ Damage to the environment

☐ Increased exhaust emissions

The emphasis is on hazard awareness and planning ahead. By looking well ahead, you'll have plenty of time to deal with hazards safely and won't need to brake sharply. This will also reduce damage to the environment.

3.70 You're checking your trailer tyres. What's the legal minimum tread depth over the central three-quarters of its breadth?

□ 1 mm   □ 1.6 mm   □ 2 mm   □ 2.6 mm

Trailers and caravans may be left in storage over the winter months, and tyres can deteriorate. It's important to check their tread depth and also their pressures and general condition. The legal tread depth of 1.6 mm applies to the central three-quarters of a tyre's breadth, over its entire circumference.

3.71 Fuel consumption is at its highest when you're doing what?

□ Braking   □ Coasting

□ Accelerating   □ Steering

Accelerating uses a lot of fuel, so always try to use the accelerator smoothly. Taking your foot off the accelerator allows the momentum of the car to take you forward, especially when going downhill. This can save a considerable amount of fuel without any loss of control over the vehicle.

3.72 When is it acceptable for a passenger to travel in a car without wearing wearing a seat belt?

□ When they're under 14 years old

□ When they're under 1.5 metres (5 feet) in height

□ When they're sitting in the rear seat

□ When they're exempt for medical reasons

If you have adult passengers, it's their responsibility to wear a seat belt, but you should still remind them to use one as they get in the car. It's your responsibility to make sure that all children in your car are secured with an appropriate restraint. Exemptions are allowed for those with a medical exemption certificate.

3.73 You're driving a friend's children home from school. They're both under 14 years old. Who's responsible for making sure they wear a seat belt or approved child restraint where required?

□ An adult passenger   □ The children

□ You, the driver   □ Your friend

Passengers should always be secured and safe. Children should be encouraged to fasten their seat belts or approved restraints themselves from an early age, so that it becomes a matter of routine. As the driver, you must check that they're fastened securely. It's your responsibility.

3.74 You have too much oil in your engine. What could this cause?

□ Low oil pressure □ Engine overheating

□ Chain wear   □ Oil leaks

Too much oil in the engine will create excess pressure and could damage engine seals and cause oil leaks. Any excess oil should be drained off.

3.75 You're carrying a five-year-old child in the back seat of your car. They're under 1.35 metres (4 feet 5 inches) tall. A correct child restraint isn't available. How should you seat them?

□ Behind the passenger seat

□ Using an adult seat belt

□ Sharing a belt with an adult

□ Between two other children

Usually, a correct child restraint must be used. In cases where one isn't available, an adult seat belt must be used instead. In a collision, unrestrained objects and people can cause serious injury or even death.

3.76   You're carrying an 11-year-old child in the back seat of your car. They're under 1.35 metres (4 feet 5 inches) tall. What must you make sure of?

☐ That they sit between two belted people

☐ That they can fasten their own seat belt

☐ That a suitable child restraint is available

☐ That they can see clearly out of the front window

As the driver, it's your responsibility to make sure that children are secure and safe in your vehicle. Make yourself familiar with the rules. In a few very exceptional cases when a child restraint isn't available, an adult seat belt must be used.

3.77   You're parked at the side of the road. You'll be waiting some time for a passenger. What should you do?

☐ Switch off the engine

☐ Apply the steering lock

☐ Switch off the radio

☐ Use your headlights

If your vehicle is stationary and is likely to remain so for some time, switch off the engine. We should all try to reduce global warming and pollution.

3.78   You want to put a rear-facing baby seat on the front passenger seat, which is protected by a frontal airbag. What must you do before setting off?

☐ Deactivate the airbag

☐ Turn the seat to face sideways

☐ Ask a passenger to hold the baby

☐ Put the child in an adult seat belt

It's illegal to fit a rear-facing baby seat into a passenger seat protected by an active frontal airbag. If the airbag activates, it could cause serious injury or even death to the child. You must secure it in a different seat or deactivate the relevant airbag. Follow the manufacturer's advice when fitting a baby seat.

3.79   You're leaving your vehicle parked on a road and unattended. When may you leave the engine running?

☐ If you'll be parking for less than five minutes

☐ If the battery keeps going flat

☐ When parked in a 20 mph zone

☐ Never if you're away from the vehicle

When you leave your vehicle parked on a road, switch off the engine and secure the vehicle. Make sure no valuables are visible, shut all the windows, lock the vehicle, and set the alarm the vehicle has one.

Section 4 Safety Margins

4.1 By how much can stopping distances increase in icy conditions?

☐ Two times   ☐ Three times

☐ Five times   ☐ Ten times

Tyre grip is greatly reduced in icy conditions. For this reason, you need to allow up to ten times the stopping distance you would allow on dry roads.

4.2 In windy conditions, which activity requires extra care?

☐ Using the brakes

☐ Moving off on a hill

☐ Turning into a narrow road

☐ Passing pedal cyclists

Always give cyclists plenty of room when overtaking them. You need to give them even more room when it's windy. A sudden gust could easily blow them off course and into your path.

4.3 When approaching a right-hand bend, you should keep well to the left. Why is this?

☐ To improve your view of the road

☐ To overcome the effect of the road's slope

☐ To let faster traffic from behind overtake

☐ To be positioned safely if you skid

Doing this will give you an earlier view around the bend and enable you to see any hazards sooner. It also reduces the risk of collision with an oncoming vehicle that may have drifted over the centre line while taking the bend.

4.4 You've just gone through deep water. What should you do to make sure your brakes are working properly?

☐ Accelerate and keep to a high speed for a short time

☐ Go slowly while gently applying the brakes

☐ Avoid using the brakes at all for a few miles

☐ Stop for at least an hour to allow them time to dry

Water on the brakes will act as a lubricant, causing them to work less efficiently. Using the brakes lightly as you go along will quickly dry them out.

4.5 In very hot weather the road surface can become soft. What will this affect?

☐ The suspension

☐ The exhaust emissions

☐ The fuel consumption

☐ The tyre grip

If the road surface becomes very hot, it can soften. Tyres are unable to grip a soft surface as well as they can a firm dry one. Take care when cornering and braking.

4.6 Where are you most likely to be affected by side winds?

☐ On a narrow country lane

☐ On an open stretch of road

☐ On a busy stretch of road

☐ On a long, straight road

In windy conditions, care must be taken on exposed roads. A strong gust of wind can blow you off course. Watch out for other road users who are particularly likely to be affected, such as cyclists, motorcyclists, high-sided lorries and vehicles towing trailers.

4.7   In good conditions, what's the typical stopping distance at 70 mph?

☐ 53 metres (175 feet) ☐ 60 metres (197 feet)

☐ 73 metres (240 feet) ☐ 96 metres (315 feet)

Note that this is the typical stopping distance. It will take at least this distance to think, brake and stop in good conditions. In poor conditions, it will take much longer.

4.8   What's the shortest overall stopping distance on a dry road at 60 mph?

☐ 53 metres (175 feet) ☐ 58 metres (190 feet)

☐ 73 metres (240 feet) ☐ 96 metres (315 feet)

This distance is the equivalent of 18 car lengths. Try pacing out 73 metres and then look back. It's probably further than you think.

4.9   You're following a vehicle at a safe distance on a wet road. Another driver overtakes you and pulls into the gap you've left. What should you do?

☐ Flash your headlights as a warning

☐ Try to overtake safely as soon as you can

☐ Drop back to regain a safe distance

☐ Stay close to the other vehicle until it moves on

Wet weather will affect the time it takes for you to stop and can affect your control. Your speed should allow you to stop safely and in good time. If another vehicle pulls into the gap you've left, ease back until you've regained your stopping distance.

4.10   You're travelling at 50 mph on a good, dry road. What's your typical overall stopping distance?

☐ 36 metres (118 feet) ☐ 53 metres (175 feet)

☐ 75 metres (245 feet) ☐ 96 metres (315 feet)

Even in good conditions, it will usually take you further than you think to stop. Don't just learn the figures; make sure you understand how far the distance is.

4.11   You're on a good, dry road surface. Your brakes and tyres are good. What's the typical overall stopping distance at 40 mph?

☐ 23 metres (75 feet). ☐ 36 metres (118 feet)

☐ 53 metres (175 feet) ☐ 96 metres (315 feet)

Stopping distances are affected by a number of variables. These include the type, model and condition of your vehicle, the road and weather conditions, and your reaction time. Look well ahead for hazards and leave enough space between you and the vehicle in front. This should allow you to pull up safely if you have to, without braking sharply.

4.12   What should you do when overtaking a motorcyclist in strong winds?

☐ Pass closely.   ☐ Pass very slowly

☐ Pass wide   ☐ Pass immediately

In strong winds, riders of two-wheeled vehicles are particularly vulnerable. When you overtake them, allow plenty of room. Always check to the left as you pass.

4.13   Overall stopping distance is made up of thinking distance and braking distance. You're on a good, dry road surface, with good brakes and tyres. What's the typical braking distance from 50 mph?

☐ 14 metres (46 feet). ☐ 24 metres (80 feet)

☐ 38 metres (125 feet) ☐ 55 metres (180 feet)

Be aware that this is just the braking distance. You need to add the thinking distance to this to give the overall stopping distance. At 50 mph, the typical thinking distance will be 15 metres (50 feet), plus a braking distance of 38 metres (125 feet), giving an overall stopping distance of 53 metres (175 feet). The stopping distance could be greater than this, depending on your attention and response to any hazards. These figures are a general guide.

4.14 In heavy motorway traffic, the vehicle behind you is following too closely. How can you lower the risk of a collision?

☐ Increase your distance from the vehicle in front

☐ Brake sharply

☐ Switch on your hazard warning lights

☐ Move onto the hard shoulder and stop

On busy roads, traffic may still travel at high speeds despite being close together. Don't follow the vehicle in front too closely. If a driver behind seems to be 'pushing' you, gradually increase your distance from the vehicle in front by slowing down gently. This will give you more space in front if you have to brake, and will reduce the risk of a collision involving several vehicles.

4.15 You're following other vehicles in fog. You have your lights on. What else can you do to reduce the chances of being in a collision?

☐ Keep close to the vehicle in front

☐ Use your main beam instead of dipped headlights

☐ Keep up with the faster vehicles

☐ Reduce your speed and increase the gap in front

When it's foggy, use dipped headlights. This will help you see and be seen by other road users. If visibility is seriously reduced, consider using front and rear fog lights if you have them. Keep to a sensible speed and don't follow the vehicle in front too closely. If the road is wet and slippery, you'll need to allow twice the normal stopping distance.

4.16 You're using a contraflow system. What should you do?

☐ Choose an appropriate lane in good time

☐ Switch lanes at any time to make progress

☐ Increase speed to pass through quickly

☐ Follow other motorists closely to avoid long queues

In a contraflow system, you'll be travelling close to oncoming traffic and sometimes in narrow lanes. You should get into the correct lane in good time, obey any temporary speed-limit signs and keep a safe separation distance from the vehicle ahead.

4.17 You're driving on an icy road. How can you avoid wheel spin?

☐ Drive at a slow speed in as high a gear as possible

☐ Use the handbrake if the wheels start to slip

☐ Brake gently and repeatedly

☐ Drive in a low gear at all times

If you're travelling on an icy road, extra caution will be required to avoid loss of control. Keeping your speed down and using the highest gear possible will reduce the risk of the tyres losing their grip on this slippery surface.

4.18 What's the main cause of skidding?

☐ The weather

☐ The driver

☐ The vehicle

☐ The road

Skidding is usually caused by driver error. You should always adjust your driving to take account of the road and weather conditions.

4.19 You're driving in freezing conditions. What should you do when approaching a sharp bend?

☐ Coast into the bend

☐ Gently apply your handbrake

☐ Firmly use your footbrake

☐ Slow down before you reach the bend

Harsh use of the accelerator, brakes or steering is likely to lead to skidding, especially on slippery surfaces. Avoid steering and braking at the same time. In icy conditions it's very important that you constantly assess what's ahead, so that you can take appropriate action in plenty of tIme.

4.20 You're turning left on a slippery road. What should you do if the back of your vehicle slides to the right?

☐ Brake firmly and don't turn the steering wheel

☐ Steer carefully to the left

☐ Steer carefully to the right

☐ Brake firmly and steer to the left

To correct a skid, you need to steer into it. However, be careful not to overcorrect with too much steering, as this may cause a skid in the opposite direction. Skids don't just happen; they're caused – usually by the driver. Factors increasing the likelihood of a skid include the condition of the vehicle (especially its tyres) and the road and weather conditions.

4.21 What should you clear of ice and snow before starting a journey in freezing weather?

☐ The aerial

☐ The windows

☐ The bumper

☐ The boot

Driving in bad weather increases your risk of having a collision. If you absolutely have to travel, clear your lights, mirrors, number plates and windows of any snow or ice, so that you can see and be seen.

4.22 What will help when you're trying to move off on snow?

☐ Use the car's lowest gear

☐ Use a higher gear than normal

☐ Use a high engine speed

☐ Use the handbrake and footbrake together

If you attempt to move off in a low gear, there will be more torque (turning force) at the driven wheels than if you use a higher gear. More torque makes it easier for the tyres to lose grip and so spin the wheels.

4.23 What should you do when you're driving in snowy conditions?

☐ Brake firmly and quickly

☐ Be ready to steer sharply

☐ Use sidelights only

☐ Brake gently in plenty of time

In snowy conditions, be careful with the steering, accelerator and brakes. Braking sharply while you're driving on snow is likely to make your car skid.

4.24 What's the main benefit of driving a four-wheel-drive vehicle?

☐ Improved grip on the road

☐ Lower fuel consumption

☐ Shorter stopping distances

☐ Improved passenger comfort

By driving all four wheels, the vehicle has maximum grip on the road. This grip is especially helpful when travelling on slippery or uneven surfaces. However, having four-wheel drive doesn't replace the skills you need to drive safely.

4.25 You're about to go down a steep hill. What should you do to control the speed of your vehicle?

☐ Select a high gear and use the brakes carefully

☐ Select a high gear and use the brakes firmly

☐ Select a low gear and use the brakes carefully

☐ Select a low gear and avoid using the brakes

When driving down a steep hill, gravity will cause your vehicle to speed up. This will make it more difficult for you to stop. To help keep your vehicle's speed under control, select a lower gear to give you more engine braking and make careful use of the brakes.

4.26 What should you do when parking your vehicle facing downhill?

☐ Turn the steering wheel towards the kerb

☐ Park close to the bumper of another car

☐ Park with two wheels on the kerb

☐ Turn the steering wheel away from the kerb

Turning the wheels towards the kerb will allow them to act as a chock, preventing any forward movement of the vehicle. It will also help to leave your car in gear, or select 'Park' if you have an automatic.

4.27 You're driving in a built-up area that has traffic-calming measures. What should you do when you approach a road hump?

☐ Move across to the left-hand side of the road

☐ Wait for any pedestrians to cross

☐ Check your mirror and slow down

☐ Stop and check both pavements

Many towns have road humps as part of traffic-calming measures, designed to slow down traffic. Reduce your speed when driving over them. If you go too fast, you could lose control or damage your car. Look out for pedestrians or cyclists while you're driving in these areas.

4.28 Anti-lock brakes reduce the chances of skidding. When is this particularly important?

☐ When you're driving down steep hills

☐ When you're braking during normal driving

☐ When you're braking in an emergency

☐ When you're driving on good road surfaces

The anti-lock braking system (ABS) will operate when the brakes have been applied harshly and the wheels are about to lock, such as during an emergency. ABS will reduce the likelihood of your car skidding, but it isn't a substitute for safe and responsible driving.

4.29 On what type of road surface may anti-lock brakes not work effectively?

☐ Dry   ☐ Loose   ☐ Firm   ☐ Smooth

Poor contact with the road surface could cause one or more of the tyres to lose grip on the road. This is more likely to happen when braking in poor weather conditions and when the road has a loose, slippery or uneven surface.

4.30 When are anti-lock brakes of most use to you?

☐ When you're braking gently

☐ When you're braking on rural roads

☐ When you're braking harshly

☐ When you're braking on a motorway

Anti-lock brakes won't be needed when you're braking normally. Looking well down the road and anticipating possible hazards could prevent you from having to brake late and harshly. Knowing that you have anti-lock brakes isn't an excuse to drive in a careless or reckless way.

4.31 What does driving a vehicle with anti-lock brakes allow you to do?

☐ Brake harder because it's impossible to skid

☐ Drive at higher speeds

☐ Steer and brake harshly at the same time

☐ Pay less attention to the road ahead

If the wheels of your vehicle lock, they won't grip the road and you'll lose steering control. In good conditions, the anti-lock braking system (ABS) will prevent the wheels from locking and you'll keep control of your steering. In poor weather conditions or on loose surfaces, the ABS may be less effective.

4.32 You're driving a vehicle that has anti-lock brakes. How should you apply the footbrake when you need to stop in an emergency?

☐ Slowly and gently. ☐ Slowly but firmly

☐ Rapidly and gently. ☐ Rapidly and firmly

You may have to stop in an emergency due to a misjudgement by another driver or a hazard arising suddenly, such as a child running out into the road. If your vehicle has anti-lock brakes, you should apply the brakes immediately and keep them firmly applied until you stop.

4.33 In which conditions are your anti-lock brakes most unlikely to prevent skidding?

☐ In foggy conditions

☐ At night on unlit roads

☐ On loose road surfaces

☐ On dry tarmac

Anti-lock brakes may be ineffective on gravel or loose surfaces. They may also be ineffective in very wet weather, when water can build up between the tyre and the road surface; this is known as aquaplaning.

4.34 You're driving along a country road. You see this sign. What should you do after dealing safely with the hazard?

☐ Check your tyre pressures

☐ Switch on your hazard warning lights

☐ Accelerate briskly

☐ Test your brakes

If your brakes have been thoroughly soaked, you should check that they're working properly before you build up speed again. Before you do this, remember to check your mirrors and consider what's behind you.

4.35 What would suggest you're driving on ice?

☐ There's less wind noise

☐ There's less tyre noise

☐ There's less transmission noise

☐ There's less engine noise

Drive extremely carefully when the roads are icy. When travelling on ice, tyres make virtually no noise and the steering feels light and unresponsive.

In icy conditions, be very gentle when braking, accelerating and steering.

4.36 You're driving along a wet road. How can you tell if your vehicle's tyres are losing their grip on the surface?

☐ The engine will stall

☐ The steering will feel very heavy

☐ The engine noise will increase

☐ The steering will feel very light

If you drive at speed in very wet conditions, your steering may suddenly feel lighter than usual. This means that the tyres have lifted off the surface of the road and are skating on the surface of the water. This is known as aquaplaning. Reduce speed but don't brake until your steering returns to normal.

4.37 In which conditions will your overall stopping distance increase?

☐ In the rain ☐ In fog

☐ At night ☐ In strong winds

Extra care should be taken in wet weather. On wet roads, your stopping distance could be double that in dry conditions.

4.38 You're driving on an open road in dry weather. What should the distance be between you and the vehicle in front?

☐ A two-second time gap

☐ One car length

☐ Two metres (6 feet 6 inches)

☐ Two car lengths

One way of checking there's a safe distance between you and the vehicle in front is to use the two-second rule. To check for a two-second time gap, choose a stationary object ahead, such as a bridge or road sign. When the car in front passes the object, say 'Only a fool breaks the two-second rule'. If you reach the object before you finish saying the phrase, you're too close and need to increase the gap.

4.39 How can you use your vehicle's engine as a brake?

☐ By changing to a lower gear

☐ By selecting reverse gear

☐ By changing to a higher gear

☐ By selecting neutral gear

When driving on downhill stretches of road, selecting a lower gear gives increased engine braking. This will prevent excessive use of the brakes, which become less effective if they overheat.

4.40 When are anti-lock brakes (ABS) most effective?

☐ When you keep pumping the foot brake to prevent skidding

☐ When you brake normally but grip the steering wheel tightly

☐ When you brake promptly and firmly until you've stopped

☐ When you apply the handbrake to reduce the stopping distance

If you have ABS and need to stop in an emergency, keep your foot firmly on the brake pedal until the vehicle has stopped. When the ABS operates, you may hear a grating sound and feel vibration through the brake pedal. This is normal and you should maintain pressure on the brake pedal until the vehicle stops.

4.41 When will anti-lock brakes take effect?

☐ When you don't brake quickly enough

☐ When the wheels are about to lock

☐ When you haven't seen a hazard ahead

☐ When you're speeding on a slippery road surface

If your car is fitted with anti-lock brakes, they'll only activate when they sense that the wheels are about to lock. By preventing the wheels from locking, you'll be able to steer to avoid the hazard, while maximum braking is also applied.

4.42   You're driving on a wet motorway with surface spray. What lights should you use?

☐ Hazard warning lights ☐ Dipped headlights

☐ Rear fog lights   ☐ Sidelights

When surface spray reduces visibility, switch on your dipped headlights. This will help other road users to see you.

4.43   What can result when you travel for long distances in neutral (known as coasting)?

☐ Improvement in control

☐ Easier steering

☐ Reduction in control

☐ Increased fuel consumption

Coasting is the term used when the clutch is held down, or the gear lever is in neutral, and the vehicle is allowed to freewheel. This reduces the driver's control of the vehicle. When you coast, the engine can't drive the wheels to stabilise you through a corner, or give the assistance of engine braking to help slow the car.

4.44   What should you do when driving in fog?

☐ Use sidelights only

☐ Position close to the centre line

☐ Allow more time for your journey

☐ Keep close to the car in front

Don't venture out if your journey isn't necessary. If you have to travel and someone is expecting you at the other end, let them know that you'll be taking longer than usual for your journey. This will stop them worrying if you don't turn up on time and will also take the pressure off you, so you don't feel you have to rush.

Section 5 Hazard Awareness

5.1 Where would you expect to see these markers?

☐ On a motorway sign

☐ On a railway bridge

☐ On a large goods vehicle

☐ On a diversion sign

These markers must be fitted to vehicles over 13 metres long, large goods vehicles, and rubbish skips placed in the road. They're reflective to make them easier to see in the dark.

5.2 What's the main hazard shown in this picture?

☐ Vehicles turning right

☐ Vehicles doing U-turns

☐ The cyclist crossing the road

☐ Parked cars around the corner

Look at the picture carefully and try to imagine you're there. The cyclist in this picture appears to be trying to cross the road. You must be able to deal with the unexpected, especially when you're approaching a hazardous junction. Look well ahead to give yourself time to deal with any hazards.

5.3 Which road user has caused a hazard?

☐ The parked car (arrowed A)

☐ The pedestrian waiting to cross (arrowed B)

☐ The moving car (arrowed C)

☐ The car turning (arrowed D)

The car arrowed A is parked within the area marked by zigzag lines at the pedestrian crossing. Parking here is illegal. It also

• blocks the view for pedestrians wishing to cross the road

• restricts the view of the crossing for approaching traffic."

5.4 What should the driver of the car approaching the crossing do?

☐ Continue at the same speed

☐ Sound the horn

☐ Drive through quickly

☐ Slow down and get ready to stop

Look well ahead to see whether any hazards are developing. This will give you more time to deal with them in the correct way. The man in the picture is clearly intending to cross the road. You should be travelling at a speed that allows you to check your mirror, slow down and stop in good time. You shouldn't have to brake harshly.

5.5   What should the driver of the grey car (arrowed) be especially aware of?

☐ The uneven road surface

☐ Traffic following behind

☐ Doors opening on parked cars

☐ Empty parking spaces

When passing parked cars, there's a risk that a driver or passenger may not check before opening the door into the road. A defensive driver will drive slowly and be looking for people who may be about to get out of their car.

5.6   You see this sign ahead. What should you expect?

☐ The road will go steeply uphill

☐ The road will go steeply downhill

☐ The road will bend sharply to the left

☐ The road will bend sharply to the right

This sign indicates that the road will bend sharply to the left. Slow down in plenty of time and select the correct gear before you start to turn. Braking hard and late, while also sharply changing direction, is likely to cause a skid.

5.7   You're approaching this cyclist. What should you do?

☐ Overtake before the cyclist gets to the junction

☐ Flash your headlights at the cyclist

☐ Slow down and allow the cyclist to turn

☐ Overtake the cyclist on the left-hand side

Keep well back and give the cyclist time and room to turn safely. Don't intimidate them by getting too close or trying to squeeze past.

5.8   Why must you take extra care when turning right at this junction?

☐ The road surface is poor

☐ The footpaths are narrow

☐ The road markings are faint

☐ The view is restricted

You may have to pull forward slowly until you can see up and down the road. Be aware that the traffic approaching the junction can't see you either. If you don't know that it's clear, don't go.

5.9   Which type of vehicle should you be ready to give way to as you approach this bridge?

☐ Bicycles   ☐ Buses

☐ Motorcycles   ☐ Cars

A double-deck bus or high-sided lorry will have to take a position in the centre of the road to clear the bridge. There's normally a sign to show this. Look well ahead, past the bridge and be ready to stop and give way to large oncoming vehicles.

5.10 What type of vehicle could you expect to meet in the middle of the road?

□ Lorry □ Bicycle □ Car □ Motorcycle

The highest point of the bridge is in the centre, so a large vehicle might have to move to the centre of the road to have enough room to pass under the bridge.

5.11 What must you do at this junction?

□ Stop behind the line, then edge forward to see clearly

□ Stop beyond the line, at a point where you can see clearly

□ Stop only if there's traffic on the main road

□ Stop only if you're turning right

The 'stop' sign has been put here because the view into the main road is poor. You must stop because it won't be possible to take proper observation while you're moving.

5.12 A driver pulls out of a side road in front of you, causing you to brake hard. What should you do?

□ Ignore the error and stay calm

□ Flash your lights to show your annoyance

□ Sound your horn to show your annoyance

□ Overtake as soon as possible

Be tolerant if a vehicle emerges and you have to brake quickly. Anyone can make a mistake, so don't react aggressively. Be alert where there are side roads and be especially careful where there are parked vehicles, because these can make it difficult for emerging drivers to see you.

5.13 How would age affect an elderly person's driving ability?

□ They won't be able to obtain car insurance

□ They'll need glasses to read road signs

□ They'll take longer to react to hazards

□ They won't signal at junctions

Be tolerant of older drivers. They may take longer to react to a hazard and they may be hesitant in some situations – for example, at a junction.

5.14 You've just passed these warning lights. What hazard would you expect to see next?

□ A level crossing with no barrier

□ An ambulance station

□ A school crossing patrol

□ An opening bridge

These lights warn that children may be crossing the road to a nearby school. Slow down so that you're ready to stop if necessary.

5.15 You're planning a long journey. Do you need to plan rest stops?

☐ Yes, you should plan to stop every half an hour

☐ Yes, regular stops help concentration

☐ No, you'll be less tired if you get there as soon as possible

☐ No, only fuel stops will be needed

Try to plan your journey so that you can take rest stops. It's recommended that you take a break of at least 15 minutes after every two hours of driving or riding. This should help to maintain your concentration.

5.16 The red lights are flashing. What should you do when approaching this level crossing?

☐ Go through quickly

☐ Go through carefully

☐ Stop before the barrier

☐ Switch on hazard warning lights

At level crossings, the red lights flash before and while the barrier is down. At most crossings, an amber light will precede the red lights. You must stop behind the white line unless you've already crossed it when the amber light comes on. Never zigzag around half-barriers.

5.17 You're approaching a crossroads. The traffic lights have failed. What should you do?

☐ Brake and stop only for large vehicles

☐ Brake sharply to a stop before looking

☐ Be prepared to brake sharply to a stop

☐ Be prepared to stop for any traffic

When approaching a junction where the traffic lights have failed, you should proceed with caution. Treat the situation as an unmarked junction and be prepared to stop.

5.18 What should the driver of the red car (arrowed) do?

☐ Wave towards the pedestrians who are waiting to cross

☐ Wait for the pedestrian in the road to cross

☐ Quickly drive behind the pedestrian in the road

☐ Tell the pedestrian in the road she shouldn't have crossed

Some people might take a long time to cross the road. They may be older or have a disability. Be patient and don't hurry them by showing your impatience. If pedestrians are standing at the side of the road, don't signal or wave them to cross. Other road users might not have seen your signal and this could lead the pedestrians into a hazardous situation.

5.19 You're following a slower-moving vehicle on a narrow country road. There's a junction just ahead on the right. What should you do?

☐ Overtake after checking your mirrors and signalling

☐ Only consider overtaking when you're past the junction

☐ Accelerate quickly to pass before the junction

☐ Slow down and prepare to overtake on the left

You should never overtake as you approach a junction. If a vehicle emerged from the junction while you were overtaking, a dangerous situation could develop very quickly.

5.20 What should you do as you approach this overhead bridge?

□ Move out to the centre of the road before going through

□ Find another route; this one is only for high vehicles

□ Be prepared to give way to large vehicles in the middle of the road

□ Move across to the right-hand side before going through

Oncoming large vehicles may need to move to the middle of the road to pass safely under the bridge. There won't be enough room for you to continue, so you should be ready to stop and wait.

5.21 Why are mirrors often slightly curved (convex)?

□ They give a wider field of vision

□ They totally cover blind spots

□ They make it easier to judge the speed of following traffic

□ They make following traffic look bigger

Although a convex mirror gives a wide view of the scene behind, you should be aware that it won't show you everything behind or to the side of your vehicle. Before you move off, you'll need to look over your shoulder to check for anything not visible in the mirrors.

5.22 A slow-moving lorry showing this sign is travelling in the middle lane of a three-lane motorway. How should you pass it?

□ Cautiously approach the lorry, then pass on either side

□ Don't pass the lorry and leave the motorway at the next exit

□ Use the right-hand lane and pass the lorry normally

□ Approach with care and pass on the left of the lorry

This sign is found on slow-moving or stationary works vehicles. If you wish to overtake, do so on the left, as indicated. Be aware that there might be workmen in the area.

5.23 You think the driver of the vehicle in front has forgotten to cancel their right indicator. What should you do?

□ Flash your lights to alert the driver

□ Sound your horn before overtaking

□ Overtake on the left if there's room

□ Stay behind and don't overtake

Be cautious and don't attempt to overtake. The driver may be unsure of the location of a junction and may turn suddenly.

5.24 What's the main hazard the driver of the red car (arrowed) should be aware of?

□ Glare from the sun may affect the driver's vision

□ The black car may stop suddenly

□ The bus may move out into the road

□ Oncoming vehicles will assume the driver is turning right

If you can do so safely, give way to buses signalling to move off at bus stops. Try to anticipate the actions of other road users around you. The driver of the red car should be prepared for the bus pulling out. As you approach a bus stop, look to see how many passengers are waiting to board. If the last one has just got on, the bus is likely to move off.

5.25 What type of vehicle displays this yellow sign?

□ A broken-down vehicle

□ A school bus

□ An ice-cream van

□ A private ambulance

Buses which carry children to and from school may stop at places other than scheduled bus stops. Be aware that they might pull over at any time to allow children to get on or off. This will normally be when traffic is heavy during rush hour.

5.26 What hazard should you be aware of when travelling along this street?

□ Glare from the sun

□ Lack of road markings

□ Children running out between vehicles

□ Large goods vehicles

On roads where there are many parked vehicles, you might not be able to see children between parked cars and they may run out into the road without looking.

5.27 What's the main hazard you should be aware of when following this cyclist?

□ The cyclist may move to the left and dismount

□ The cyclist may swerve into the road

□ The contents of the cyclist's carrier may fall onto the road

□ The cyclist may wish to turn right at the end of the road

When following a cyclist, be aware that they have to deal with the hazards around them. They may wobble or swerve to avoid a pothole in the road or see a potential hazard and change direction suddenly. Don't follow them too closely or rev your engine impatiently.

5.28 A driver's behaviour has upset you. What can you do to safely get over this incident?

☐ Stop and take a break

☐ Shout abusive language

☐ Gesture to them with your hand

☐ Follow them, flashing your headlights

If you feel yourself becoming tense or upset, stop in a safe place and take a break. Tiredness can make things worse and may cause a different reaction to upsetting situations.

5.29 How should you drive in areas with traffic-calming measures?

☐ At a reduced speed

☐ At the speed limit

☐ In the centre of the road

☐ With headlights on dipped beam

Traffic-calming measures such as road humps, chicanes and narrowings are intended to slow drivers down to protect vulnerable road users. Don't speed up until you reach the end of the traffic-calmed zone.

5.30 When approaching this hazard, why should you slow down?

☐ Because of the level crossing

☐ Because it's hard to see to the right

☐ Because of approaching traffic

☐ Because of animals crossing

You should be slowing down and selecting the correct gear in case you have to stop at the level crossing. Look for the signals and be prepared to stop if necessary.

5.31 Why are place names painted on the road surface?

☐ To restrict the flow of traffic

☐ To warn you of oncoming traffic

☐ To enable you to change lanes early

☐ To prevent you changing lanes

The names of towns and cities may be painted on the road at busy junctions and complex road systems. Their purpose is to let you move into the correct lane in good time, allowing traffic to flow more freely.

5.32 Some two-way roads are divided into three lanes. Why are these particularly dangerous?

☐ Traffic in both directions can use the middle lane to overtake

☐ Traffic can travel faster in poor weather conditions

☐ Traffic can overtake on the left

☐ Traffic uses the middle lane for emergencies only

If you intend to overtake, you must consider that approaching traffic could be planning the same manoeuvre. When you've considered the situation and decided it's safe, indicate your intentions early. This will show the approaching traffic that you intend to pull out.

5.33 You're on a dual carriageway. Ahead, you see a vehicle with an amber flashing light. What could this be?

☐ An ambulance

☐ A fire engine

☐ A doctor on call

☐ A disabled person's vehicle

An amber flashing light on a vehicle indicates that it's slow-moving. Battery-powered vehicles used by disabled people are limited to 8 mph. It isn't advisable for them to be used on dual carriageways where the speed limit exceeds 50 mph. If they are, then an amber flashing light must be used.

5.34 What does this signal from a police officer mean to oncoming traffic?

☐ Go ahead ☐ Stop ☐ Turn left ☐ Turn right

Police officers may need to direct traffic; for example, at a junction where the traffic lights have broken down. Check your copy of The Highway Code for the signals that they use.

5.35 Why should you be cautious when going past this stationary bus?

☐ There is traffic approaching in the distance

☐ The driver may open the door

☐ People may cross the road in front of it

☐ The road surface will be slippery

A stationary bus at a bus stop can hide pedestrians who might try to cross the road just in front of it. Drive at a speed that will enable you to respond safely if you have to.

5.36 Where shouldn't you overtake?

☐ On a single carriageway

☐ On a one-way street

☐ Approaching a junction

☐ Travelling up a long hill

You should overtake only when it's really necessary and you can see it's clear ahead. Look out for road signs and markings that show it's illegal or would be unsafe to overtake; for example, approaching junctions or bends. In many cases, overtaking is unlikely to significantly improve your journey time.

5.37 What's an effect of drinking alcohol?

☐ Poor judgement of speed

☐ A loss of confidence

☐ Faster reactions

☐ Greater awareness of danger

Alcohol will severely reduce your ability to drive or ride safely and there are serious consequences if you're caught over the drink-drive limit. It's known that alcohol can

• affect your judgement

• cause overconfidence

• reduce coordination and control.

5.38 What does the solid white line at the side of the road indicate?

☐ Traffic lights ahead

☐ Edge of the carriageway

☐ Footpath on the left

☐ Cycle path

The continuous white line shows the edge of the carriageway. It can be especially useful when visibility is restricted, such as at night or in bad weather. It's discontinued in some places; for example, at junctions, lay-bys, entrances or other openings.

5.39 You're driving towards this level crossing. What would be the first warning of an approaching train?

☐ Both half-barriers down

☐ A steady amber light

☐ One half-barrier down

☐ Twin flashing red lights

The steady amber light will be followed by twin flashing red lights that mean you must stop. An alarm will also sound to alert you to the fact that a train is approaching.

5.40 You're behind this cyclist. When the traffic lights change, what should you do?

☐ Try to move off before the cyclist

☐ Allow the cyclist time and room

☐ Turn right but give the cyclist room

☐ Tap your horn and drive through first

Hold back and allow the cyclist to move off. Some junctions have special areas marked across the front of the traffic lane. These allow cyclists to wait for the lights to change and move off ahead of other traffic.

5.41 What should the white car do when the traffic lights change to green?

☐ Wait for the cyclist to pull away

☐ Move off quickly and turn in front of the cyclist

☐ Move up close to the cyclist to beat the lights

☐ Sound their horn to warn the cyclist

If you're waiting at traffic lights, check all around you before you move away, as cyclists often filter through waiting traffic. Allow the cyclist to move off safely.

5.42 You intend to turn left at the traffic lights. What should you do just before turning?

☐ Check your right mirror

☐ Move up close to the white car

☐ Straddle the lanes

☐ Check for bicycles on your left

Check your nearside for cyclists before moving away. This is especially important if you've been in a queue of traffic and are about to move off, as cyclists often filter past on the nearside of stationary vehicles.

5.43 Why should you reduce your speed when driving along this road?

☐ A staggered junction is ahead

☐ A low bridge is ahead

☐ The road surface changes ahead

☐ The road narrows ahead

Traffic could be turning off or pulling out ahead of you, to the left or right. Vehicles turning left will be slowing down before the junction, and any vehicles turning right may have to stop to allow oncoming traffic to clear. Be prepared for this, as you might have to slow down or stop behind them.

5.44 What might you expect to happen in this situation?

☐ Traffic will move into the right-hand lane

☐ Traffic speed will increase

☐ Traffic will move into the left-hand lane

☐ Traffic won't need to change position

Be courteous and allow the traffic to merge into the left-hand lane.

5.45 You're driving on a road with several lanes. You see these signs above the lanes. What do they mean?

☐ The two right lanes are open

☐ The two left lanes are open

☐ Traffic in the left lanes should stop

☐ Traffic in the right lanes should stop

If you see a red cross above your lane, it means that there's an obstruction ahead. You'll have to move into one of the lanes that's showing a green light. If all the lanes are showing a red cross, then you must stop.

5.46 You're invited to a pub lunch. You know that you'll have to drive in the evening. What's your best course of action?

☐ Avoid mixing your alcoholic drinks

☐ Don't drink any alcohol at all

☐ Have some milk before drinking alcohol

☐ Eat a hot meal with your alcoholic drinks

Alcohol will stay in your body for several hours and may make you unfit to drive later in the day. Drinking during the day will also affect your performance at work or study.

5.47 You've been convicted of driving while unfit through drink or drugs. You'll find this is likely to cause the cost of one of the following to rise considerably. Which one?

☐ Road fund licence

☐ Insurance premiums

☐ Vehicle test certificate

☐ Driving licence

You've shown that you're a risk to yourself and others on the road. For this reason, insurance companies may charge you a higher premium.

5.48 What advice should you give to a driver who has had a few alcoholic drinks at a party?

☐ Have a strong cup of coffee and then drive home

☐ Drive home carefully and slowly

☐ Go home by public transport

☐ Wait a short while and then drive home

Drinking black coffee or waiting a few hours won't make any difference. Alcohol takes time to leave the body.

A driver who has been drinking should go home by public transport or taxi. They might even be unfit to drive the following morning."

5.49 You've been taking medicine that causes drowsiness. You begin to feel better, but you still need to take the medicine. What should you do about driving?

☐ Only drive if your journey is necessary

☐ Drive on quiet roads

☐ Ask someone to come with you

☐ Avoid driving and check with your doctor

You aren't fit to drive if you're taking medicine that makes you drowsy. Check with your doctor if you're unsure. You must not put other road users, your passengers or yourself at risk.

5.50 You're about to drive home from holiday when you become ill. A doctor prescribes drugs that are likely to affect your driving. What should you do?

☐ Only drive if someone is with you

☐ Avoid driving on motorways

☐ Get someone else to drive

☐ Never drive at more than 30 mph

You shouldn't drive if you're taking medicine that could cause you to feel drowsy at the wheel. Ask someone else to drive or, if that isn't possible, find another way to get home.

5.51 During periods of illness, your ability to drive may be impaired. What must you do?

☐ See your doctor each time before you drive

☐ Take smaller doses of any medicines

☐ Make sure you're medically fit to drive

☐ Take all your medicines with you when you drive

Only drive if you're fit to do so. Driving when you're ill or taking some medicines can affect your concentration and judgement. It may also cause you to become drowsy or even fall asleep.

5.52 What should you do if you begin to feel drowsy while you're driving?

☐ Stop and rest as soon as possible

☐ Turn the heater up to keep you warm and comfortable

☐ Close the car windows to help you concentrate

☐ Continue with your journey but drive more slowly

You'll be putting other road users at risk if you continue to drive when you're drowsy. Pull over and stop in a safe place for a rest. Caffeinated drinks and a short nap can temporarily help counter sleepiness. If you're driving a long distance, think about finding some accommodation so you can rest for longer before continuing your journey.

5.53   What should you do if you become tired while you're driving on a motorway?

☐ Pull up on the hard shoulder and change drivers

☐ Leave the motorway at the next exit and rest

☐ Increase your speed and turn up the radio volume

☐ Close all your windows and set the heating to warm

If you feel yourself becoming tired or sleepy, you should leave the motorway at the next exit or services and stop for a rest. If you have to drive a long way, leave earlier and plan your journey to include rest stops. That way, you're less likely to become tired while driving and you'll still arrive in good time.

5.54   You're about to drive home. You feel very tired and have a severe headache. What should you do?

☐ Wait until you're fit and well before driving

☐ Drive home, but take a tablet for headaches

☐ Drive home if you can stay awake for the journey

☐ Wait for a short time, then drive home slowly

All of your concentration should be on your driving. Any pain you feel will distract you, and you should avoid driving when drowsy. The safest course of action is to wait until you've rested and are feeling better before starting your journey.

5.55   You're driving on a long journey. What can you do to help prevent tiredness?

☐ Eat a large meal before driving

☐ Take regular refreshment breaks

☐ Play loud music in the car

☐ Complete the journey without stopping

Long-distance driving can be boring. This, coupled with a stuffy, warm vehicle, can make you feel tired and sleepy. Make sure you take rest breaks to help you stay awake and alert. Stop in a safe place before you get to the stage of fighting sleep.

5.56   You take some cough medicine given to you by a friend. What should you do before driving?

☐ Ask your friend if taking the medicine affected their driving

☐ Drink some strong coffee one hour before driving

☐ Check the label to see if the medicine will affect your driving

☐ Drive a short distance to see if the medicine is affecting your driving

If you've taken medicine, never drive without first checking what the side effects might be; they might affect your judgement and perception, and therefore endanger lives.

5.57   You take the wrong route and find you're on a one-way street. What should you do?

☐ Reverse out of the road

☐ Turn around in a side road

☐ Continue to the end of the road

☐ Reverse into a driveway

Never reverse or turn your vehicle around in a one-way street. It's illegal and could even cause a collision. If you've taken a wrong turn, carry on along the one-way street and find another route, checking the direction signs as you drive. Stop in a safe place if you need to check a map.

5.58   What will be a serious distraction from driving?

□ Looking at road maps

□ Switching on your demister

□ Using your windscreen washers

□ Looking in your door mirror

Looking at road maps while driving is very dangerous. If you aren't sure of your route, stop in a safe place and check the map. You must not allow anything to take your attention away from the road while you're driving.

5.59   You're driving along this road. The driver on the left is reversing from a driveway. What should you do?

□ Move to the opposite side of the road

□ Drive through as you have priority

□ Sound your horn and be prepared to stop

□ Speed up and drive through quickly

White lights at the rear of a car show that the driver has selected reverse gear. Sound your horn to warn the other driver of your presence, and reduce your speed as a precaution.

5.60   You've been involved in an argument that has made you feel angry. What should you do before starting your journey?

□ Open a window

□ Turn on your radio

□ Have an alcoholic drink

□ Calm down

If you're feeling upset or angry, you'll find it much more difficult to concentrate on your driving. You should wait until you've calmed down before starting a journey.

5.61   You're driving on this dual carriageway. Why may you need to slow down?

□ There's a broken white line in the centre

□ There are solid white lines on either side

□ There are roadworks ahead of you

□ There are no footpaths

Look well ahead and read any road signs as you drive. They're there to inform you of what's ahead. In this case, you may need to slow down and change direction.

Check your mirrors so you know what's happening around you before you change speed or direction.

5.62   You've just been overtaken by this motorcyclist, who has cut in sharply. What should you do?

□ Sound the horn

□ Brake firmly

□ Keep a safe gap

□ Flash your lights

If another vehicle cuts in sharply, ease off the accelerator and drop back to allow a safe separation distance. Try not to overreact by braking sharply or swerving, as you could lose control. If vehicles behind you are too close or unprepared, it could lead to a crash.

5.63 You're about to drive home. You can't find the glasses you need to wear. What should you do?

□ Drive home slowly, keeping to quiet roads

□ Borrow a friend's glasses and use those

□ Drive home at night, so that the lights will help you

□ Find a way of getting home without driving

If you need to wear glasses for driving, it's illegal to drive without them. You must be able to see clearly when you're driving.

5.64 What's a common effect of drinking alcohol?

□ Colour blindness

□ Increased confidence

□ Faster reactions

□ Increased concentration

Alcohol can increase confidence to a point where a driver's behaviour might become 'out of character'. Someone who normally behaves sensibly might suddenly enjoy taking risks. Never let yourself or your friends get into this situation.

5.65 Your doctor has given you a course of medicine. Why should you ask how it will affect you?

□ Drugs make you a better driver by quickening your reactions

□ You'll have to let your insurance company know about the medicine

□ Some types of medicine can cause your reactions to slow down

□ The medicine you take may affect your hearing

Always check the label or information leaflet for any medication you take. The medicine might affect your driving. If you aren't sure, ask your doctor or pharmacist.

5.66 You find that you need glasses to read vehicle number plates at the required distance. When must you wear them?

□ Only in bad weather conditions

□ At all times when driving

□ Only when you think it's necessary

□ Only in bad light or at night time

Have your eyesight tested before you start your practical training. Then, throughout your driving life, have checks periodically, as your vision may change.

5.67 Which of the following types of glasses shouldn't be worn when driving at night?

□ Half-moon □ Round □ Bifocal □ Tinted

If you're driving at night or in poor visibility, tinted lenses will reduce the efficiency of your vision by reducing the amount of light reaching your eyes.

5.68 What can seriously affect your ability to concentrate?

□ Drugs   □ Busy roads

□ Tinted windows □ Contact lenses

Both recreational drugs and prescribed medicine can affect your concentration. It's also now an offence to drive with certain drugs in your body and a positive test could lead to a conviction.

5.69 You find that your eyesight has become very poor and your optician cannot help you. By law, who should you tell?

□ The driver licensing authority

□ Your own doctor

□ The local police

□ Another optician

Having very poor eyesight will have a serious effect on your ability to drive safely. If you can't meet the driver's eyesight requirements, you must tell DVLA (or DVA in Northern Ireland).

5.70 When should you use hazard warning lights?

☐ When you're double-parked on a two-way road

☐ When your direction indicators aren't working

☐ When warning oncoming traffic that you intend to stop

☐ When your vehicle has broken down and is causing an obstruction

Hazard warning lights are an important safety feature and should be used if you've broken down and are causing an obstruction. Don't use them as an excuse to park illegally. You may also use them on motorways to warn traffic behind you of danger ahead.

5.71 You want to turn left at this junction. Your view of the main road is restricted. What should you do?

☐ Stay well back and wait to see if anything comes

☐ Build up your speed so that you can emerge quickly

☐ Stop and apply the handbrake even if the road is clear

☐ Approach slowly and edge out until you can see more clearly

You should slow right down, and stop if necessary, at any junction where your view is restricted. Edge forward until you can see properly. Only then can you decide whether it's safe to go.

5.72 When driving a car fitted with automatic transmission, what would you use 'kick down' for?

☐ Cruise control   ☐ Quick acceleration

☐ Slow braking   ☐ Fuel economy

'Kick down' selects a lower gear, enabling the vehicle to accelerate faster.

5.73 You're driving along this motorway. It's raining. What should you do when following this lorry?

☐ Allow at least a two-second gap

☐ Move left and drive on the hard shoulder

☐ Move right and stay in the right-hand lane

☐ Be aware of spray reducing your vision

The usual two-second time gap increases to four seconds when the roads are wet. If you stay well back, you'll

• be able to see past the vehicle

• be out of the spray thrown up by the lorry's tyres

• give yourself more time to stop if the need arises

• increase your chances of being seen by the lorry driver.

5.74 You're driving towards this left-hand bend. What dangers should you be aware of?

□ A vehicle overtaking you

□ No white lines in the centre of the road

□ No sign to warn you of the bend

□ Pedestrians walking towards you

Pedestrians walking on a road with no pavement should walk against the direction of the traffic. You can't see around this bend: there may be hidden dangers. Always keep this in mind and give yourself time to react if a hazard does appear.

5.75 Ahead of you, traffic in the left-hand lane is slowing. What should you do?

□ Slow down, keeping a safe separation distance

□ Accelerate past the vehicles in the left-hand lane

□ Pull up on the left-hand verge

□ Move across and continue in the right-hand lane

Allow the traffic to merge into the left-hand lane. Leave enough room so that you can maintain a safe separation distance, even if vehicles pull in ahead of you.

5.76 In which circumstances may you use hazard warning lights?

□ When driving on a motorway to warn traffic behind of a hazard ahead

□ When you're double-parked on a two-way road

□ When your direction indicators aren't working

□ When warning oncoming traffic that you intend to stop

Hazard warning lights are an important safety feature. Use them when driving on a motorway to warn traffic behind you of danger ahead.

You should also use them if your vehicle has broken down and is causing an obstruction.

5.77 You're waiting to emerge at a junction. Your view is restricted by parked vehicles. What can help you to see traffic on the road you're joining?

□ Looking for traffic behind you

□ Reflections of traffic in shop windows

□ Making eye contact with other road users

□ Checking for traffic in your interior mirror

You must be completely sure it's safe to emerge. Try to look for traffic through the windows of the parked cars or in the reflections in shop windows. Keep looking in all directions as you slowly edge forwards until you can see it's safe.

5.78 After passing your driving test, you suffer from ill health. This affects your driving. What must you do?

□ Inform your local police

□ Avoid using motorways

□ Always drive accompanied

□ Inform the licensing authority

You must tell DVLA (or DVA in Northern Ireland) if your health is likely to affect your ability to drive. The licensing authority will investigate your situation and then make a decision on whether or not to take away your licence.

5.79   Why should the junction on the left be kept clear?

☐ To allow vehicles to enter and emerge

☐ To allow the bus to reverse

☐ To allow vehicles to make a U-turn

☐ To allow vehicles to park

You should always try to keep junctions clear. If you're in queuing traffic, make sure that when you stop you leave enough space for traffic to flow into and out of the junction.

5.80   Your motorway journey is boring and you feel drowsy. What should you do?

☐ Stop on the hard shoulder for a sleep

☐ Open a window and stop as soon as it's safe and legal

☐ Speed up to arrive at your destination sooner

☐ Slow down and let other drivers overtake

Never stop on the hard shoulder to rest. If there's no service area for several miles, leave the motorway at the next exit and find somewhere safe and legal to pull over.

Section 6 Vulnerable Road Users

6.1   Which sign means that there may be people walking along the road?

Always check the road signs. Triangular signs are warning signs: they inform you about hazards ahead and help you to anticipate any problems. There are a number of different signs showing pedestrians. Learn the meaning of each one.

6.2   You're turning left at a junction where pedestrians have started to cross. What should you do?

☐ Go around them, leaving plenty of room

☐ Stop and wave at them to cross

☐ Sound your horn and proceed

☐ Give way to them

When you're turning into a side road, pedestrians who are crossing have priority. You should wait to allow them to finish crossing safely. Be patient if they're slow or unsteady. Don't try to rush them by sounding your horn, flashing your lights, revving your engine or giving any other inappropriate signal.

6.3   You're turning left into a side road. What hazard should you be especially aware of?

☐ One-way street   ☐ Pedestrians

☐ Traffic congestion ☐ Parked vehicles

Make sure that you've reduced your speed and are in the correct gear for the turn. Look into the road before you turn and always give way to any pedestrians who are crossing.

6.4   You intend to turn right into a side road. Why should you check for motorcyclists just before turning?

☐ They may be overtaking on your left

☐ They may be following you closely

☐ They may be emerging from the side road

☐ They may be overtaking on your right

Never attempt to change direction to the right without first checking your right-hand mirror and blind spot. A motorcyclist might not have seen your signal and could be hidden by other traffic. This observation should become a matter of routine.

6.5   Why is a toucan crossing different from other crossings?

☐ Moped riders can use it

☐ It's controlled by a traffic warden

☐ It's controlled by two flashing lights

☐ Cyclists can use it

Toucan crossings are shared by pedestrians and cyclists, who are permitted to cycle across. They're shown the green light together. The signals are push-button-operated and there's no flashing amber phase.

6.6 How will a school crossing patrol signal you to stop?

☐ By pointing to children on the opposite pavement

☐ By displaying a red light

☐ By displaying a 'stop' sign

☐ By giving you an arm signal

If a school crossing patrol steps out into the road with a 'stop' sign, you must stop. Don't wave anyone across the road and don't get impatient or rev your engine.

6.7 Where would you see this sign?

☐ In the window of a car taking children to school

☐ At the side of the road

☐ At playground areas

☐ On the rear of a school bus or coach

Vehicles that are used to carry children to and from school will be travelling at busy times of the day. If you're following a vehicle with this sign, be prepared for it to make frequent stops. It might pick up or set down passengers in places other than normal bus stops.

6.8 What does this sign mean?

☐ No route for pedestrians and cyclists

☐ A route for pedestrians only

☐ A route for cyclists only

☐ A route for pedestrians and cyclists

This sign shows a shared route for pedestrians and cyclists: when it ends, the cyclists will be rejoining the main road.

6.9 You see a pedestrian carrying a white stick with a red band. What does this tell you?

☐ They have limited mobility

☐ They're deaf

☐ They're blind

☐ They're deaf and blind

When someone is deaf as well as blind, they may carry a white stick with a red reflective band. They may not be aware that you're approaching and they may not be able to hear anything; so, for example, your horn would be ineffective as a warning to them.

6.10 What action would you take when elderly people are crossing the road?

☐ Wave them across so they know that you've seen them

☐ Be patient and allow them to cross in their own time

☐ Rev the engine to let them know that you're waiting

☐ Tap the horn in case they're hard of hearing

Be aware that older people might take a long time to cross the road. They might also be hard of hearing and not hear you approaching. Don't hurry older people across the road by getting too close to them or revving your engine.

6.11   What should you do when you see two elderly pedestrians about to cross the road ahead?

☐ Expect them to wait for you to pass

☐ Speed up to get past them quickly

☐ Stop and wave them across the road

☐ Be careful; they may misjudge your speed

Older people may have impaired hearing, vision, concentration and judgement. They may also walk slowly and so could take a long time to cross the road.

6.12   You're coming up to a roundabout. A cyclist is signalling to turn right. What should you do?

☐ Overtake on the right

☐ Give a warning with your horn

☐ Signal the cyclist to move across

☐ Give the cyclist plenty of room

If you're following a cyclist who's signalling to turn right at a roundabout, leave plenty of room. Give them space and time to get into the correct lane.

6.13   Which of these should you allow extra room when overtaking?

☐ Lorry   ☐ Tractor

☐ Bicycle   ☐ Road-sweeping vehicle

Don't pass cyclists too closely, as they may

• need to veer around a pothole or other obstacle

• be buffeted by side wind

• be made unsteady by your vehicle.

Always leave as much room as you would for a car, and don't cut in front of them.

6.14   Why should you look particularly for motorcyclists and cyclists at junctions?

☐ They may want to turn into the side road

☐ They may slow down to let you turn

☐ They're harder to see

☐ They might not see you turn

Cyclists and motorcyclists are smaller than other vehicles and so are more difficult to see. They can easily be hidden from your view by cars parked near a junction.

6.15   You're waiting to come out of a side road. Why should you look carefully for motorcycles?

☐ Motorcycles are usually faster than cars

☐ Police patrols often use motorcycles

☐ Motorcycles can easily be hidden behind obstructions

☐ Motorcycles have right of way

If you're waiting to emerge from a side road, look carefully for motorcycles: they can be difficult to see. Be especially careful if there are parked vehicles or other obstructions restricting your view.

6.16   In daylight, an approaching motorcyclist is using dipped headlights. Why?

☐ So that the rider can be seen more easily

☐ To stop the battery overcharging

☐ To improve the rider's vision

☐ The rider is inviting you to proceed

A motorcycle can be lost from sight behind another vehicle. The use of the headlights helps to make it more conspicuous and therefore more easily seen.

6.17 Why should motorcyclists wear bright clothing?

☐ They must do so by law

☐ It helps keep them cool in summer

☐ The colours are popular

☐ Drivers often do not see them

Motorcycles and scooters are generally smaller than other vehicles and can be difficult to see. Wearing bright clothing makes it easier for other road users to see a motorcyclist approaching, especially at junctions.

6.18 You're unsure what a slow-moving motorcyclist ahead of you is going to do. What should you do?

☐ Pass on the left ☐ Pass on the right

☐ Stay behind   ☐ Move closer

When a motorcyclist is travelling slowly, it's likely that they're looking for a turning or entrance. Be patient and stay behind them in case they stop or change direction suddenly.

6.19 Why will a motorcyclist look round over their right shoulder just before turning right?

☐ To listen for following traffic

☐ Motorcycles don't have mirrors

☐ It helps them balance as they turn

☐ To check for traffic in their blind area

When you see a motorcyclist take a glance over their shoulder, they're probably about to change direction. Recognising a clue like this helps you to anticipate their next action. This can improve road safety for you and others.

6.20 Which is the most vulnerable road user at road junctions?

☐ Car driver   ☐ Tractor driver

☐ Lorry driver   ☐ Motorcyclist

Pedestrians and riders on two wheels can be harder to see than other road users. Make sure you look for them, especially at junctions. Effective observation, coupled with appropriate action, can save lives.

6.21 You're approaching a roundabout. There are horses just ahead of you. What should you do?

☐ Sound your horn as a warning

☐ Treat them like any other vehicle

☐ Give them plenty of room

☐ Accelerate past as quickly as possible

Horse riders often keep to the outside of the roundabout even if they're turning right. Give them plenty of room and remember that they may have to cross lanes of traffic.

6.22 As you approach a pelican crossing, the lights change to green. What should you do if elderly people are halfway across?

☐ Wave them to cross as quickly as they can

☐ Rev your engine to make them hurry

☐ Flash your lights in case they haven't noticed you

☐ Wait patiently because they'll probably take longer to cross

If the lights turn to green, wait for any pedestrians to clear the crossing. Allow them to finish crossing the road in their own time, and don't try to hurry them by revving your engine.

6.23 There are flashing amber lights under a school warning sign. What action should you take?

☐ Reduce speed until you're clear of the area

☐ Keep up your speed and sound the horn

☐ Increase your speed to clear the area quickly

☐ Wait at the lights until they change to green

The flashing amber lights are switched on to warn you that children may be crossing near a school. Slow down and take extra care, as you may have to stop.

6.24 Why must these road markings be kept clear?

☐ To allow schoolchildren to be dropped off

☐ To allow teachers to park

☐ To allow schoolchildren to be picked up

☐ To allow a clear view of the crossing area

The markings are there to show that the area must be kept clear. This is to allow an unrestricted view for

• approaching drivers and riders

• children wanting to cross the road.

6.25 Where would you see this sign?

☐ Near a school crossing

☐ At a playground entrance

☐ On a school bus

☐ At a 'pedestrians only' area

Watch out for children crossing the road from the other side of the bus.

6.26 You're following two cyclists. They approach a roundabout in the left-hand lane. In which direction should you expect the cyclists to go?

☐ Left

☐ Right

☐ Any direction

☐ Straight ahead

Cyclists approaching a roundabout in the left-hand lane may be turning right but may not have been able to get into the correct lane due to heavy traffic. They may also feel safer keeping to the left all the way around the roundabout. Be aware of them and give them plenty of room.

6.27 You're travelling behind a moped. What should you do when you want to turn left just ahead?

☐ Overtake the moped before the junction

☐ Pull alongside the moped and stay level until just before the junction

☐ Sound your horn as a warning and pull in front of the moped

☐ Stay behind until the moped has passed the junction

Passing the moped and turning into the junction could mean that you cut across the front of the rider. This might force them to slow down, stop or even lose control. Stay behind the moped until it has passed the junction and then you can turn without affecting the rider.

6.28 You see a horse rider as you approach a roundabout. What should you do if they're signalling right but keeping well to the left?

☐ Proceed as normal

☐ Keep close to them

☐ Cut in front of them

☐ Stay well back

Allow the horse rider to enter and exit the roundabout in their own time. They may feel safer keeping to the left all the way around the roundabout. Don't get up close behind or alongside them, because that would probably upset the horse and create a dangerous situation.

6.29 How would you react to drivers who appear to be inexperienced?

☐ Sound your horn to warn them of your presence

☐ Be patient and prepare for them to react more slowly

☐ Flash your headlights to indicate that it's safe for them to proceed

☐ Overtake them as soon as possible

Learners might not have confidence when they first start to drive. Allow them plenty of room and don't react adversely to their hesitation. We all learn from experience, but new drivers will have had less practice in dealing with all the situations that might occur.

6.30 What should you do when you're following a learner driver who stalls at a junction?

☐ Be patient, as you expect them to make mistakes

☐ Stay very close behind and flash your headlights

☐ Start to rev your engine if they take too long to restart

☐ Immediately steer around them and drive on

Learning to drive is a process of practice and experience. Try to understand this and tolerate those who make mistakes while they're learning.

6.31 You're on a country road. What should you expect to see coming towards you on your side of the road?

☐ Motorcycles

☐ Bicycles

☐ Pedestrians

☐ Horse riders

On a quiet country road, always be aware that there may be a hazard just around the next bend, such as a slow-moving vehicle or pedestrians. Pedestrians are advised to walk on the right-hand side of the road if there's no pavement, so they may be walking towards you on your side of the road.

6.32 What should you do when following a car driven by an elderly driver?

☐ Expect the driver to drive badly

☐ Flash your lights and overtake

☐ Be aware that their reactions may be slower than yours

☐ Stay very close behind but be careful

You must show consideration to other road users. The reactions of older drivers may be slower and they might need more time to deal with a situation. Be tolerant and don't lose patience or show annoyance.

6.33 You're following a cyclist. What should you do when you wish to turn left just ahead?

☐ Overtake the cyclist before you reach the junction

☐ Pull alongside the cyclist and stay level until after the junction

☐ Hold back until the cyclist has passed the junction

☐ Go around the cyclist on the junction

Make allowances for cyclists, and give them plenty of room. Don't overtake and then immediately turn left. Be patient and turn behind them when they've passed the junction.

6.34 A horse rider is in the left-hand lane approaching a roundabout. Where should you expect the rider to go?

☐ In any direction ☐ To the right

☐ To the left ☐ Straight ahead

Horses and their riders move more slowly than other road users. They might not have time to cut across heavy traffic to take up a position in the right-hand lane. For this reason, a horse and rider may approach a roundabout in the left-hand lane even though they're turning right.

6.35 Powered vehicles used by disabled people are small and hard to see. How do they give early warning when on a dual carriageway?

☐ They'll have a flashing red light

☐ They'll have a flashing green light

☐ They'll have a flashing blue light

☐ They'll have a flashing amber light

Powered vehicles used by disabled people are small, low, hard to see and travel very slowly. On a dual carriageway, a flashing amber light will warn other road users.

6.36 Where should you never overtake a cyclist?

☐ Just before you turn left

☐ On a left-hand bend

☐ On a one-way street

☐ On a dual carriageway

If you want to turn left and there's a cyclist in front of you, hold back. Wait until the cyclist has passed the junction and then turn left behind them. Don't try to intimidate them by driving too closely.

6.37 What does a flashing amber beacon mean when it's on a moving vehicle?

☐ The vehicle is slow moving

☐ The vehicle has broken down

☐ The vehicle is a doctor's car

☐ The vehicle belongs to a school crossing patrol

Different coloured beacons warn of different types of vehicle needing special attention. Blue beacons are used on emergency vehicles that need priority. Green beacons are found on doctors' cars. Amber beacons generally denote slower moving vehicles, which are often large. These vehicles are usually involved in road maintenance or local amenities and make frequent stops.

6.38 What does this sign mean?

☐ Contraflow cycle lane

☐ With-flow cycle lane

☐ Cycles and buses only

☐ No cycles or buses

Usually, a picture of a cycle will also be painted on the road, and sometimes the lane will have a different coloured surface. Leave these areas clear for cyclists and don't pass too closely when you overtake.

6.39 You notice horse riders in front. What should you do first?

☐ Pull out to the middle of the road

☐ Slow down and be ready to stop

☐ Accelerate around them

☐ Signal right

Be particularly careful when approaching horse riders – slow down and be prepared to stop. Always pass wide and slowly, and look out for signals given by the riders. Horses are unpredictable: always treat them as potential hazards and take great care when passing them.

6.40 What's the purpose of these road markings?

☐ To ensure children can see and be seen when crossing the road

☐ To enable teachers to have clear access to the school

☐ To ensure delivery vehicles have easy access to the school

☐ To enable parents to pick up or drop off children safely

These markings are found on the road outside schools. Don't stop or park on them, even to set down or pick up children. The markings are there to ensure that drivers, riders, children and other pedestrians have a clear view of the road in all directions.

6.41 The left-hand pavement is closed due to street repairs. What should you do?

☐ Watch out for pedestrians walking in the road

☐ Use your right-hand mirror more often

☐ Speed up to get past the roadworks more quickly

☐ Position close to the left-hand kerb

Where street repairs have closed off pavements, proceed carefully and slowly, as pedestrians might have to walk in the road.

6.42 What should you do when you're following a motorcyclist along a road that has a poor surface?

☐ Follow closely so they can see you in their mirrors

☐ Overtake immediately to avoid delays

☐ Allow extra room in case they swerve to avoid potholes

☐ Allow the same room as normal to avoid wasting road space

To avoid being unbalanced, a motorcyclist might swerve to avoid potholes and bumps in the road. Be prepared for this and allow them extra space.

6.43 What does this sign tell you?

☐ No cycling. ☐ Cycle route ahead

☐ Cycle parking only ☐ End of cycle route

With people's concern today for the environment, cycle routes are being extended in our towns and cities.

Respect the presence of cyclists on the road and give them plenty of room if you need to pass.

6.44 You're approaching this roundabout and see the cyclist signal right. Why is the cyclist keeping to the left?

❏ It's a quicker route for the cyclist

❏ The cyclist is going to turn left instead

❏ The cyclist thinks The Highway Code doesn't apply to bicycles

❏ The cyclist is slower and more vulnerable

Cycling in today's heavy traffic can be hazardous. Some cyclists may not feel happy about crossing the path of traffic to take up a position in an outside lane. Be aware of this and understand that, although they're in the left-hand lane, the cyclist might be turning right.

6.45 What should you do when approaching this crossing?

❏ Prepare to slow down and stop

❏ Stop and wave the pedestrians across

❏ Speed up and pass by quickly

❏ Continue unless the pedestrians step out

Be courteous and prepare to stop. Don't wave people across, because this could be dangerous if another vehicle is approaching the crossing.

6.46 You see a pedestrian with a dog wearing a yellow or burgundy coat. What does this indicate?

❏ The pedestrian is elderly

❏ The pedestrian is a dog trainer

❏ The pedestrian is colour-blind

❏ The pedestrian is deaf

Dogs trained to help deaf people have a yellow or burgundy coat. If you see one, you should take extra care, as the pedestrian may not be aware of vehicles approaching.

6.47 Who may use toucan crossings?

❏ Motorcyclists and cyclists

❏ Motorcyclists and pedestrians

❏ Only cyclists

❏ Cyclists and pedestrians

There are some crossings where cycle routes lead cyclists to cross at the same place as pedestrians. These are called toucan crossings. Always look out for cyclists, as they're likely to be approaching faster than pedestrians.

6.48 Some junctions controlled by traffic lights have a marked area between two stop lines. What's this for?

❏ To allow taxis to position in front of other traffic

❏ To allow people with disabilities to cross the road

❏ To allow cyclists and pedestrians to cross the road together

❏ To allow cyclists to position in front of other traffic

These are known as advanced stop lines. When the lights are red (or about to become red), you should stop at the first white line. However, if you've crossed that line as the lights change, you must stop at the second line even if it means you're in the area reserved for cyclists.

6.49 When you're overtaking a cyclist, you should leave as much room as you would give to a car. What's the main reason for this?

☐ The cyclist might speed up

☐ The cyclist might get off their bike

☐ The cyclist might swerve

☐ The cyclist might have to make a left turn

Before overtaking, assess the situation. Look well ahead to see whether the cyclist will need to change direction. Be especially aware of a cyclist approaching parked vehicles, as they'll need to alter course. Don't pass too closely or cut in sharply.

6.50 What should you do when passing sheep on a road?

☐ Briefly sound your horn

☐ Go very slowly

☐ Pass quickly but quietly

☐ Herd them to the side of the road

Slow down and be ready to stop if you see animals in the road ahead. Animals are easily frightened by noise and vehicles passing too close to them. Stop if signalled to do so by the person in charge.

6.51 At night, you see a pedestrian wearing reflective clothing and carrying a bright red light. What does this mean?

☐ You're approaching roadworks

☐ You're approaching an organised walk

☐ You're approaching a slow-moving vehicle

☐ You're approaching a traffic danger spot

The people on the walk should be keeping to the left, but don't assume this. Pass carefully, making sure you have time to do so safely. Be aware that the pedestrians have their backs to you and may not know that you're there.

6.52 You've just passed your test. How can you reduce your risk of being involved in a collision?

☐ By always staying close to the vehicle in front

☐ By never going over 40 mph

☐ By staying in the left-hand lane on all roads

☐ By taking further training

New drivers and riders are often involved in a collision or incident early in their driving career. Due to a lack of experience, they may not react to hazards appropriately. Approved training courses are offered by driver and rider training schools for people who have passed their test but want extra training.

6.53 You want to reverse into a side road, but you aren't sure that the area behind your car is clear. What should you do?

☐ Look through the rear window only

☐ Get out and check

☐ Check the mirrors only

☐ Carry on, assuming it's clear

If you can't tell whether there's anything behind you, it's always safest to check before reversing. There may be a small child or a low obstruction close behind your car.

6.54 You're about to reverse into a side road. A pedestrian is waiting to cross behind you. What should you do?

☐ Wave to the pedestrian to stop

☐ Give way to the pedestrian

☐ Sound your horn to warn the pedestrian

☐ Reverse before the pedestrian starts to cross

If you need to reverse into a side road, try to find a place that's free from traffic and pedestrians. Look all around before and during the manoeuvre. Stop and give way to any pedestrians who want to cross behind you. Avoid waving them across, sounding the horn, flashing your lights or giving any signals that could mislead them and create a dangerous situation.

6.55 Who's especially in danger of not being seen as you reverse your car?

☐ Motorcyclists   ☐ Car drivers

☐ Cyclists   ☐ Children

It may not be possible to see a small child through the rear windscreen of your vehicle. Be aware of this before you reverse. If there are children about, get out and check that it's clear before reversing.

6.56 You want to turn right from a junction but your view is restricted by parked vehicles. What should you do?

☐ Move out quickly, but be prepared to stop

☐ Sound your horn and pull out if there's no reply

☐ Stop, then move forward slowly until you have a clear view

☐ Stop, get out and look along the main road to check

If you want to turn right from a junction and your view is restricted, stop. Ease forward until you can see – something might be approaching.

If you don't know, don't go.

6.57 You're at the front of a queue of traffic waiting to turn right into a side road. Why is it important to check your right mirror just before turning?

☐ To look for pedestrians about to cross

☐ To check for overtaking vehicles

☐ To make sure the side road is clear

☐ To check for emerging traffic

A motorcyclist could be riding along the outside of the queue. Always check your mirror before turning, as situations behind you can change in the time you've been waiting to turn.

6.58 What must a driver do at a pelican crossing when the amber light is flashing?

☐ Signal the pedestrian to cross

☐ Always wait for the green light before proceeding

☐ Give way to any pedestrians on the crossing

☐ Wait for the red-and-amber light before proceeding

The flashing amber light allows pedestrians already on the crossing to get to the other side before a green light shows to the traffic. Be aware that some pedestrians, such as elderly people and young children, need longer to cross. Let them do this at their own pace.

6.59 You've stopped at a pelican crossing. A disabled person is crossing slowly in front of you when the lights change to green. What should you do?

☐ Wait for them to finish crossing

☐ Drive in front of them

☐ Edge forward slowly

☐ Sound your horn

At a pelican crossing, the green light means you may proceed as long as the crossing is clear. If someone hasn't finished crossing, be patient and wait for them, whether they're disabled or not.

6.60 You're driving past a line of parked cars. You notice a ball bouncing out into the road ahead. What should you do?

☐ Continue driving at the same speed and sound your horn

☐ Continue driving at the same speed and flash your headlights

☐ Slow down and be prepared to stop for children

☐ Stop and wave the children across to fetch their ball

Beware of children playing in the street and running out into the road. If a ball bounces out from the pavement, slow down and be prepared to stop. Don't encourage anyone to retrieve it. Other road users may not see your signal and you might lead a child into a dangerous situation.

6.61 You want to turn right from a main road into a side road. What should you do just before turning?

☐ Cancel your right-turn signal

☐ Select first gear

☐ Check for traffic overtaking on your right

☐ Stop and set the handbrake

In some circumstances, your indicators may be difficult to see and another road user may not realise you're about to turn. A final check in your mirror and blind spot can help you to see an overtaking vehicle, so that you can avoid turning across their path.

6.62 You're driving in a slow-moving queue of traffic. Just before changing lane, what should you do?

☐ Sound the horn and flash your lights

☐ Look for motorcyclists filtering through the traffic

☐ Give a 'slowing down' arm signal

☐ Change down to first gear

In queuing traffic, motorcyclists could be passing you on either side. Use your mirrors and check your blind area before changing lanes or changing direction.

6.63 You're driving in town. There's a bus at the bus stop on the other side of the road. Why should you be careful?

☐ The bus might have broken down

☐ Pedestrians might come from behind the bus

☐ The bus might move off suddenly

☐ The bus might remain stationary

If you see a bus ahead, watch out for pedestrians. They might not be able to see you if they're crossing from behind the bus.

6.64 How should you overtake horse riders?

☐ Drive up close and overtake as soon as possible

☐ Speed isn't important but allow plenty of room

☐ Use your horn just once to warn them

☐ Drive slowly and leave plenty of room

When you decide to overtake a horse rider, make sure you can do so safely before you move out. Leave them plenty of room and pass slowly. Passing too closely at speed could startle the horse and unseat the rider.

6.65   Why should you allow extra room when overtaking a motorcyclist on a windy day?

☐ The rider may turn off suddenly to get out of the wind

☐ The rider may be blown across in front of you

☐ The rider may stop suddenly

☐ The rider may be travelling faster than normal

If you're driving in high winds, be aware that the conditions might force a motorcyclist or cyclist to swerve or wobble. Take this into consideration if you're following or wish to overtake a two-wheeled vehicle.

6.66   Where should you take particular care to look for motorcyclists and cyclists?

☐ On dual carriageways

☐ At junctions

☐ At zebra crossings

☐ On one-way streets

Motorcyclists and cyclists are often more difficult to see at junctions. They're easily hidden from view and you may not be able to see them approaching a junction if your view is partially blocked; for example, by other traffic.

6.67   The road outside this school is marked with yellow zigzag lines. What do these lines mean?

☐ You may park on the lines when dropping off schoolchildren

☐ You may park on the lines when picking up schoolchildren

☐ You mustn't wait or park your vehicle here at all

☐ You must stay with your vehicle if you park here

Parking here would block other road users' view of the school entrance and would endanger the lives of children on their way to and from school.

6.68   You're driving past parked cars. You notice a bicycle wheel sticking out between them. What should you do?

☐ Accelerate past quickly and sound your horn

☐ Slow down and wave the cyclist across

☐ Brake sharply and flash your headlights

☐ Slow down and be prepared to stop for a cyclist

Scan the road as you drive. Try to anticipate hazards by being aware of the places where they're likely to occur. You'll then be able to react in good time.

6.69   You're dazzled at night by a vehicle behind you. What should you do?

☐ Set your mirror to the anti-dazzle position

☐ Set your mirror to dazzle the other driver

☐ Brake sharply to a stop

☐ Switch your rear lights on and off

The interior mirror of most vehicles can be set to an anti-dazzle position. You'll still be able to see the lights of the traffic behind you, but the dazzle will be greatly reduced.

6.70   You're driving towards a zebra crossing. A person in a wheelchair is waiting to cross. What should you do?

☐ Continue on your way

☐ Wave to the person to cross

☐ Wave to the person to wait

☐ Be prepared to stop

You should slow down and be prepared to stop, as you would for an able-bodied person. Don't wave them across, as other traffic may not stop.

Section 7 Other Types of Vehicle

7.1 You're about to overtake a slow-moving motorcyclist. Which one of these signs would make you take special care?

☐ ☐

☐ ☐

In windy weather, watch out for motorcyclists and also cyclists, as they can be blown sideways into your path. When you pass them, leave plenty of room and check their position in your mirror before pulling back in.

7.2 You're waiting to emerge left from a minor road. A large vehicle is approaching from the right. You have time to turn, but you should wait. Why?

☐ The large vehicle can easily hide an overtaking vehicle

☐ The large vehicle can turn suddenly

☐ The large vehicle is difficult to steer in a straight line

☐ The large vehicle can easily hide vehicles from the left

Large vehicles can hide other vehicles that are overtaking – especially motorcycles, which may be filtering past queuing traffic. You need to be aware of the possibility of hidden vehicles and not assume that it's safe to emerge.

7.3 You're following a long vehicle. As it approaches a crossroads, it signals left but moves out to the right. What should you do?

☐ Get closer in order to pass it quickly

☐ Stay well back and give it room

☐ Assume the signal is wrong and that it's turning right

☐ Overtake it as it starts to slow down

A long vehicle may need to swing out in the opposite direction as it approaches a turn, to allow the rear wheels to clear the kerb. Don't try to filter through if you see a gap; as the lorry turns, the gap will close.

7.4 You're following a long vehicle approaching a crossroads. The driver signals right but moves close to the left-hand kerb. What should you do?

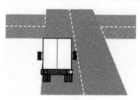

☐ Warn the driver about the wrong signal

☐ Wait behind the long vehicle

☐ Report the driver to the police

☐ Overtake on the right-hand side

When a long vehicle is going to turn right, it may need to keep close to the left-hand kerb. This is to prevent the rear end of the trailer cutting the corner. You need to be aware of how long vehicles behave in such situations. Don't overtake the lorry, because it could turn as you're alongside. Stay behind and wait for it to turn.

7.5 You're approaching a mini-roundabout. What should you do when you see the long vehicle in front signalling left but positioned over to the right?

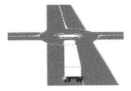

□ Sound your horn

□ Overtake on the left

□ Follow the same course as the lorry

□ keep well back

At mini-roundabouts, there isn't much room for a long vehicle to manoeuvre. It will have to swing out wide so that it can complete the turn safely. Keep well back and don't try to move up alongside it.

7.6 Before overtaking a large vehicle, you should keep well back. Why is this?

□ To give acceleration space to overtake quickly on blind bends

□ To get the best view of the road ahead

□ To leave a gap in case the vehicle stops and rolls back

□ To offer other drivers a safe gap if they want to overtake you

When following a large vehicle, keep well back. If you're too close, you won't be able to see the road ahead and the driver of the long vehicle might not be able to see you in their mirrors.

7.7 You're travelling behind a bus that pulls up at a bus stop. What should you do?

□ Accelerate past the bus

□ Watch carefully for pedestrians

□ Sound your horn

□ Pull in closely behind the bus

There might be pedestrians crossing from in front of the bus. Look out for them if you intend to pass. Consider how many people are waiting to get on the bus - check the queue if you can. The bus might move off straight away if no-one is waiting to get on.

If a bus is signalling to pull out, give it priority if it's safe to do so.

7.8 You're following a lorry on a wet road. What should you do when spray makes it difficult to see the road ahead?

□ Drop back until you can see better

□ Put your headlights on full beam

□ Keep close to the lorry, away from the spray

□ Speed up and overtake quickly

Large vehicles throw up a lot of spray when it's wet. This makes it difficult for following drivers to see the road ahead. You'll be able to see more by dropping back further, out of the spray. This will also increase your separation distance, giving you more room to stop if you have to.

7.9 You keep well back while waiting to overtake a large vehicle. What should you do if a car moves into the gap?

□ Sound your horn

□ Drop back further

□ Flash your headlights

□ Start to overtake

Sometimes your separation distance is shortened by a driver moving into the gap you've allowed. When this happens, react positively, stay calm and drop further back to re-establish a safe following distance.

7.10 What should you do when you're approaching a bus that's signalling to move away from a bus stop?

☐ Get past before it moves

☐ Allow it to pull away, if it's safe to do so

☐ Flash your headlights as you approach

☐ Signal left and wave the bus on

Try to give way to buses if you can do so safely, especially when the driver signals to pull away from a bus stop. Look out for people getting off the bus or running to catch it, because they may cross the road without looking. Don't accelerate to get past the bus, and don't flash your lights, as this could mislead other road users.

7.11 How should you overtake a long, slow-moving vehicle on a busy road?

☐ Follow it closely and keep moving out to see the road ahead

☐ Flash your headlights for the oncoming traffic to give way

☐ Stay behind until the driver waves you past

☐ Keep well back until you can see that it's clear

When you're following a long vehicle, stay well back so that you can get a better view of the road ahead. The closer you get, the less you'll be able to see of the road. Be patient and don't take a gamble. Only overtake when you're certain that you can complete the manoeuvre safely.

7.12 Which of these is least likely to be affected by side winds?

☐ Cyclists ☐ Motorcyclists

☐ High-sided vehicles ☐ Cars

Although cars are the least likely to be affected, side winds can take anyone by surprise. This is most likely to happen after overtaking a large vehicle, when passing gaps between hedges or buildings, and on exposed sections of road.

7.13 What should you do as you approach this lorry?

☐ Slow down and be prepared to wait

☐ Make the lorry wait for you

☐ Flash your lights at the lorry

☐ Move to the right-hand side of the road

When turning, long vehicles need much more room on the road than other vehicles. At junctions, they may take up the whole of the road space, so be patient and allow them the room they need.

7.14 You're following a large vehicle approaching a crossroads. The driver signals to turn left. What should you do?

☐ Overtake if you can leave plenty of room

☐ Overtake only if there are no oncoming vehicles

☐ Don't overtake until the vehicle begins to turn

☐ Don't overtake as you approach or at the junction

Hold back and wait until the vehicle has turned before proceeding. Don't overtake, because the vehicle turning left could hide a vehicle emerging from the same junction.

7.15   What's the maximum speed of powered wheelchairs or scooters used by disabled people?

□ 8 mph   □ 12 mph   □ 16 mph   □ 20 mph

Some powered wheelchairs and mobility scooters are designed for use on the pavement only and cannot exceed 4 mph (6 km/h). Others can go on the road as well, and this category cannot exceed 8 mph (12 km/h). Take great care around these vehicles. They're extremely vulnerable because of their low speed and small size.

7.16   Why is it more difficult to overtake a large vehicle than a car?

□ It will take longer to pass one

□ It will be fitted with a speed limiter

□ It will have air brakes

□ It will be slow climbing hills

Depending on relative speed, it will usually take you longer to pass a lorry than other vehicles. Hazards to watch for include oncoming traffic, junctions ahead, bends or dips that could restrict your view, and signs or road markings that prohibit overtaking. Make sure you can see that it's safe to complete the manoeuvre before you start to overtake.

7.17   It's very windy. You're behind a motorcyclist who's overtaking a high-sided vehicle. What should you do?

□ Overtake the motorcyclist immediately

□ Keep well back

□ Stay level with the motorcyclist

□ Keep close to the motorcyclist

Windy weather affects motorcyclists more than other vehicles. In windy conditions, high-sided vehicles cause air turbulence. You should keep well back, as the motorcyclist could be blown off course.

7.18   You're driving in town. Ahead of you a bus is at a bus stop. Which of the following should you do?

□ Flash your lights to warn the driver of your presence

□ Continue at the same speed but sound your horn as a warning

□ Watch carefully for the sudden appearance of pedestrians

□ Pass the bus as quickly as you possibly can

As you approach, look out for any signal the driver might make. If you pass the vehicle, watch out for pedestrians attempting to cross the road from behind the bus. They'll be hidden from view until the last moment.

7.19   You're driving along this road. What should you be prepared to do?

□ Sound your horn and continue

□ Slow down and give way

□ Report the driver to the police

□ Squeeze through the gap

Sometimes, large vehicles may need more space than other road users. If a vehicle needs more time and space to turn, be prepared to stop and wait.

7.20   As a driver, why should you be more careful where trams operate?

□ Because they don't have a horn

□ Because they can't stop for cars

□ Because they don't have lights

□ Because they can't steer to avoid you

You should take extra care when you first encounter trams. You'll have to get used to dealing with a different traffic system.

Be aware that trams can accelerate and travel very quickly, and they can't change direction to avoid obstructions.

7.21   You're towing a caravan. Which is the safest type of rear-view mirror to use?

□ Interior wide-angle mirror

□ Extended-arm side mirrors

□ Ordinary door mirrors

□ Ordinary interior mirror

Towing a large trailer or caravan can greatly reduce your view of the road behind. You may need to fit extended-arm side mirrors so that you can see clearly behind and down both sides of the caravan or trailer.

7.22   You're driving in heavy traffic on a wet road. Spray makes it difficult to be seen. What lights should you use?

□ Full-beam headlights

□ Sidelights only

□ Rear fog lights if visibility is more than 100 metres (328 feet)

□ Dipped headlights

You must make sure that other road users can see you, but you don't want to dazzle them. Use your dipped headlights during the day if visibility is poor. If visibility falls below 100 metres (328 feet), you may use your rear fog lights, but don't forget to turn them off when the visibility improves.

7.23   It's a very windy day and you're about to overtake a cyclist. What should you do?

□ Overtake very slowly

□ Keep close as you pass

□ Sound your horn repeatedly

□ Allow extra room

Cyclists, and motorcyclists, are very vulnerable in high winds. They can easily be blown well off course and veer into your path. Always allow plenty of room when overtaking them. Passing too close could cause a draught and unbalance the rider.

Section 8 Road Conditons and Vehicle Handling

8.1 When may you overtake another vehicle on the left?

□ When you're in a one-way street

□ When approaching a motorway slip road where you'll be turning off

□ When the vehicle in front is signalling to turn left

□ When a slower vehicle is travelling in the right-hand lane of a dual carriageway

You may pass slower vehicles on their left while travelling along a one-way street. Be aware of drivers who may need to change lanes and may not expect faster traffic passing on their left.

8.2 You're travelling in very heavy rain. How is this likely to affect your overall stopping distance?

□ It will be doubled

□ It will be halved

□ It will be ten times greater

□ It will be no different

The road will be very wet and spray from other vehicles will reduce your visibility. Tyre grip will also be reduced, increasing your stopping distance. You should at least double your separation distance.

8.3 What should you do when you're overtaking at night?

□ Wait until a bend so that you can see oncoming headlights

□ Sound your horn twice before moving out

□ Put your headlights on full beam

□ Beware of bends in the road ahead

Don't overtake if there's a possibility of a road junction, bend or brow of a bridge or hill ahead. There are many hazards that are difficult to see in the dark. Only overtake if you're certain that the road ahead is clear. Don't take a chance.

8.4 When may you wait in a box junction?

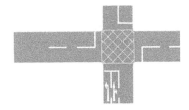

□ When you're stationary in a queue of traffic

□ When approaching a pelican crossing

□ When approaching a zebra crossing

□ When oncoming traffic prevents you turning right

The purpose of a box junction is to keep the junction clear by preventing vehicles from stopping in the path of crossing traffic.

You mustn't enter a box junction unless your exit is clear. However, you may enter the box and wait if you want to turn right and are only prevented from doing so by oncoming traffic.

8.5   Which of these plates normally appears with this road sign?

☐

Humps for ½ mile

☐

Hump Bridge

☐

Low Bridge

☐

Soft Verge

Road humps are used to slow down traffic. They're found in places where there are often pedestrians, such as

• shopping areas

• near schools

• residential areas.

Watch out for people close to the kerb or crossing the road.

8.6   What do traffic-calming measures do?

☐ Stop road rage

☐ Make overtaking easier

☐ Slow traffic down

☐ Make parking easier

Traffic-calming measures make the roads safer for vulnerable road users, such as cyclists, pedestrians and children. These can be designed as chicanes, road humps or other obstacles that encourage drivers and riders to slow down.

8.7   You're on a motorway in fog. The left-hand edge of the motorway can be identified by reflective studs. What colour are they?

☐ Green ☐ Amber ☐ Red ☐ White

"Be especially careful if you're on a motorway in fog. Reflective studs are there to help you in poor visibility. Different colours are used so that you'll know which lane you're in. These are

• red on the left-hand edge of the carriageway

• white between lanes

• amber on the right-hand edge of the carriageway

• green between the carriageway and slip roads.

8.8   What's a rumble device designed to do?

☐ Give directions

☐ Prevent cattle escaping

☐ Alert you to low tyre pressure

☐ Alert you to a hazard

A rumble device consists of raised markings or strips across the road, designed to give drivers an audible, visual and tactile warning. These devices are used in various locations, including in the line separating the hard shoulder and the left-hand lane on the motorway and on the approach to some hazards, to alert drivers to the need to slow down.

8.9 What should you do when making a journey in foggy conditions?

□ Follow other vehicles' tail lights closely

□ Avoid using dipped headlights

□ Leave plenty of time for your journey

□ Keep two seconds behind the vehicle ahead

If you're planning to make a journey when it's foggy, listen to the weather reports. If visibility is very poor, avoid making unnecessary journeys. If you do travel, leave plenty of time – and if someone is waiting for you to arrive, let them know that your journey will take longer than normal. This will also take off any pressure you may feel to rush.

8.10 What must you do when overtaking a car at night?

□ Flash your headlights before overtaking

□ Select a higher gear

□ Switch your lights to full beam before overtaking

□ Make sure you don't dazzle other road users

To prevent your lights from dazzling the driver of the car in front, wait until you've passed them before switching to full beam.

8.11 You're travelling on a road that has speed humps. What should you do when the driver in front is travelling more slowly than you?

□ Sound your horn

□ Overtake as soon as you can

□ Flash your headlights

□ Slow down and stay behind

Be patient and stay behind the car in front. You shouldn't normally overtake other vehicles in areas subject to traffic calming. If you overtake here, you may easily exceed the speed limit, defeating the purpose of the traffic-calming measures.

8.12 You see these markings on the road. Why are they there?

□ To show a safe distance between vehicles

□ To keep the area clear of traffic

□ To make you aware of your speed

□ To warn you to change direction

These lines may be painted on the road on the approach to a roundabout, a village or a particular hazard. The lines are raised and painted yellow, and their purpose is to make you aware of your speed. Reduce your speed in good time so that you avoid having to brake harshly over the last few metres before reaching the junction.

8.13 How would you identify a section of road used by trams?

□ There would be metal studs around it

□ There would be zigzag markings alongside it

□ There would be a different surface texture

□ There would be yellow hatch markings around it

Trams may run on roads used by other vehicles and pedestrians. The section of road used by trams is known as the reserved area and should be kept clear. It usually has a different surface, edged with white lane markings.

8.14 What should you do when you meet an oncoming vehicle on a single-track road?

☐ Reverse back to the main road

☐ Carry out an emergency stop

☐ Stop at a passing place

☐ Switch on your hazard warning lights

Take care when using single-track roads. It can be difficult to see around bends, because of hedges or fences, so expect to meet oncoming vehicles. Drive carefully and be ready to pull into or stop opposite a passing place, where you can pass each other safely.

8.15 The road is wet. Why might a motorcyclist steer round drain covers on a bend?

☐ To avoid puncturing the tyres on the edge of the drain covers

☐ To prevent the motorcycle sliding on the metal drain covers

☐ To help judge the bend using the drain covers as marker points

☐ To avoid splashing pedestrians on the pavement

Other drivers or riders may have to change course due to the size or characteristics of their vehicle. Understanding this will help you to anticipate their actions. Motorcyclists and cyclists will be checking the road ahead for uneven or slippery surfaces, especially in wet weather. They may need to move across their lane to avoid surface hazards such as potholes and drain covers.

8.16 After this hazard you should test your brakes. Why is this?

☐ You'll be on a slippery road

☐ Your brakes will be soaking wet

☐ You'll be going down a long hill

☐ You'll have just crossed a long bridge

A ford is a crossing over a stream that's shallow enough to drive or ride through. After you've gone through a ford or deep puddle, your brakes will be wet and they won't work as well as usual. To dry them out, apply a light brake pressure while moving slowly. Don't travel at normal speeds until you're sure your brakes are working properly again.

8.17 Why should you always reduce your speed when travelling in fog?

☐ The brakes don't work as well

☐ You'll be dazzled by other headlights

☐ The engine will take longer to warm up

☐ It's more difficult to see what's ahead

You won't be able to see as far ahead in fog as you can on a clear day. You'll need to reduce your speed so that, if a hazard looms out of the fog, you have the time and space to take avoiding action.

Travelling in fog is hazardous. If you can, try to delay your journey until it has cleared.

8.18 How will your vehicle be affected when you drive up steep hills?

☐ The higher gears will pull better

☐ The steering will feel heavier

☐ Overtaking will be easier

☐ The engine will work harder

The engine will need more power to pull the vehicle up the hill. When approaching a steep hill you should select a lower gear to help maintain your speed. You should do this without hesitation, so that you don't lose too much speed before engaging the lower gear.

8.19 You're driving on the motorway in windy conditions. What should you do as you pass a high-sided vehicle?

☐ Increase your speed

☐ Be wary of a sudden gust

☐ Drive alongside very closely

☐ Expect normal conditions

The draught caused by other vehicles – particularly those with high sides – could be strong enough to push you out of your lane. Be prepared for a sudden gust of wind as you pass large vehicles. Keep both hands on the steering wheel to help you keep full control.

8.20 What should you do to correct a rear-wheel skid?

☐ Not steer at all

☐ Steer away from it

☐ Steer into it

☐ Apply your handbrake

If your car skids and the rear wheels slide to the right, you need to steer into the skid (ie to the right), until the front and rear wheels are brought into line. Don't oversteer or you'll cause a skid in the opposite direction and this will make the situation worse.

8.21 You're driving in fog. Why should you keep well back from the vehicle in front?

☐ In case it changes direction suddenly

☐ In case its fog lights dazzle you

☐ In case it stops suddenly

☐ In case its brake lights dazzle you

If you're following another road user in fog, stay well back. The driver in front won't be able to see hazards until they're close and might need to brake suddenly. Also, the road surface is likely to be wet and could be slippery.

8.22 What should you do if you park on the road when it's foggy?

☐ Leave sidelights switched on

☐ Leave dipped headlights and fog lights switched on

☐ Leave dipped headlights switched on

☐ Leave main-beam headlights switched on

If you have to park your vehicle in foggy conditions, try to find a place to park off the road. If this isn't possible, park on the road facing in the same direction as the traffic. Leave your sidelights switched on and make sure they're clean.

8.23 You're driving at night and are dazzled by vehicle headlights coming towards you. What should you do?

☐ Pull down your sun visor

☐ Slow down or stop

☐ Flash your main-beam headlights

☐ Shade your eyes with your hand

If the headlights of an oncoming vehicle dazzle you, slow down or, if necessary, stop. Don't close your eyes or swerve, as you'll increase your chances of having a collision. Don't flash your headlights either, as this could dazzle other drivers and make the situation worse.

8.24 When may front fog lights be used?

☐ When visibility is seriously reduced

☐ When they're fitted above the bumper

☐ When they aren't as bright as the headlights

☐ When an audible warning device is used

Your fog lights must only be used when visibility is reduced to 100 metres (328 feet) or less. You need to be familiar with the layout of your dashboard so you're aware if your fog lights have been switched on in error, or you've forgotten to switch them off.

8.25 You're driving with your front fog lights switched on. Earlier fog has now cleared. What should you do?

□ Leave them on if other drivers have their lights on

□ Switch them off as long as visibility remains good

□ Flash them to warn oncoming traffic that it's foggy

□ Drive with them on instead of your headlights

Switch off your fog lights if the weather improves, but be prepared to use them again if visibility reduces to less than 100 metres (328 feet).

8.26 Why should you switch off your rear fog lights when the fog has cleared?

□ To allow your headlights to work

□ To stop draining the battery

□ To stop the engine losing power

□ To prevent dazzling following drivers

Don't forget to switch off your fog lights when the weather improves. You could be prosecuted for driving with them on in good visibility. The high intensity of rear fog lights can dazzle following drivers and make your brake lights difficult to notice.

8.27 What will happen if you use rear fog lights in good conditions?

□ They'll make it safer when towing a trailer

□ They'll protect you from larger vehicles

□ They'll dazzle other drivers

□ They'll make following drivers keep back

Rear fog lights shine more brightly than normal rear lights, so that they show up in reduced visibility. When the visibility improves, you must switch them off; this stops them dazzling the driver behind.

8.28 What can fitting chains to your wheels help to prevent?

□ Damage to the road surface

□ Wear to the tyres

□ Skidding in deep snow

□ The brakes locking

Chains can be fitted to your wheels in snowy conditions. They can help you to move off without wheelspin, or to keep moving in deep snow. You'll still need to adjust your driving to suit these conditions.

8.29 How can you use your vehicle's engine to control your speed?

□ By changing to a lower gear

□ By selecting reverse gear

□ By changing to a higher gear

□ By selecting neutral

You should brake and slow down before selecting a lower gear. The gear can then be used to keep the speed low and help you control the vehicle. This is particularly helpful on long downhill stretches, where brake fade can occur if the brakes overheat.

8.30 Why could it be dangerous to keep the clutch down, or select neutral, for long periods of time while you're driving?

□ Fuel spillage will occur

□ Engine damage may be caused

□ You'll have less steering and braking control

□ It will wear tyres out more quickly

Letting your vehicle roll or coast in neutral reduces your control over steering and braking. This can be dangerous on downhill slopes, where your vehicle could pick up speed very quickly.

8.31 You're driving on an icy road. What distance from the car in front should you drive?

☐ Four times the normal distance

☐ Six times the normal distance

☐ Eight times the normal distance

☐ Ten times the normal distance

Don't travel in icy or snowy weather unless your journey is essential.

Drive extremely carefully when roads are or may be icy. Stopping distances can be ten times greater than on dry roads.

8.32 You're driving on a well-lit motorway on a clear night. What must you do?

☐ Use only your sidelights

☐ Use your headlights

☐ Use rear fog lights

☐ Use front fog lights

If you're driving on a motorway at night or in poor visibility, you must always use your headlights, even if the road is well lit. Other road users must be able to see you, but you should avoid causing dazzle.

8.33 You're on a motorway at night, with other vehicles just ahead of you. Which lights should you have on?

☐ Front fog lights

☐ Main-beam headlights

☐ Sidelights only

☐ Dipped headlights

If you're driving behind other traffic on the motorway at night, use dipped headlights. Main-beam headlights will dazzle the other drivers. Your headlights' dipped beam should fall short of the vehicle in front.

8.34 What will affect your vehicle's stopping distance?

☐ The speed limit

☐ The street lighting

☐ The time of day

☐ The condition of the tyres

Having tyres correctly inflated and in good condition will ensure they have maximum grip on the road; how well your tyres grip the road has a significant effect on your car's stopping distance.

8.35 You're driving on a motorway at night. When may you switch off your headlights?

☐ When there are vehicles close in front of you

☐ When you're travelling below 50 mph

☐ When the motorway is lit

☐ When your vehicle is broken down on the hard shoulder

Always use your headlights at night on a motorway unless you've had to stop on the hard shoulder. If you break down and have to use the hard shoulder, switch off your headlights but leave your sidelights on, so that other road users can see your vehicle.

8.36 When will you feel the effects of engine braking?

☐ When you only use the handbrake

☐ When you're in neutral

☐ When you change to a lower gear

☐ When you change to a higher gear

When you take your foot off the accelerator, engines have a natural resistance to turn, caused mainly by the cylinder compression. Changing to a lower gear requires the engine to turn faster and so it will have greater resistance than when it's made to turn more slowly. When going downhill, changing to a lower gear will therefore help to keep the vehicle's speed in check.

8.37 Daytime visibility is poor but not seriously reduced. Which lights should you switch on?

☐ Headlights and fog lights

☐ Front fog lights

☐ Dipped headlights

☐ Rear fog lights

Only use your fog lights when visibility is seriously reduced. Use dipped headlights in poor conditions because this helps other road users to see you without the risk of causing dazzle.

8.38 Why are vehicles fitted with rear fog lights?

☐ To make them more visible when driving at high speed

☐ To show when they've broken down in a dangerous position

☐ To make them more visible in thick fog

☐ To warn drivers following closely to drop back

Rear fog lights make it easier to spot a vehicle ahead in foggy conditions. Avoid the temptation to use other vehicles' lights as a guide, as they may give you a false sense of security.

8.39 While you're driving in fog, it becomes necessary to use front fog lights. What should you remember?

☐ Only use them in heavy traffic conditions

☐ Don't use them on motorways

☐ Only use them on dual carriageways

☐ Switch them off when visibility improves

It's illegal to use your fog lights in conditions other than when visibility is seriously reduced; that is, less than 100 metres (328 feet). Fog lights are very bright and, if you use them when visibility has improved, you could dazzle other drivers.

8.40 What should you do when there's been a heavy fall of snow?

☐ Drive with your hazard warning lights on

☐ Don't drive unless you have a mobile phone

☐ Only drive when your journey is short

☐ Don't drive unless it's essential

Consider whether the increased risk is worth it. If the weather conditions are bad and your journey isn't essential, then don't drive.

8.41 You're driving down a long, steep hill. You suddenly notice that your brakes aren't working as well as normal. What's the usual cause of this?

☐ The brakes overheating

☐ Air in the brake fluid

☐ Oil on the brakes

☐ Badly adjusted brakes

This is more likely to happen on vehicles fitted with drum brakes, but it can apply to disc brakes as well. Using a lower gear will assist the braking and help you to keep control of your vehicle.

8.42 You have to make a journey in fog. What should you do before you set out?

☐ Top up the radiator with anti-freeze

☐ Make sure that you have a warning triangle in the vehicle

☐ Make sure that the windows are clean

☐ Check the battery

If you have to drive in fog, switch your dipped-beam headlights on and keep your windscreen clear. You should always be able to pull up within the distance you can see ahead.

8.43 You've just driven out of fog. What must you do now that visibility has improved?

☐ Switch off your fog lights

☐ Keep your rear fog lights switched on

☐ Keep your front fog lights switched on

☐ Leave your fog lights switched on in case the fog returns

You must turn off your fog lights if visibility is more than 100 metres (328 feet). Be prepared for the fact that the fog may be patchy and you may need to turn them on again if the fog returns.

8.44 Why is it dangerous to leave rear fog lights on when they're not needed?

☐ They may be confused with brake lights

☐ The bulbs would fail

☐ Electrical systems could be overloaded

☐ Direction indicators may not work properly

If your rear fog lights are left on when it isn't foggy, the glare they cause makes it difficult for road users behind to know whether you're braking or you've just forgotten to turn off your rear fog lights. This can be a particular problem on wet roads and on motorways. If you leave your rear fog lights on at night, road users behind you are likely to be dazzled and this could put them at risk.

8.45 What will happen if you hold the clutch pedal down or roll in neutral for too long?

☐ It will use more fuel

☐ It will cause the engine to overheat

☐ It will reduce your control

☐ It will improve tyre wear

Holding the clutch down or staying in neutral for too long will cause your vehicle to freewheel. This is known as 'coasting' and it's dangerous because it reduces your control of the vehicle.

8.46 You're driving down a steep hill. Why could it be dangerous to keep the clutch down or roll in neutral for too long?

☐ Fuel consumption will be higher

☐ Your vehicle will pick up speed

☐ It will damage the engine

☐ It will wear tyres out more quickly

Driving in neutral or with the clutch down for long periods is known as 'coasting'. There will be no engine braking and your vehicle will pick up speed on downhill slopes. Coasting can be very dangerous because it reduces steering and braking control.

8.47 Why is it bad technique to coast when driving downhill?

☐ The fuel consumption will increase

☐ The engine will overheat

☐ The tyres will wear more quickly

☐ The vehicle will gain speed

Coasting is when you allow the vehicle to freewheel in neutral or with the clutch pedal depressed. Speed will increase as you lose the benefits of engine braking and have less control. You shouldn't coast, especially when approaching hazards such as junctions or bends and when travelling downhill.

8.48 What should you do when dealing with this hazard?

☐ Switch on your hazard warning lights

☐ Use a low gear and drive slowly

☐ Use a high gear to prevent wheelspin

☐ Switch on your windscreen wipers

In normal conditions, a ford can be crossed quite safely by driving through it slowly. The water may affect your brakes, so when you're clear of the ford, test them before you resume normal driving.

8.49 Why is travelling in neutral for long distances (known as coasting) wrong?

☐ It will cause the car to skid

☐ It will make the engine stall

☐ The engine will run faster

☐ There won't be any engine braking

Try to look ahead and read the road. Plan your approach to junctions and select the correct gear in good time. This will give you the control you need to deal with any hazards that occur.

You'll coast a little every time you change gear. This can't be avoided, but it should be kept to a minimum.

8.50 When must you use dipped headlights during the day?

☐ All the time   ☐ On narrow streets

☐ In poor visibility   ☐ When parking

You must use dipped headlights when daytime visibility is seriously reduced, generally to 100 metres (328 feet) or less. You may also use front or rear fog lights, but they must be switched off when visibility improves.

8.51 You're braking on a wet road. Your vehicle begins to skid. It doesn't have anti-lock brakes. What's the first thing you should do?

☐ Quickly pull up the handbrake

☐ Release the footbrake

☐ Push harder on the brake pedal

☐ Gently use the accelerator

If the skid has been caused by braking too hard for the conditions, release the brake. You may then need to reapply and release the brake again. You may need to do this a number of times. This will allow the wheels to turn and so some steering should also be possible.

Section 9 Motorway Rules

9.1 What should you do when you're joining a motorway?

☐ Use the hard shoulder

☐ Stop at the end of the acceleration lane

☐ Slow to a stop before joining the motorway

☐ Give way to traffic already on the motorway

You should give way to traffic already on the motorway. Where possible, traffic may move over to let you in, but don't force your way into the traffic stream. Traffic could be travelling at high speed, so try to match your speed to filter in without affecting the traffic flow.

9.2 What's the national speed limit on motorways for cars and motorcycles?

☐ 30 mph ☐ 50 mph ☐ 60 mph ☐ 70 mph

Travelling at the national speed limit doesn't allow you to hog the right-hand lane. Always use the left-hand lane whenever possible. When leaving a motorway, get into the left-hand lane well before your exit. Reduce your speed on the slip road and look out for sharp bends or curves and traffic queuing at roundabouts.

9.3 Which vehicles should use the left-hand lane on a three-lane motorway?

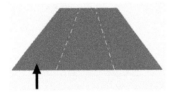

☐ Any vehicle

☐ Large vehicles only

☐ Emergency vehicles only

☐ Slow vehicles only

On a motorway, all traffic should use the left-hand lane unless overtaking. When overtaking a number of slower vehicles, move back to the left-hand lane when you're safely past. Check your mirrors frequently and don't stay in the middle or right-hand lane if the left-hand lane is free.

9.4 Which of these isn't allowed to travel in the right-hand lane of a three-lane motorway?

☐ A small delivery van

☐ A motorcycle

☐ A vehicle towing a trailer

☐ A motorcycle and sidecar

A vehicle with a trailer is restricted to 60 mph. For this reason, it isn't allowed in the right-hand lane, as it might hold up faster-moving traffic that wishes to overtake in that lane.

9.5 You break down on a motorway. You need to call for help. Why may it be better to use an emergency roadside telephone rather than a mobile phone?

☐ It connects you to a local garage

☐ Using a mobile phone will distract other drivers

☐ It allows easy location by the emergency services

☐ Mobile phones don't work on motorways

On a motorway, it's best to use a roadside emergency telephone so that the emergency services are able to find you easily. The location of the nearest telephone is shown by an arrow on marker posts at the edge of the hard shoulder. If you use a mobile, the operator will need to know your exact location. Before you call, find out the number on the nearest marker post. This number will identify your exact location.

9.6 You've had a breakdown on the hard shoulder of a motorway. When the problem has been fixed, how should you rejoin the main carriageway?

☐ Move out onto the carriageway, then build up your speed

☐ Move out onto the carriageway using your hazard warning lights

☐ Gain speed on the hard shoulder before moving out onto the carriageway

☐ Wait on the hard shoulder until someone flashes their headlights at you

Signal your intention and build up sufficient speed on the hard shoulder so that you can filter into a safe gap in the traffic. Don't push your way in, causing other traffic to alter speed or direction.

9.7 You're travelling along a motorway. Where would you find a crawler or climbing lane?

☐ On a steep gradient

☐ Before a service area

☐ Before a junction

☐ Along the hard shoulder

Large, slow-moving vehicles can hinder the progress of other traffic. On a steep gradient, an extra crawler lane may be provided for slow-moving vehicles to allow faster-moving traffic to flow more easily.

9.8 What do these motorway signs show?

☐ They're countdown markers to a bridge

☐ They're distance markers to the next telephone

☐ They're countdown markers to the next exit

☐ They warn of a police control ahead

The exit from a motorway is indicated by countdown markers. These are positioned 90 metres (100 yards) apart, the first being 270 metres (300 yards) from the start of the slip road. Move into the left-hand lane well before you reach the start of the slip road.

9.9 On which part of a motorway are amber reflective studs found?

☐ Between the hard shoulder and the carriageway

☐ Between the acceleration lane and the carriageway

☐ Between the central reservation and the carriageway

☐ Between each pair of lanes

On motorways, reflective studs of various colours are fixed in the road between the lanes. These help you to identify which lane you're in when it's dark or in poor visibility. Amber-coloured studs are found on the right-hand edge of the main carriageway, next to the central reservation.

9.10 What colour are the reflective studs between the lanes on a motorway?

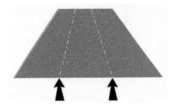

☐ Green ☐ Amber ☐ White ☐ Red

White studs are found between the lanes on motorways. They reflect back the light from your headlights. This is especially useful in bad weather, when visibility is restricted.

9.11 What colour are the reflective studs between a motorway and its slip road?

☐ Amber ☐ White ☐ Green ☐ Red

The studs between the carriageway and the hard shoulder are normally red. These change to green where there's a slip road, helping you to identify slip roads when visibility is poor or when it's dark.

9.12 You've broken down on a motorway. In which direction should you walk to find the nearest emergency telephone?

☐ With the traffic flow

☐ Facing oncoming traffic

☐ In the direction shown on the marker posts

☐ In the direction of the nearest exit

Along the hard shoulder there are marker posts at 100-metre intervals. These will direct you to the nearest emergency telephone.

9.13 You're joining a motorway. Why is it important to make full use of the slip road?

☐ Because there is space available to turn round if you need to

☐ To allow you direct access to the overtaking lanes

☐ To build up a speed similar to traffic on the motorway

☐ Because you can continue on the hard shoulder

Try to join the motorway without affecting the progress of the traffic already travelling on it. Always give way to traffic already on the motorway. At busy times you may have to slow down to merge into slow-moving traffic.

9.14 How should you use the emergency telephone on a motorway?

☐ Stay close to the carriageway

☐ Face the oncoming traffic

☐ Keep your back to the traffic

☐ Stand on the hard shoulder

Traffic is passing you at speed. If the draught from a large lorry catches you by surprise, it could blow you off balance and even onto the carriageway. By facing the oncoming traffic, you can see approaching lorries and so be prepared for their draught. You'll also be in a position to see other hazards approaching.

9.15 You're on a motorway. What colour are the reflective studs on the left of the carriageway?

☐ Green ☐ Red ☐ White ☐ Amber

Red studs are placed between the edge of the carriageway and the hard shoulder. Where slip roads leave or join the motorway, the studs are green.

9.16   On a three-lane motorway, which lane should you normally use?

☐ Left   ☐ Right

☐ Centre   ☐ Either the right or centre

On a three-lane motorway, you should travel in the left-hand lane unless you're overtaking. This applies regardless of the speed at which you're travelling.

9.17   What should you do when going through a contraflow system on a motorway?

☐ Ensure that you don't exceed 30 mph

☐ Keep a good distance from the vehicle ahead

☐ Switch lanes to keep the traffic flowing

☐ Stay close to the vehicle ahead to reduce queues

At roadworks, and especially where a contraflow system is operating, a speed restriction is likely to be in place. Keep to the lower speed limit and don't

• switch lanes

• get too close to the vehicle in front of you.

Be aware that there will be no permanent barrier between you and the oncoming traffic.

9.18   You're on a three-lane motorway. There are red reflective studs on your left and white ones to your right. Which lane are you in?

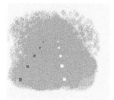

☐ In the right-hand lane   ☐ In the middle lane

☐ On the hard shoulder   ☐ In the left-hand lane

The colours of the reflective studs on the motorway and their locations are

• red – between the hard shoulder and the carriageway

• white – between lanes

• amber – between the carriageway and the central reservation

• green – along slip-road exits and entrances

• bright green/yellow – at roadworks and contraflow systems.

9.19   You're approaching roadworks on a motorway. What should you do?

☐ Speed up to clear the area quickly

☐ Always use the hard shoulder

☐ Obey all speed limits

☐ Stay very close to the vehicle in front

Collisions often happen at roadworks. Be aware of the speed limits, slow down in good time and keep your distance from the vehicle in front.

9.20   Which vehicles are prohibited from using the motorway?

☐ Powered mobility scooters

☐ Motorcycles over 50 cc

☐ Double-deck buses

☐ Cars with automatic transmission

Motorways mustn't be used by pedestrians, cyclists, motorcycles under 50 cc, certain slow-moving vehicles without permission, and powered wheelchairs/mobility scooters.

9.21 What should you do when driving or riding along a motorway?

□ Look much further ahead than you would on other roads

□ Travel much faster than you would on other roads

□ Maintain a shorter separation distance than you would on other roads

□ Concentrate more than you would on other roads

Traffic on motorways usually travels faster than on other roads. You need to be looking further ahead to give yourself more time to react to any hazard that may develop.

9.22 What should you do immediately after joining a motorway?

□ Try to overtake

□ Re-adjust your mirrors

□ Position your vehicle in the centre lane

□ Keep in the left-hand lane

Stay in the left-hand lane long enough to get used to the higher speeds of motorway traffic before considering overtaking.

9.23 What's the right-hand lane used for on a three-lane motorway?

□ Emergency vehicles only

□ Overtaking

□ Vehicles towing trailers

□ Coaches only

You should keep to the left and only use the right-hand lane if you're passing slower-moving traffic.

9.24 What should you use the hard shoulder of a motorway for?

□ Stopping in an emergency

□ Leaving the motorway

□ Stopping when you're tired

□ Joining the motorway

Don't use the hard shoulder for stopping unless it's an emergency. If you want to stop for any other reason, go to the next exit or service station.

9.25 You're in the right-hand lane of a three-lane motorway. What do these overhead signs mean?

□ Move to the left and reduce your speed to 50 mph

□ There are roadworks 50 metres (55 yards) ahead

□ Use the hard shoulder until you've passed the hazard

□ Leave the motorway at the next exit

You must obey these signs even if there appear to be no problems ahead. There could be queuing traffic or another hazard which you can't yet see.

9.26 When are you allowed to stop on a motorway?

☐ When you need to walk and get fresh air

☐ When you wish to pick up hitchhikers

☐ When you're signalled to do so by flashing red lights

☐ When you need to use a mobile telephone

You must stop if overhead gantry signs show flashing red lights above every lane on the motorway. If any of the other lanes doesn't show flashing red lights or a red cross, you may move into that lane and continue if it's safe to do so.

9.27 You're travelling in the left-hand lane of a three-lane motorway. How should you react to traffic joining from a slip road?

☐ Race the other vehicles

☐ Move to another lane

☐ Maintain a steady speed

☐ Switch on your hazard warning lights

Plan well ahead when approaching a slip road. If you see traffic joining the motorway, move to another lane if it's safe to do so. This can help the flow of traffic joining the motorway, especially at peak times.

9.28 What basic rule applies when you're using a motorway?

☐ Use the lane that has the least traffic

☐ Keep to the left-hand lane unless overtaking

☐ Overtake on the side that's clearest

☐ Try to keep above 50 mph to prevent congestion

You should normally travel in the left-hand lane unless you're overtaking a slower-moving vehicle. When you've finished overtaking, move back into the left-hand lane, but don't cut across in front of the vehicle that you've overtaken.

9.29 You're travelling along a motorway. When are you allowed to overtake on the left?

☐ When you can see well ahead that the hard shoulder is clear

☐ When the traffic in the right-hand lane is signalling right

☐ When you warn drivers behind by signalling left

☐ When in queues and traffic to your right is moving more slowly than you are

Never overtake on the left, unless the traffic is moving in queues and the queue on your right is moving more slowly than the one you're in.

9.30 On a motorway, what's an emergency refuge area used for?

☐ In cases of emergency or breakdown

☐ If you think you'll be involved in a road rage incident

☐ For a police patrol to park and watch traffic

☐ For construction and road workers to store emergency equipment

Emergency refuge areas are built at the side of the hard shoulder. If you break down, try to get your vehicle into the refuge, where there's an emergency telephone. The phone connects directly to a control centre. Remember to take care when rejoining the motorway, especially if the hard shoulder is being used as a running lane.

9.31 Traffic officers operate on motorways and some primary routes in England. What are they authorised to do?

□ Stop and arrest drivers who break the law

□ Repair broken-down vehicles on the motorway

□ Issue fixed penalty notices

□ Stop and direct anyone on a motorway

Traffic officers don't have enforcement powers but are able to stop and direct people on motorways and some 'A' class roads. They only operate in England and work in partnership with the police at incidents, providing a highly trained and visible service. They're recognised by an orange-and-yellow jacket and their vehicle has yellow-and-black markings.

9.32 You're on a motorway. A red cross is displayed above the hard shoulder. What does this mean?

□ Pull up in this lane to answer your mobile phone

□ Use this lane as a running lane

□ This lane can be used if you need a rest

□ You shouldn't travel in this lane

Active traffic management operates on some motorways. Within these areas, at certain times, the hard shoulder will be used as a running lane. A red cross above the hard shoulder shows that this lane should only be used for emergencies and breakdowns.

9.33 You're on a smart motorway. A mandatory speed limit is displayed above the hard shoulder. What does this mean?

□ You shouldn't travel in this lane

□ The hard shoulder can be used as a running lane

□ You can park on the hard shoulder if you feel tired

□ You can pull up in this lane to answer a mobile phone

A mandatory speed-limit sign above the hard shoulder shows that this part of the road can be used as a running lane between junctions. You must stay within the speed limit. Look out for vehicles that may have broken down and could be blocking the hard shoulder.

9.34 What's the aim of a smart motorway?

□ To prevent overtaking

□ To reduce rest stops

□ To prevent tailgating

□ To reduce congestion

Smart motorway schemes are intended to reduce congestion and make journey times more reliable. In these areas, the hard shoulder may be used as a running lane to ease congestion at peak times or in the event of an incident. Variable speed limits are used to help keep the traffic moving and to avoid bunching.

9.35 You're using a smart motorway. What happens when it's operating?

☐ Speed limits above lanes are advisory

☐ The national speed limit will apply

☐ The speed limit is always 30 mph

☐ You must obey the speed limits shown

When a smart motorway is operating, you must follow the mandatory signs on the gantries above each lane, including the hard shoulder. Variable speed limits help keep the traffic moving and also help to prevent bunching.

9.36 Why can it be an advantage for traffic speed to stay constant over a longer distance?

☐ You'll do more stop–start driving

☐ You'll use far more fuel

☐ You'll be able to use more direct routes

☐ Your overall journey time will normally improve

When traffic travels at a constant speed over a longer distance, journey times normally improve. You may feel that you could travel faster for short periods, but this generally leads to bunching and increased overall journey time.

9.37 You shouldn't normally travel on the hard shoulder of a motorway. When can you use it?

☐ When taking the next exit

☐ When traffic is stopped

☐ When signs direct you to

☐ When traffic is slow moving

Normally, you should only use the hard shoulder for emergencies and breakdowns, and at roadworks when signs direct you to do so. Smart motorways use active traffic management to ease congestion. In these areas, the hard shoulder may be used as a running lane when speed-limit signs are shown directly above.

9.38 What's used to reduce traffic bunching on a motorway?

☐ Variable speed limits ☐ Contraflow systems

☐ National speed limits ☐ Lane closures

Congestion can be reduced by keeping traffic at a constant speed. At busy times, maximum speed limits are displayed on overhead gantries. These can be varied quickly, depending on the amount of traffic. By keeping to a constant speed on busy sections of motorway, overall journey times are normally improved.

9.39 When may you stop on a motorway?

☐ If you have to read a map

☐ When you're tired and need a rest

☐ If your mobile phone rings

☐ In an emergency or breakdown

You shouldn't normally stop on a motorway, but there may be occasions when you need to do so. If you're unfortunate enough to break down, make every effort to pull up on the hard shoulder.

9.40 Unless signs show otherwise, what's the national speed limit for a car or motorcycle on a motorway?

☐ 50 mph

☐ 60 mph

☐ 70 mph

☐ 80 mph

The national speed limit for a car or motorcycle on a motorway is 70 mph. Lower speed limits may be in force; for example, at roadworks. Variable speed limits also operate in some areas when the motorway is very busy. Cars or motorcycles towing trailers are subject to a lower speed limit.

9.41 You're on a motorway and there are red flashing lights above every lane. What must you do?

☐ Pull onto the hard shoulder

☐ Slow down and watch for further signals

☐ Leave at the next exit

☐ Stop and wait

Red flashing lights above all lanes mean you must stop and wait. You'll also see a red cross lit up. Don't change lanes, don't continue and don't pull onto the hard shoulder (unless in an emergency).

9.42 You're on a three-lane motorway. A red cross is showing above the hard shoulder and mandatory speed limits above all other lanes. What does this mean?

☐ The hard shoulder can be used as a rest area if you feel tired

☐ The hard shoulder is for emergency or breakdown use only

☐ The hard shoulder can be used as a normal running lane

☐ The hard shoulder has a speed limit of 50 mph

A red cross above the hard shoulder shows that it's closed as a running lane and should only be used for emergencies or breakdowns. On a smart motorway, the hard shoulder may be used as a running lane at busy times. This will be shown by a mandatory speed limit on the gantry above the hard shoulder.

9.43 On a three-lane motorway, what does this sign mean?

☐ Use any lane except the hard shoulder

☐ Use the hard shoulder only

☐ Use the three right-hand lanes only

☐ Use all the lanes, including the hard shoulder

You must obey mandatory speed-limit signs above motorway lanes, including the hard shoulder. In this case, you can use the hard shoulder as a running lane but you should look for any vehicles that may have broken down and may be blocking the hard shoulder.

9.44 You're travelling along a motorway and feel tired. Where should you stop to rest?

☐ On the hard shoulder

☐ At the nearest service area

☐ On a slip road

☐ On the central reservation

If you feel tired, stop at the nearest service area. If that's too far away, leave the motorway at the next exit and find a safe place to stop. You mustn't stop on the carriageway or hard shoulder of a motorway except in an emergency, when in a traffic queue, or when signalled to do so by a police officer, a traffic officer or traffic signals. Plan your journey so that you have regular rest stops.

9.45 You're towing a trailer on a motorway. What's the speed limit for a car towing a trailer on this road?

☐ 40 mph ☐ 50 mph ☐ 60 mph ☐ 70 mph

Don't forget that you're towing a trailer. If you're towing a small, light trailer, it won't reduce your vehicle's performance by very much. However, strong winds or buffeting from large vehicles might cause the trailer to snake from side to side. Be aware of your speed and don't exceed the reduced speed limit imposed on vehicles towing trailers.

9.46 What should the left-hand lane of a motorway be used for?

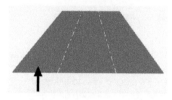

☐ Breakdowns and emergencies only

☐ Overtaking slower traffic in the other lanes

☐ Slow vehicles only

☐ Normal driving

You should drive in the left-hand lane whenever possible. Only use the other lanes for overtaking or when directed to do so by signals. Using other lanes when the left-hand lane is empty can frustrate drivers behind you.

9.47 You're driving on a motorway and have to slow down quickly due to a hazard ahead. How can you warn drivers behind of the hazard?

☐ Switch on your hazard warning lights

☐ Switch on your headlights

☐ Sound your horn

☐ Flash your headlights

Using your hazard warning lights, as well as your brake lights, will give following traffic an extra warning of the problem ahead. Only use them for long enough for your warning to be seen.

9.48 Your car gets a puncture while you're driving on the motorway. You get it onto the hard shoulder. What should you do?

☐ Carefully change the wheel yourself

☐ Use an emergency telephone and call for help

☐ Try to wave down another vehicle for help

☐ Only change the wheel if you have a passenger to help you

Park as far to the left as you can and leave the vehicle by the nearside door. Don't attempt even simple repairs. Instead, walk to an emergency telephone on your side of the road and phone for help. While waiting for help to arrive, stay by your car, keeping well away from the carriageway and hard shoulder.

9.49 You're driving on a motorway. By mistake, you go past the exit that you wanted to take. What should you do?

☐ Carefully reverse on the hard shoulder

☐ Carry on to the next exit

☐ Carefully reverse in the left-hand lane

☐ Make a U-turn at a gap in the central reservation

It's illegal to reverse, cross the central reservation or drive against the traffic flow on a motorway. If you miss your exit, carry on until you reach the next one. Ask yourself why you missed your exit – if you think that your concentration is fading, take a break before completing your journey.

9.50 Your vehicle has broken down on a motorway. You aren't able to stop on the hard shoulder. What should you do?

☐ Switch on your hazard warning lights

☐ Stop following traffic and ask for help

☐ Attempt to repair your vehicle quickly

☐ Stand behind your vehicle to warn others

If you can't get your vehicle onto the hard shoulder, use your hazard warning lights to warn others. Leave your vehicle only when you can safely get clear of the carriageway. Don't try to repair the vehicle or attempt to place any warning device on the carriageway.

9.51 Why is it particularly important to carry out a check on your vehicle before making a long motorway journey?

☐ You'll have to do more harsh braking on motorways

☐ Motorway service stations don't deal with breakdowns

☐ The road surface will wear down the tyres faster

☐ Continuous high speeds increase the risk of your vehicle breaking down

Before you start your journey, make sure that your vehicle can cope with the demands of high-speed driving. You should check a number of things, the main ones being oil, water and tyres. You also need to plan rest stops if you're making a long journey.

9.52 You're driving on a motorway. The car in front shows its hazard warning lights for a short time. What does this tell you?

☐ The driver wants you to overtake

☐ The other car is going to change lanes

☐ Traffic ahead is slowing or stopping suddenly

☐ There's a police speed check ahead

If the vehicle in front shows its hazard warning lights, there may be an incident, stopped traffic or queuing traffic ahead. By keeping a safe distance from the vehicle in front, you're able to look beyond it and see any hazards well ahead.

9.53 You're driving on the motorway. Well before you reach your intended exit, where should you position your vehicle?

☐ In the middle lane

☐ In the left-hand lane

☐ On the hard shoulder

☐ In any lane

You'll see the first advance direction sign one mile from a motorway exit. If you're travelling at 60 mph in the right-hand lane, you'll only have about 50 seconds before you reach the countdown markers. There'll be another sign at the half-mile point. Move to the left-hand lane in good time. Don't cut across traffic at the last moment and don't risk missing your exit.

9.54 What restrictions apply to new drivers holding a provisional driving licence?

☐ They can't drive over 30 mph

☐ They can't drive at night

☐ They can't drive unaccompanied

☐ They can't drive with more than one passenger

You won't be able to drive unaccompanied until you've passed your practical driving test. When you've passed, it's a good idea to ask your instructor to take you for a lesson on the motorway. Alternatively, you could take part in the Pass Plus scheme. This has been created for new drivers and includes motorway driving. Ask your instructor for details.

9.55 Your vehicle breaks down on the hard shoulder of a motorway. You need to use your mobile phone to call for help. What should you do?

☐ Stand at the rear of the vehicle while making the call

☐ Phone a friend and ask them to come and collect you

☐ Open the bonnet to help the emergency services know you've broken down

☐ Check your location from the marker posts on the left

You should use an emergency telephone when you break down on the motorway; only use your mobile if this isn't possible. The emergency services need to know your exact location so they can reach you as quickly as possible. Look for a number on the nearest marker post beside the hard shoulder. Give this number when you call the emergency services.

9.56   You're towing a trailer along a three-lane motorway. When may you use the right-hand lane?

☐ When there are lane closures

☐ When there's slow-moving traffic

☐ When you can maintain a high speed

☐ When large vehicles are in the left and centre lanes

If you're towing a caravan or trailer, you mustn't use the right-hand lane of a motorway with three or more lanes except in certain specified circumstances, such as when lanes are closed.

9.57   You're on a motorway. There's a contraflow system ahead. What would you expect to find?

☐ Temporary traffic lights

☐ Lower speed limits

☐ Wider lanes than normal

☐ Speed humps

When approaching a contraflow system, reduce speed in good time and obey all speed limits. You may be travelling in a narrower lane than normal, with no permanent barrier between you and the oncoming traffic. Be aware that the hard shoulder may be used for traffic and the road ahead could be obstructed by slow-moving or broken-down vehicles.

9.58   When may you stop on the hard shoulder of a motorway?

☐ In an emergency

☐ If you feel tired and need to rest

☐ If you miss the exit that you wanted

☐ To pick up a hitchhiker

You should only stop on the hard shoulder in a genuine emergency. Don't stop there to have a rest or picnic, pick up hitchhikers, answer a mobile phone or check a map. If you miss your intended exit, carry on to the next. Never reverse along the hard shoulder.

Section 10 Rules of the Road

10.1   What's the meaning of this sign?

□ Local speed limit applies

□ No waiting on the carriageway

□ National speed limit applies

□ No entry for vehicles

This sign doesn't tell you the speed limit in figures. You should know the speed limit for the type of road that you're on and the type of vehicle that you're driving. Study your copy of The Highway Code.

10.2   What's the national speed limit for cars and motorcycles on a dual carriageway?

□ 30 mph □ 50 mph □ 60 mph □ 70 mph

Make sure that you know the speed limit for the road that you're on. The speed limit on a dual carriageway or motorway is 70 mph for cars and motorcycles, unless signs indicate otherwise. The speed limits for different types of vehicle are listed in The Highway Code.

10.3   There are no speed-limit signs on the road. How is a 30 mph limit indicated?

□ By hazard warning lines

□ By street lighting

□ By pedestrian islands

□ By double or single yellow lines

There's a 30 mph speed limit where there are street lights unless signs show another limit.

10.4   You see street lights but no speed-limit signs. What will the speed limit usually be?

□ 30 mph □ 40 mph □ 50 mph □ 60 mph

The presence of street lights generally indicates that there's a 30 mph speed limit, unless signs tell you otherwise.

10.5   What does this sign mean?

□ Minimum speed 30 mph

□ End of maximum speed

□ End of minimum speed

□ Maximum speed 30 mph

The red slash through the sign indicates that the restriction has ended. In this case, the restriction was a minimum speed limit of 30 mph.

10.6   There's a tractor ahead. You want to overtake but you aren't sure whether it's safe. What should you do?

□ Follow another vehicle as it overtakes the tractor

□ Sound your horn to make the tractor pull over

□ Speed past, flashing your lights at oncoming traffic

□ Stay behind the tractor if you're in any doubt

Following a tractor can be frustrating, but never overtake if you're unsure whether it's safe. Ask yourself: 'Can I see far enough down the road to ensure that I can complete the manoeuvre safely?' It's better to be delayed for a minute or two than to take a chance that may cause a collision.

10.7 Which vehicle is most likely to take an unusual course at a roundabout?

- ☐ Estate car
- ☐ Delivery van
- ☐ Milk float
- ☐ Long lorry

Long vehicles might have to take a slightly different position when approaching the roundabout or going around it. This is to stop the rear of the vehicle cutting in and mounting the kerb.

10.8 When mustn't you stop on a clearway?

- ☐ At any time
- ☐ When it's busy
- ☐ In the rush hour
- ☐ During daylight hours

Clearways are in place so that traffic can flow without the obstruction of parked vehicles. Just one parked vehicle can cause an obstruction for all other traffic. You mustn't stop where a clearway is in force, not even to pick up or set down passengers.

10.9 What's the meaning of this sign?

- ☐ No entry
- ☐ Waiting restrictions
- ☐ National speed limit
- ☐ School crossing patrol

This sign indicates that there are waiting restrictions. It's normally accompanied by details of when the restrictions are in force.

Details of most signs in common use are shown in The Highway Code. For more comprehensive coverage, see Know Your Traffic Signs.

10.10 When can you park on the right-hand side of a road at night?

- ☐ When you're in a one-way street
- ☐ When you have your sidelights on
- ☐ When you're more than 10 metres (32 feet) from a junction
- ☐ When you're under a lamppost

Red rear reflectors show up when headlights shine on them. These are useful when you're parked at night, but they'll only reflect if you park in the same direction as the traffic flow. Normally you should park on the left, but in a one-way street you may also park on the right-hand side.

10.11 On a three-lane dual carriageway, what can the right-hand lane be used for?

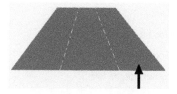

- ☐ Overtaking only, never turning right
- ☐ Overtaking or turning right
- ☐ Fast-moving traffic only
- ☐ Turning right only, never overtaking

You should normally use the left-hand lane on any dual carriageway unless you're overtaking or turning right.

When overtaking on a dual carriageway, look for vehicles ahead that are turning right. They may be slowing or stopped. You need to see them in good time so that you can take appropriate action.

10.12 You're approaching a busy junction. What should you do when, at the last moment, you realise you're in the wrong lane?

☐ Continue in that lane

☐ Force your way across

☐ Stop until the area has cleared

☐ Use clear arm signals to cut across

There are times when road markings are obscured by queuing traffic, or you're unsure which lane to use. If, at the last moment, you find you're in the wrong lane, don't cut across or bully other drivers to let you in. Follow the lane you're in and find somewhere safe to turn around and rejoin your route.

10.13 Where may you overtake on a one-way street?

☐ Only on the left-hand side

☐ Overtaking isn't allowed

☐ Only on the right-hand side

☐ On either the right or the left

You can overtake other traffic on either side when travelling in a one-way street. Make full use of your mirrors and ensure it's clear all around before you attempt to overtake. Look for signs and road markings, and use the most suitable lane for your destination.

10.14 How should you signal when going straight ahead at a roundabout?

☐ Indicate left before leaving the roundabout

☐ Don't indicate at any time

☐ Indicate right when approaching the roundabout

☐ Indicate left when approaching the roundabout

When going straight ahead at a roundabout, don't signal as you approach it. Indicate left just after passing the exit before the one you wish to take.

10.15 Which vehicle might have to take a different course from normal at roundabouts?

☐ Sports car

☐ Van

☐ Estate car

☐ Long vehicle

A long vehicle may have to straddle lanes either on or approaching a roundabout so that the rear wheels don't hit the kerb.

If you're following a long vehicle, stay well back and give it plenty of room.

10.16 On which occasion may you enter a box junction?

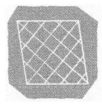

☐ When there are fewer than two vehicles ahead

☐ When signalled by another road user

☐ When your exit road is clear

☐ When traffic signs direct you

Yellow box junctions are marked on the road to prevent the road becoming blocked. Don't enter the box unless your exit road is clear. You may wait in the box if you want to turn right and your exit road is clear but oncoming traffic or other vehicles waiting to turn right are preventing you from making the turn.

10.17 When may you stop and wait in a box junction?

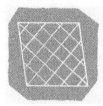

☐ When oncoming traffic prevents you from turning right

☐ When you're in a queue of traffic turning left

☐ When you're in a queue of traffic going ahead

☐ When you're on a roundabout

The purpose of yellow box markings is to keep junctions clear of queuing traffic. You may only wait in the marked area when you're turning right and your exit lane is clear but you can't complete the turn because of oncoming traffic or other traffic waiting to turning right.

10.18 Which person's signal to stop must you obey?

☐ A motorcyclist   ☐ A pedestrian

☐ A police officer   ☐ A bus driver

You must obey signals to stop given by police and traffic officers, traffic wardens and school crossing patrols. Failure to do so is an offence and could lead to prosecution.

10.19 You see a pedestrian waiting at a zebra crossing. What should you normally do?

☐ Go on quickly before they step onto the crossing

☐ Stop before you reach the zigzag lines and let them cross

☐ Stop to let them cross and wait patiently

☐ Ignore them as they're still on the pavement

By standing on the pavement, the pedestrian is showing an intention to cross. By looking well ahead, you'll give yourself time to see the pedestrian, check your mirrors and respond safely.

10.20 Who can use a toucan crossing?

☐ Cars and motorcycles

☐ Cyclists and pedestrians

☐ Buses and lorries

☐ Trams and trains

Toucan crossings are similar to pelican crossings but there's no flashing amber phase. Cyclists share the crossing with pedestrians and are allowed to cycle across when the green cycle symbol is shown.

10.21 You're waiting at a pelican crossing. What does it mean when the red light changes to flashing amber?

☐ Wait for pedestrians on the crossing to clear

☐ Move off immediately without any hesitation

☐ Wait for the green light before moving off

☐ Get ready and go when the continuous amber light shows

This light allows pedestrians already on the crossing to get to the other side in their own time, without being rushed. Don't rev your engine or start to move off while they're still crossing.

10.22 When can you park on the left opposite these road markings?

☐ If the line nearest to you is broken

☐ When there are no yellow lines

☐ To pick up or set down passengers

☐ During daylight hours only

You mustn't park or stop on a road marked with double white lines (even where one of the lines is broken) except to pick up or set down passengers.

10.23 You're turning right at a crossroads. An oncoming driver is also turning right. What's the advantage of turning behind the oncoming vehicle?

☐ You'll have a clearer view of any approaching traffic

☐ You'll use less fuel because you can stay in a higher gear

☐ You'll have more time to turn

☐ You'll be able to turn without stopping

When turning right at a crossroads where oncoming traffic is also turning right, it's generally safer to turn behind the approaching vehicle. This allows you a clear view of approaching traffic and is called 'turning offside to offside'. However, some junctions, usually controlled by traffic-light filters - are marked for vehicles to turn nearside to nearside.

10.24 You're travelling along a street with parked vehicles on the left-hand side. Why should you keep your speed down?

☐ So that oncoming traffic can see you more clearly

☐ You may set off car alarms

☐ There may be delivery lorries on the street

☐ Children may run out from between the vehicles

Travel slowly and carefully near parked vehicles. Beware of
• vehicles pulling out, especially bicycles and motorcycles
• pedestrians, especially children, who may run out from between cars
• drivers opening their doors.

10.25 What should you do when you meet an obstruction on your side of the road?

☐ Carry on, as you have priority

☐ Give way to oncoming traffic

☐ Wave oncoming vehicles through

☐ Accelerate to get past first

Take care if you have to pass a parked vehicle on your side of the road. Give way to oncoming traffic if there isn't enough room for you both to continue safely.

10.26 You're on a two-lane dual carriageway. Why would you use the right-hand lane?

☐ To overtake slower traffic

☐ For normal progress

☐ When staying at the minimum allowed speed

☐ To keep driving at a constant high speed

Normally you should travel in the left-hand lane and only use the right-hand lane for overtaking or turning right. Move back into the left lane as soon as it's safe but don't cut in across the path of the vehicle you've just passed.

10.27 Who has priority at an unmarked crossroads?

☐ The larger vehicle

☐ No-one has priority

☐ The faster vehicle

☐ The smaller vehicle

Practise good observation in all directions before you emerge or make a turn. Proceed only when you're sure it's safe to do so.

10.28 What's the nearest you may park to a junction?

☐ 10 metres (32 feet)

☐ 12 metres (39 feet)

☐ 15 metres (49 feet)

☐ 20 metres (66 feet)

Don't park within 10 metres (32 feet) of a junction (unless in an authorised parking place). This is to allow drivers emerging from, or turning into, the junction a clear view of the road they're joining. It also allows them to see hazards such as pedestrians or cyclists at the junction.

10.29 Where shouldn't you park?

☐ On a road with a 40 mph speed limit

☐ At or near a bus stop

☐ Where there's no pavement

☐ Within 20 metres (65 feet) of a junction

It may be tempting to park where you shouldn't while you run a quick errand. Careless parking is a selfish act and could endanger other road users. It's important not to park at or near a bus stop, as this could inconvenience passengers and may put them at risk as they get on or off the bus.

10.30 You're waiting at a level crossing. A train passes but the lights keep flashing. What must you do?

☐ Carry on waiting

☐ Phone the signal operator

☐ Edge over the stop line and look for trains

☐ Park and investigate

If the lights at a level crossing keep flashing after a train has passed, you should continue to wait, because another train might be coming. Time seems to pass slowly when you're held up in a queue. Be patient and wait until the lights stop flashing.

10.31 What does this sign tell you?

☐ No through road

☐ End of traffic-calming zone

☐ Free-parking zone ends

☐ No-waiting zone ends

The blue-and-red circular sign on its own means that waiting restrictions are in force. This sign shows that you're leaving the controlled zone and waiting restrictions no longer apply.

10.32 What must you do when entering roadworks where a temporary speed limit is displayed?

☐ Obey the speed limit

☐ Obey the limit, but only during rush hour

☐ Ignore the displayed limit

☐ Use your own judgment; the limit is only advisory

Where there are extra hazards, such as at roadworks, it's often necessary to slow traffic down by imposing a lower speed limit. These speed limits aren't advisory; they must be obeyed.

10.33 You're on a well-lit road at night, in a built-up area. How will using dipped headlights help?

☐ You can see further along the road

☐ You can go at a much faster speed

☐ You can switch to main beam quickly

☐ You can be easily seen by others

You may be difficult to see when you're travelling at night, even on a well-lit road. If you use dipped headlights rather than sidelights, other road users should be able to see you more easily.

10.34 The dual carriageway you're turning right onto has a very narrow central reservation. What should you do?

☐ Proceed to the central reservation and wait

☐ Wait until the road is clear in both directions

☐ Stop in the first lane so that other vehicles give way

☐ Emerge slightly to show your intentions

When the central reservation is narrow, you should treat a dual carriageway as one road. Wait until the road is clear in both directions before emerging to turn right. If you try to treat it as two separate roads and wait in the middle, you're likely to cause an obstruction and possibly a collision.

10.35   What's the national speed limit on a single carriageway road for cars and motorcycles?

☐ 30 mph   ☐ 50 mph   ☐ 60 mph   ☐ 70 mph

Exceeding the speed limit is dangerous and can result in you receiving penalty points on your licence. It isn't worth it. You should know the speed limit for the road that you're on by observing the road signs. Different speed limits apply if you're towing a trailer.

10.36   You park at night on a road with a 40 mph speed limit. What should you do?

☐ Park facing the traffic

☐ Park with parking lights on

☐ Park with dipped headlights on

☐ Park near a street light

You must use parking lights when parking at night on a road or in a lay-by on a road with a speed limit greater than 30 mph. You must also park in the direction of the traffic flow and not close to a junction.

10.37   Where will you see these red and white markers?

☐ Approaching the end of a motorway

☐ Approaching a concealed level crossing

☐ Approaching a concealed speed-limit sign

☐ Approaching the end of a dual carriageway

If there's a bend just before a level crossing, you may not be able to see the level-crossing barriers or waiting traffic. These signs give you an early warning that you may find these hazards just around the bend.

10.38   You're travelling on a motorway in England. You must stop when signalled to do so by which of these?

☐ Flashing amber lights above your lane

☐ A traffic officer

☐ Pedestrians on the hard shoulder

☐ A driver who has broken down

You'll find traffic officers on England's motorways. They work in partnership with the police, helping to keep traffic moving and helping to make your journey as safe as possible. It's an offence not to comply with the directions given by a traffic officer.

10.39   You're going straight ahead at a roundabout. How should you signal?

☐ Signal right on the approach and then left to leave the roundabout

☐ Signal left after you leave the roundabout and enter the new road

☐ Signal right on the approach to the roundabout and keep the signal on

☐ Signal left just after you pass the exit before the one you're going to take

To go straight ahead at a roundabout, you should normally approach in the left-hand lane, but check the road markings. At some roundabouts, the left lane on approach is marked 'left turn only', so make sure you use the correct lane to go ahead. You won't normally need to signal as you approach, but signal before you leave the roundabout, as other road users need to know your intentions.

10.40   When may you drive over a footpath?

☐ To overtake slow-moving traffic

☐ When the pavement is very wide

☐ If there are no pedestrians nearby

☐ To get onto a property

It's illegal to drive on or over a footpath, except to gain access to a property. If you need to cross a pavement, give priority to pedestrians.

10.41 A single carriageway road has this sign. What's the maximum permitted speed for a car towing a trailer?

☐ 30 mph ☐ 40 mph ☐ 50 mph ☐ 60 mph

When you're towing a trailer, a reduced speed limit also applies on dual carriageways and motorways. These lower speed limits apply to vehicles pulling all sorts of trailers, including caravans and horse boxes.

10.42 What's the speed limit for a car towing a small caravan along a dual carriageway?

☐ 50 mph ☐ 40 mph ☐ 70 mph ☐ 60 mph

The speed limit for cars towing caravans or trailers on dual carriageways or motorways is 60 mph. Due to the increased weight and size of the combination, you should plan further ahead. Take care in windy weather, as a strong side wind can make a caravan or large trailer unstable.

10.43 You want to park and you see this sign. What should you do on the days and times shown?

☐ Park in a bay and not pay

☐ Park on yellow lines and pay

☐ Park on yellow lines and not pay

☐ Park in a bay and pay

Parking restrictions apply in a variety of places and situations. Make sure you know the rules and understand where and when restrictions apply. Controlled parking areas will be indicated by signs and road markings. Parking in the wrong place could cause an obstruction and danger to other traffic. It can also result in a fine.

10.44 A cycle lane, marked by a solid white line, is in operation. What does this mean for car drivers?

☐ The lane may be used for parking your car

☐ You may drive in the lane at any time

☐ The lane may be used when necessary

☐ You mustn't drive in that lane

Leave the lane free for cyclists. At other times, when the lane isn't in operation, you should still be aware that there may be cyclists about. Give them plenty of room as you pass and allow for their movement from side to side, especially in windy weather or on a bumpy road.

10.45 You intend to turn left from a main road into a minor road. What should you do as you approach it?

☐ Keep just left of the middle of the road

☐ Keep in the middle of the road

☐ Swing out to the right just before turning

☐ Keep well to the left of the road

Your road position can help other road users to anticipate your actions. Keep to the left as you approach a left turn and don't swing out into the centre of the road in order to make the turn easier. This could endanger oncoming traffic and may cause other road users to misunderstand your intentions.

10.46 You're waiting at a level crossing. The red warning lights continue to flash after a train has passed by. What should you do?

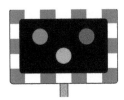

☐ Get out and investigate

☐ Telephone the signal operator

☐ Continue to wait

☐ Drive across carefully

At a level crossing, flashing red lights mean you must stop. If the train passes but the lights keep flashing, wait. Another train may be coming.

10.47 You're driving over a level crossing. The warning lights come on and a bell rings. What should you do?

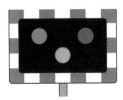

☐ Get everyone out of the vehicle immediately

☐ Stop and reverse back to clear the crossing

☐ Keep going and clear the crossing

☐ Stop immediately and use your hazard warning lights

Keep going; don't stop on the crossing. If the amber warning lights come on as you're approaching the crossing, you must stop unless it's unsafe to do so. Red flashing lights together with an audible signal mean you must stop.

10.48 You're on a busy main road and find that you're travelling in the wrong direction. What should you do?

☐ Turn into a side road on the right and reverse into the main road

☐ Make a U-turn in the main road

☐ Make a 'three-point' turn in the main road

☐ Turn around in a side road

Don't turn around in a busy street or reverse from a side road into a main road. Find a quiet side road and choose a place where you won't obstruct an entrance or exit. Look out for pedestrians and cyclists as well as other traffic.

10.49 During which manoeuvre may you remove your seat belt?

☐ Reversing   ☐ Hill start

☐ Emergency stop   ☐ Driving slowly

You may remove your seat belt while you're carrying out a manoeuvre that includes reversing. However, you must remember to put it back on again before you resume driving.

10.50 Over what distance are you allowed to reverse?

☐ No further than is necessary

☐ No more than a car's length

☐ As far as it takes to reverse around a corner

☐ The length of a residential street

You mustn't reverse further than is necessary. You may decide to turn your vehicle around by reversing into an opening or side road. When you reverse, always look all around you, and watch for pedestrians. Don't reverse from a side road into a main road.

10.51   What should you do when you're unsure whether it's safe to reverse your vehicle?

☐ Sound your horn   ☐ Rev your engine

☐ Get out and check   ☐ Reverse slowly

A small child could be hidden directly behind you, so, if you can't see all around your vehicle, get out and have a look. You could also ask someone reliable outside the vehicle to guide you.

10.52   When may you reverse from a side road into a main road?

☐ Only if both roads are clear of traffic

☐ Not at any time

☐ At any time

☐ Only if the main road is clear of traffic

Don't reverse into a main road from a side road. The main road is likely to be busy and the traffic on it moving quickly.

10.53   You want to turn right at a box junction. There's oncoming traffic. What should you do?

☐ Wait in the box junction if your exit is clear

☐ Wait before the junction until it's clear of all traffic

☐ Drive on; you can't turn right at a box junction

☐ Drive slowly into the box junction when signalled by oncoming traffic

You can wait in the box junction as long as your exit is clear. At some point there'll be a gap in the oncoming traffic, or the traffic lights will change, allowing you to proceed.

10.54   You're reversing your vehicle into a side road. When would the greatest hazard to passing traffic occur?

☐ After you've completed the manoeuvre

☐ Just before you actually begin to manoeuvre

☐ After you've entered the side road

☐ When the front of your vehicle swings out

Always check in all directions before reversing into a side road. Keep a good lookout throughout the manoeuvre. Act on what you see and wait if necessary.

10.55   Where's the safest place to park your vehicle at night?

☐ In a garage

☐ On a busy road

☐ In a quiet car park

☐ Near a red route

If you have a garage, use it. Your vehicle is less likely to be a victim of car crime if it's in a garage. Also, in winter, the windows will be kept free from ice and snow.

10.56   When may you stop on an urban clearway?

☐ To set down and pick up passengers

☐ To use a mobile telephone

☐ To ask for directions

☐ To load or unload goods

Urban clearways have their times of operation clearly signed. You may stop only for as long as is reasonable to pick up or set down passengers. You should ensure that you're not causing an obstruction for other traffic.

10.57   You're looking for somewhere to park your vehicle. The area is full except for spaces marked 'disabled use'. What can you do?

☐ You can use these spaces when elsewhere is full

☐ You can park in one of these spaces if you stay with your vehicle

☐ You can use one of the spaces as long as one is kept free

☐ You can't park there, unless you're permitted to do so

It's illegal to park in a space reserved for disabled users unless you're permitted to do so. These spaces are provided for people with limited mobility, who may need extra space to get in and out of their vehicle.

10.58 You're on a road that's only wide enough for one vehicle. A car is coming towards you. What should you do?

☐ Pull into a passing place on your right

☐ Force the other driver to reverse

☐ Pull into a passing place if your vehicle is wider

☐ Pull into a passing place on your left

Pull into the nearest passing place on the left if you meet another vehicle on a narrow road. If the nearest passing place is on the right, wait opposite it.

10.59 You're driving at night with your headlights on full beam. A vehicle is overtaking you. When should you dip your lights?

☐ Some time after the vehicle has passed you

☐ Before the vehicle starts to pass you

☐ Only if the other driver dips their headlights

☐ As soon as the vehicle passes you

On full beam, your lights could dazzle the driver in front. Dip your lights as soon as the driver passes you and drop back so that the dipped beam falls short of the other vehicle.

10.60 When may you drive a motor car in this bus lane?

☐ Outside its hours of operation

☐ To get to the front of a traffic queue

☐ You may not use it at any time

☐ To overtake slow-moving traffic

Some bus lanes operate only during peak hours and other vehicles may use them outside these hours. Make sure you check the sign for the hours of operation before driving in a bus lane.

10.61 Other than direction indicators, how can you give signals to other road users?

☐ By using brake lights

☐ By using sidelights

☐ By using fog lights

☐ By using interior lights

Your brake lights will give an indication to traffic behind that you're slowing down. Good anticipation will allow you time to check your mirrors before slowing.

10.62 You're parked in a busy high street. What's the safest way to turn your vehicle around so you can go the opposite way?

☐ Find a quiet side road to turn around in

☐ Drive into a side road and reverse into the main road

☐ Get someone to stop the traffic

☐ Do a U-turn

Make sure you carry out the manoeuvre without causing a hazard to other vehicles. Choose a place to turn that's safe and convenient for you and for other road users.

10.63 To help keep your vehicle secure at night, where should you park?

☐ Near a police station   ☐ In a quiet road

☐ On a red route   ☐ In a well-lit area

Whenever possible, park in an area that will be well lit at night.

10.64   You're driving in the right-hand lane of a dual carriageway. You see signs showing that the right-hand lane is closed 800 yards ahead. What should you do?

☐ Keep in that lane until you reach the queue

☐ Move to the left immediately

☐ Wait and see which lane is moving faster

☐ Move to the left in good time

Keep a lookout for traffic signs. If you're directed to change lanes, do so in good time. Don't

• push your way into traffic in another lane

• try to gain advantage by delaying changing lanes.

10.65   You're driving on a road that has a cycle lane. The lane is marked by a broken white line. What does this mean?

☐ You shouldn't drive in the lane unless it's unavoidable

☐ There's a reduced speed limit for motor vehicles using the lane

☐ Cyclists can travel in both directions in that lane

☐ The lane must be used by motorcyclists in heavy traffic

Cycle lanes are marked with either a solid or a broken white line. If the line is solid, you should check the times of operation shown on the signs, and not drive or park in the lane during those times. If the line is broken, you shouldn't drive or park in the lane unless it's unavoidable.

10.66   What must you have to park in a disabled space?

☐ A Blue Badge

☐ A wheelchair

☐ An advanced driver certificate

☐ An adapted vehicle

Don't park in a space reserved for disabled people unless you or your passenger are a disabled badge holder. The badge must be displayed in your vehicle, in the bottom left-hand corner of the windscreen.

10.67   When must you stop your vehicle?

☐ If you're involved in an incident that causes damage or injury

☐ At a junction where there are 'give way' lines

☐ At the end of a one-way street

☐ Before merging onto a motorway

You must stop your vehicle when signalled to do so by a

• police or traffic officer

• traffic warden

• school crossing patrol

• red traffic light.

You must also stop if you're involved in an incident which causes damage or injury to any other person, vehicle, animal or property.

Section 11 Road and Traffic Signs

11.1 How can you identify traffic signs that give orders?

☐ They're rectangular with a yellow border

☐ They're triangular with a blue border

☐ They're square with a brown border

☐ They're circular with a red border

There are three basic types of traffic sign: those that warn, those that inform and those that give orders. Generally, triangular signs warn, rectangular signs give information or directions and circular signs give orders. An exception is the eight-sided 'stop' sign.

11.2 Traffic signs giving orders are generally which shape?

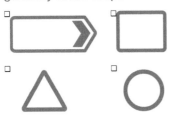

Road signs in the shape of a circle give orders. Those with a red circle are mostly prohibitive. The 'stop' sign is octagonal to give it greater prominence. Signs giving orders must always be obeyed.

11.3 Which type of sign tells you not to do something?

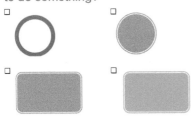

Signs in the shape of a circle give orders. A sign with a red circle means that you aren't allowed to do something. Study Know Your Traffic Signs to ensure that you understand what the different traffic signs mean.

11.4 What does this sign mean?

☐ Maximum speed limit with traffic calming

☐ Minimum speed limit with traffic calming

☐ '20 cars only' parking zone

☐ Only 20 cars allowed at any one time

If you're in a place where there are likely to be pedestrians (for example, outside a school, near a park, in a residential area or in a shopping area), you should be cautious and keep your speed down.

Many local authorities have taken steps to slow traffic down by creating traffic-calming measures such as speed humps. They're there for a reason; slow down.

11.5 Which sign means no motor vehicles are allowed?

You'll generally see this sign at the approach to a pedestrian-only zone.

11.6 What does this sign mean?

☐ New speed limit 20 mph

☐ No vehicles over 30 tonnes

☐ Minimum speed limit 30 mph

☐ End of 20 mph zone

Where you see this sign, the 20 mph restriction ends. Check all around for possible hazards and only increase your speed if it's safe to do so.

11.7 What does this sign mean?

☐ No overtaking

☐ No motor vehicles

☐ Clearway (no stopping)

☐ Cars and motorcycles only

A sign will indicate which types of vehicles are prohibited from certain roads. Make sure that you know which signs apply to the vehicle you're using.

11.8 What does this sign mean?

☐ No parking

☐ No road markings

☐ No through road

☐ No entry

'No entry' signs are used in places such as one-way streets to prevent vehicles driving against the traffic. To ignore one would be dangerous, both for yourself and for other road users, as well as being against the law.

11.9 What does this sign mean?

☐ Bend to the right

☐ Road on the right closed

☐ No traffic from the right

☐ No right turn

The 'no right turn' sign may be used to warn road users that there's a 'no entry' prohibition on a road to the right ahead.

11.10 Which sign means 'no entry'?

☐   ☐

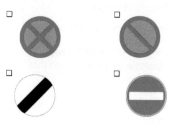

☐   ☐

Look for and obey traffic signs. Disobeying or not seeing a sign could be dangerous. It may also be an offence for which you could be prosecuted.

11.11 What does this sign mean?

☐ Route for trams only

☐ Route for buses only

☐ Parking for buses only

☐ Parking for trams only

Avoid blocking tram routes. Trams are fixed on their route and can't manoeuvre around other vehicles or pedestrians. Modern trams travel quickly and are quiet, so you might not hear them approaching.

11.12 Which type of vehicle does this sign apply to?

☐ Wide vehicles   ☐ Long vehicles

☐ High vehicles   ☐ Heavy vehicles

The triangular shapes above and below the dimensions indicate a height restriction that applies to the road ahead.

11.13 Which sign means no motor vehicles allowed?

☐   ☐

☐   ☐

This sign is used to enable pedestrians to walk free from traffic. It's often found in shopping areas.

11.14 What does this sign mean?

☐ You have priority   ☐ No motor vehicles

☐ Two-way traffic   ☐ No overtaking

Road signs that prohibit overtaking are placed in locations where passing the vehicle in front is dangerous. If you see this sign, don't attempt to overtake. The sign is there for a reason; you must obey it.

11.15 What does this sign mean?

☐ Waiting restrictions apply

☐ Waiting permitted

☐ National speed limit applies

☐ Clearway (no stopping)

There'll be a plate or additional sign to tell you when the restrictions apply.

11.16 What does this sign mean?

☐ End of restricted speed area

☐ End of restricted parking area

☐ End of clearway

☐ End of cycle route

Even though you've left the restricted area, make sure that you park where you won't endanger other road users or cause an obstruction.

11.17 Which sign means 'no stopping'?

Stopping where this clearway restriction applies is likely to cause congestion. Allow the traffic to flow by obeying the signs.

11.18 You see this sign ahead. What does it mean?

□ National speed limit applies

□ Waiting restrictions apply

□ No stopping

□ No entry

Clearways are stretches of road where you aren't allowed to stop unless it's an emergency. Stopping where these restrictions apply may be dangerous and is likely to cause an obstruction. Restrictions might apply for several miles and this may be indicated on the sign.

11.19 What does this sign mean?

□ Distance to parking place ahead

□ Distance to public telephone ahead

□ Distance to public house ahead

□ Distance to passing place ahead

If you intend to stop and rest, this sign allows you time to reduce speed and pull over safely.

11.20 What does this sign mean?

□ Vehicles may not park on the verge or footway

□ Vehicles may park on the left-hand side of the road only

□ Vehicles may park fully on the verge or footway

□ Vehicles may park on the right-hand side of the road only

In order to keep roads free from parked cars, there are some areas where you're allowed to park on the verge. Only do this where you see the sign. Parking on verges or footways anywhere else could lead to a fine.

11.21 What does this traffic sign mean?

□ No overtaking allowed

□ Give priority to oncoming traffic

□ Two-way traffic

□ One-way traffic only

Priority signs are normally shown where the road is narrow and there isn't enough room for two vehicles to pass. Examples are narrow bridges, roadworks and where there's a width restriction.

Make sure you know who has priority; don't force your way through. Show courtesy and consideration to other road users.

11.22 What's the meaning of this traffic sign?

☐ End of two-way road

☐ Give priority to vehicles coming towards you

☐ You have priority over vehicles coming towards you

☐ Bus lane ahead

Don't force your way through. Show courtesy and consideration to other road users. Although you have priority, make sure oncoming traffic is going to give way before you continue.

11.23 What shape is a 'stop' sign at a junction?

☐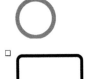

☐

☐

To make it easy to recognise, the 'stop' sign is the only sign of this shape. You must stop and take effective observation before proceeding.

11.24 At a junction, you see this sign partly covered by snow. What does it mean?

☐ Crossroads   ☐ Give way

☐ Stop   ☐ Turn right

The 'stop' sign is the only road sign that's octagonal. This is so that it can be recognised and obeyed even if it's obscured (for example, by snow).

11.25 What does this sign mean?

☐ Service area 30 miles ahead

☐ Maximum speed 30 mph

☐ Minimum speed 30 mph

☐ Lay-by 30 miles ahead

This sign is shown where slow-moving vehicles would impede the flow of traffic; for example, in tunnels. However, if you need to slow down or even stop to avoid an incident or potential collision, you should do so.

11.26 What does this sign mean?

☐ Give way to oncoming vehicles

☐ Approaching traffic passes you on both sides

☐ Turn off at the next available junction

☐ Pass either side to get to the same destination

These signs are often seen in one-way streets that have more than one lane. When you see this sign, use the route that's the most convenient and doesn't require a late change of direction.

11.27 What does this sign mean?

☐ Route for trams   ☐ Give way to trams

☐ Route for buses   ☐ Give way to buses

Take extra care when you encounter trams. Look out for road markings and signs that alert you to them. Modern trams are very quiet and you may not hear them approaching.

11.28 What does a circular traffic sign with a blue background do?

☐ Give warning of a motorway ahead

☐ Give directions to a car park

☐ Give motorway information

☐ Give an instruction

Signs with blue circles mostly give a positive instruction. These are often found in urban areas and include signs for mini-roundabouts and directional arrows.

11.29 Where would you see a contraflow bus and cycle lane?

☐ On a dual carriageway

☐ On a roundabout

☐ On an urban motorway

☐ On a one-way street

The traffic permitted to use a contraflow lane travels in the opposite direction to traffic in the other lanes on the road.

11.30 What does this sign mean?

☐ Bus station on the right

☐ Contraflow bus lane

☐ With-flow bus lane

☐ Give way to buses

There will also be markings on the road surface to indicate the bus lane. You mustn't use this lane for parking or overtaking.

11.31 What does a sign with a brown background show?

☐ Tourist directions

☐ Primary roads

☐ Motorway routes

☐ Minor roads

Signs with a brown background give directions to places of interest. They're often seen on a motorway, directing you along the easiest route to the attraction.

11.32 What does this sign mean?

☐ Tourist attraction ☐ Beware of trains

☐ Level crossing ☐ Beware of trams

These signs indicate places of interest and are designed to guide you by the easiest route. They're particularly useful when you're unfamiliar with the area.

11.33 What are triangular signs for?

☐ To give warnings ☐ To give information

☐ To give orders ☐ To give directions

This type of sign warns you of hazards ahead. Make sure you look at each sign that you pass on the road, so that you don't miss any vital instructions or information.

11.34 What does this sign mean?

☐ Turn left ahead ☐ T-junction

☐ No through road ☐ Give way

This type of sign warns you of hazards ahead. Make sure you look at each sign and road marking that you pass, so that you don't miss any vital instructions or information. This particular sign shows there's a T-junction with priority over vehicles from the right.

11.35 What does this sign mean?

☐ Multi-exit roundabout

☐ Risk of ice

☐ Six roads converge

☐ Place of historical interest

It will take up to ten times longer to stop when it's icy. Where there's a risk of icy conditions, you need to be aware of this and take extra care. If you think the road may be icy, don't brake or steer harshly, as your tyres could lose their grip on the road.

11.36 What does this sign mean?

☐ Crossroads

☐ Level crossing with gate

☐ Level crossing without gate

☐ Ahead only

The priority through the junction is shown by the broader line. You need to be aware of the hazard posed by traffic crossing or pulling out onto a major road.

11.37 What does this sign mean?

□ Ring road　　□ Mini-roundabout

□ No vehicles　　□ Roundabout

As you approach a roundabout, look well ahead and check all signs. Decide which exit you wish to take and move into the correct position as you approach the roundabout, signalling as required.

11.38 What information would be shown in a triangular road sign?

□ Road narrows　　□ Ahead only

□ Keep left　　□ Minimum speed

Warning signs are there to make you aware of potential hazards on the road ahead. Take note of the signs so you're prepared and can take whatever action is necessary.

11.39 What does this sign mean?

□ Cyclists must dismount

□ Cycles aren't allowed

□ Cycle route ahead

□ Cycle in single file

Where there's a cycle route ahead, a sign will show a bicycle in a red warning triangle. Watch out for children on bicycles and cyclists rejoining the main road.

11.40 Which sign means that pedestrians may be walking along the road?

□ 　　□

□ 　　□

When you pass pedestrians in the road, leave plenty of room. You might have to use the right-hand side of the road, so look well ahead, as well as in your mirrors, before pulling out. Take great care if a bend in the road obscures your view ahead.

11.41 Which of these signs means there's a double bend ahead?

□ 　　□

□ 　　□

Triangular signs give you a warning of hazards ahead. They're there to give you time to prepare for the hazard; for example, by adjusting your speed.

11.42 What does this sign mean?

□ Wait at the barriers

□ Wait at the crossroads

□ Give way to trams

□ Give way to farm vehicles

Obey the 'give way' signs. Trams are unable to steer around you if you misjudge when it's safe to enter the junction.

11.43 What does this sign mean?

☐ Hump bridge   ☐ Humps in the road

☐ Entrance to tunnel   ☐ Soft verges

These humps have been put in place to slow the traffic down. They're usually found in residential areas. Slow down to an appropriate speed.

11.44 Which of these signs means the end of a dual carriageway?

If you're overtaking, make sure you move back safely into the left-hand lane before you reach the end of the dual carriageway.

11.45 What does this sign mean?

☐ End of dual carriageway

☐ Tall bridge

☐ Road narrows

☐ End of narrow bridge

Don't wait until the last moment before moving into the left-hand lane. Plan ahead and don't rely on other traffic letting you in.

11.46 What does this sign mean?

☐ Side winds   ☐ Road noise

☐ Airport   ☐ Adverse camber

A warning sign with a picture of a windsock indicates that there may be strong side winds. This sign is often found on exposed roads.

11.47 What does this traffic sign mean?

☐ Slippery road ahead

☐ Tyres liable to punctures ahead

☐ Danger ahead

☐ Service area ahead

This sign is there to alert you to the likelihood of danger ahead. It may be accompanied by a plate indicating the type of hazard. Be ready to reduce your speed and take avoiding action.

11.48   You're about to overtake. What should you do when you see this sign?

Hidden dip

☐ Overtake the other driver as quickly as possible

☐ Move to the right to get a better view

☐ Switch your headlights on before overtaking

☐ Hold back until you can see clearly ahead

You won't be able to see any hazards that might be hidden in the dip. As well as oncoming traffic, the dip may conceal

• cyclists

• horse riders

• parked vehicles

• pedestrians

in the road.

11.49   What does this sign mean?

☐ Level crossing with gate or barrier

☐ Gated road ahead

☐ Level crossing without gate or barrier

☐ Cattle grid ahead

Some crossings have gates but no attendant or signals. You should stop, look both ways, listen and make sure that no train is approaching. If there's a telephone, contact the signal operator to make sure it's safe to cross.

11.50   What does this sign mean?

☐ No trams ahead

☐ Oncoming trams

☐ Trams crossing ahead

☐ Trams only

This sign tells you to beware of trams. If you don't usually drive in a town where there are trams, remember to look out for them at junctions and look for tram rails, signs and signals.

11.51   What does this sign mean?

☐ Adverse camber

☐ Steep hill downwards

☐ Uneven road

☐ Steep hill upwards

This sign gives you an early warning that the road ahead will slope downhill. Prepare to alter your speed and gear. Looking at the sign from left to right will show you whether the road slopes uphill or downhill.

11.52 What does this sign mean?

☐ Uneven road surface

☐ Bridge over the road

☐ Road ahead ends

☐ Water across the road

This sign is found where a shallow stream crosses the road. Heavy rainfall could increase the flow of water. If the water looks too deep or the stream has spread over a large distance, stop and find another route.

11.53 What does this sign mean?

☐ Turn left for parking area

☐ No through road on the left

☐ No entry for traffic turning left

☐ Turn left for ferry terminal

This sign shows you that you can't get through to another route by turning left at the junction ahead.

11.54 What does this sign mean?

☐ T-junction

☐ No through road

☐ Telephone box ahead

☐ Toilet ahead

You won't be able to find a through route to another road. Use this road only for access.

11.55 Which is the sign for a ring road?

☐   ☐

☐   ☐

Ring roads are designed to relieve congestion in towns and city centres.

11.56 What does this sign mean?

☐ The right-hand lane ahead is narrow

☐ Right-hand lane for buses only

☐ Right-hand lane for turning right

☐ The right-hand lane is closed

Yellow-and-black temporary signs may be used to inform you about roadworks or lane restrictions. Look well ahead. If you have to change lanes, do so in good time.

11.57 What does this sign mean?

☐ Change to the left lane

☐ Leave at the next exit

☐ Contraflow system

☐ One-way street

If you use the right-hand lane in a contraflow system, you'll be travelling with no permanent barrier between you and the oncoming traffic. Observe speed limits and keep a good distance from the vehicle ahead.

11.58 What does this sign mean?

☐ Leave motorway at next exit

☐ Lane for heavy and slow vehicles

☐ All lorries use the hard shoulder

☐ Rest area for lorries

Where there's a long, steep, uphill gradient on a motorway, a crawler lane may be provided. This helps the traffic to flow by diverting the slower heavy vehicles into a dedicated lane on the left.

11.59 What does a red traffic light mean?

☐ You should stop unless turning left

☐ Stop, if you're able to brake safely

☐ You must stop and wait behind the stop line

☐ Proceed with care

Whatever light is showing, you should know which light is going to appear next and be able to take appropriate action. For example, when amber is showing on its own, you'll know that red will appear next. This should give you ample time to anticipate and respond safely.

11.60 At traffic lights, what does it mean when the amber light shows on its own?

☐ Prepare to go

☐ Go if the way is clear

☐ Go if no pedestrians are crossing

☐ Stop at the stop line

When the amber light is showing on its own, the red light will follow next. The amber light means stop, unless you've already crossed the stop line or you're so close to it that stopping may cause a collision.

11.61 You're at a junction controlled by traffic lights. When shouldn't you proceed at green?

☐ When pedestrians are waiting to cross

☐ When your exit from the junction is blocked

☐ When you think the lights may be about to change

☐ When you intend to turn right

As you approach the lights, look into the road you wish to take. Only proceed if your exit road is clear. If the road is blocked, hold back, even if you have to wait for the next green signal.

11.62 You're in the left-hand lane at traffic lights, waiting to turn left. At which of these traffic lights mustn't you move on?

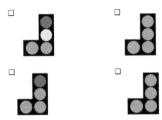

☐   ☐

☐   ☐

At some junctions, there may be separate signals for different lanes. These are called 'filter' lights. They're designed to help traffic flow at major junctions. Make sure that you're in the correct lane and proceed if the way is clear and the green light shows for your lane.

11.63   What does this sign mean?

☐ Traffic lights out of order

☐ Amber signal out of order

☐ Temporary traffic lights ahead

☐ New traffic lights ahead

You might see this sign where traffic lights are out of order. Proceed with caution, as nobody has priority at the junction.

11.64   When traffic lights are out of order, who has priority?

☐ Traffic going straight on

☐ Traffic turning right

☐ Nobody

☐ Traffic turning left

When traffic lights are out of order, you should treat the junction as an unmarked crossroads. Be cautious, as you may need to give way or stop. Look for traffic attempting to cross the junction, unaware that it doesn't have priority.

11.65   These flashing red lights mean that you must stop. Where would you find them?

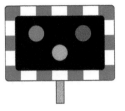

☐ Pelican crossings ☐ Motorway exits

☐ Zebra crossings ☐ Level crossings

These signals are found at level crossings, swing or lifting bridges, some airfields and emergency access sites. The flashing red lights mean stop whether or not the way seems to be clear.

11.66   What do these zigzag lines at pedestrian crossings mean?

☐ No parking at any time

☐ Parking allowed only for a short time

☐ Slow down to 20 mph

☐ Sounding horns isn't allowed

The approach to, and exit from, a pedestrian crossing is marked with zigzag lines. You mustn't park on them or overtake the leading vehicle when approaching the crossing. Parking here would block the view for pedestrians and approaching traffic.

11.67 When may you cross a double solid white line in the middle of the road?

- □ To pass traffic that's queuing back at a junction
- □ To pass a car signalling to turn left ahead
- □ To pass a road maintenance vehicle travelling at 10 mph or less
- □ To pass a vehicle that's towing a trailer

You may cross the solid white line to pass a stationary vehicle or to pass a pedal cycle, horse or road maintenance vehicle if it's travelling at 10 mph or less. You may also cross the solid white line to enter a side road or access a property.

11.68 What does this road marking mean?

- □ Don't cross the line
- □ No stopping allowed
- □ You're approaching a hazard
- □ No overtaking allowed

Road markings will warn you of a hazard ahead. A single broken line along the centre of the road, with long markings and short gaps, is a hazard warning line. Don't cross it unless you can see that the road is clear well ahead.

11.69 Where would you see this road marking?

- □ At traffic lights
- □ On road humps
- □ Near a level crossing
- □ At a box junction

Because the road has a dark colour, changes in level aren't easily seen. White triangles painted on the road surface give you an indication of where there are road humps.

11.70 Which of these is a hazard warning line?

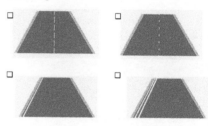

You need to know the difference between the normal centre line and a hazard warning line. If there's a hazard ahead, the markings are longer and the gaps shorter. This gives you advance warning of an unspecified hazard.

11.71 At this junction, there's a 'stop' sign and a solid white line on the road surface. Why is there a 'stop' sign here?

☐ Speed on the major road is derestricted

☐ It's a busy junction

☐ Visibility along the major road is restricted

☐ There are hazard warning lines in the centre of the road

If your view at a road junction is restricted, you must stop. There may also be a 'stop' sign. Don't emerge until you're sure no traffic is approaching. If you don't know, don't go.

11.72 You see this line across the road at the entrance to a roundabout. What does it mean?

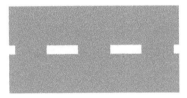

☐ Give way to traffic from the right

☐ Traffic from the left has right of way

☐ You have right of way

☐ Stop at the line

Slow down as you approach the roundabout and check for traffic from the right. If you need to stop and give way, stay behind the broken line until it's safe to emerge onto the roundabout.

11.73 How will a police officer in a patrol vehicle normally get you to stop?

☐ Flash the headlights, indicate left and point to the left

☐ Wait until you stop, then approach you

☐ Use the siren, overtake, cut in front and stop

☐ Pull alongside you, use the siren and wave you to stop

You must obey signals given by the police. If a police officer in a patrol vehicle wants you to pull over, they'll indicate this without causing danger to you or other traffic.

11.74 You're approaching a junction where the traffic lights aren't working. What should you do when a police officer gives this signal?

☐ Turn left only

☐ Turn right only

☐ Continue ahead only

☐ Stop at the stop line

When a police officer or traffic warden is directing traffic, you must obey them. They'll use the arm signals shown in The Highway Code. Learn what these signals mean and obey them.

11.75 The driver of the car in front is giving this arm signal. What does it mean?

- ☐ The driver is slowing down
- ☐ The driver intends to turn right
- ☐ The driver wishes to overtake
- ☐ The driver intends to turn left

There might be an occasion where another driver uses an arm signal. This may be because the vehicle's indicators are obscured by other traffic. In order for such signals to be effective, all drivers should know their meaning. Be aware that the 'left turn' signal might look similar to the 'slowing down' signal.

11.76 Where would you see these road markings?

- ☐ At a level crossing
- ☐ On a motorway slip road
- ☐ At a pedestrian crossing
- ☐ On a single-track road

When driving on a motorway or slip road, you mustn't enter an area marked with chevrons and bordered by a solid white line for any reason, except in an emergency.

11.77 What does this motorway sign mean?

- ☐ Change to the lane on your left
- ☐ Leave the motorway at the next exit
- ☐ Change to the opposite carriageway
- ☐ Pull up on the hard shoulder

On the motorway, signs sometimes show temporary warnings due to traffic or weather conditions. They may be used to indicate

- lane closures
- temporary speed limits
- weather warnings.

11.78 What does this motorway sign mean?

- ☐ Temporary minimum speed 50 mph
- ☐ No services for 50 miles
- ☐ Obstruction 50 metres (164 feet) ahead
- ☐ Temporary maximum speed 50 mph

Look out for signs above your lane or on the central reservation. These will give you important information or warnings about the road ahead. To allow for the high speed of motorway traffic, these signs may light up some distance from any hazard. Don't ignore the signs just because the road looks clear to you.

11.79   What does this sign mean?

☐ Through traffic to use left lane

☐ Right-hand lane T-junction only

☐ Right-hand lane closed ahead

☐ 11 tonne weight limit

You should change lanes as directed by the sign. Here, the right-hand lane is closed but the left-hand and centre lanes are available. Merging in turn is recommended when it's safe and traffic is going slowly; for example, at roadworks or a road traffic incident. When vehicles are travelling at speed, this isn't advisable and you should move into the appropriate lane in good time.

11.80   What does '25' mean on this motorway sign?

☐ The distance to the nearest town

☐ The route number of the road

☐ The number of the next junction

☐ The speed limit on the slip road

Before you set out on your journey, use a road map to plan your route. When you see an advance warning of your junction, make sure you get into the correct lane in plenty of time. Last-minute harsh braking and cutting across lanes at speed is extremely hazardous.

11.81   How should the right-hand lane of a three-lane motorway be used?

☐ As a high-speed lane

☐ As an overtaking lane

☐ As a right-turn lane

☐ As an acceleration lane

You should stay in the left-hand lane of a motorway unless you're overtaking another vehicle. The right-hand lane of a motorway is an overtaking lane; it isn't the 'fast lane'. After overtaking, move back to the left when it's safe to do so.

11.82   Where can you find reflective amber studs on a motorway?

☐ Separating the slip road from the motorway

☐ On the left-hand edge of the road

☐ On the right-hand edge of the road

☐ Separating the lanes

At night or in poor visibility, reflective studs on the road help you to judge your position on the carriageway.

11.83   Where on a motorway would you find green reflective studs?

☐ Separating driving lanes

☐ Between the hard shoulder and the carriageway

☐ At slip-road entrances and exits

☐ Between the carriageway and the central reservation

Knowing the colours of the reflective studs on the road will help you judge your position, especially at night, in foggy conditions or when visibility is poor.

11.84 What should you do when you see this sign as you travel along a motorway?

☐ Leave the motorway at the next exit

☐ Turn left immediately

☐ Change lane

☐ Move onto the hard shoulder

You'll see this sign if the motorway is closed ahead. Pull into the left-hand lane as soon as it's safe to do so. Don't wait until the last moment before you move across, because the lane may be busy and you'll have to rely on another driver making room for you.

11.85 What does this sign mean?

☐ No motor vehicles   ☐ End of motorway

☐ No through road   ☐ End of bus lane

When you leave the motorway, make sure that you check your speedometer. You may be going faster than you realise. Slow down and look for speed-limit signs.

11.86 Which of these signs means that the national speed limit applies?

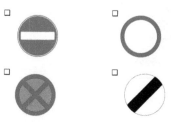

You should know the speed limit for the road on which you're travelling and the vehicle that you're driving. The different speed limits are shown in The Highway Code.

11.87 What's the maximum speed on a single carriageway road?

☐ 50 mph ☐ 60 mph ☐ 40 mph ☐ 70 mph

If you're travelling on a dual carriageway that becomes a single carriageway road, reduce your speed gradually so that you aren't exceeding the limit as you enter. There might not be a sign to remind you of the limit, so make sure you know the speed limits for different types of road and vehicle.

11.88 What does this sign mean?

☐ End of motorway

☐ End of restriction

☐ Lane ends ahead

☐ Free recovery ends

Temporary restrictions on motorways are shown on signs that have flashing amber lights. At the end of the restriction, you'll see this sign without any flashing lights.

11.89   What does this sign indicate?

☐ A diversion route

☐ A picnic area

☐ A pedestrian zone

☐ A cycle route

When a diversion route has been put in place, drivers are advised to follow a symbol, which may be a black triangle, square, circle or diamond shape on a yellow background.

11.90   What does this temporary sign indicate?

☐ The speed-limit change at the end of the motorway

☐ An advisory change of speed limit ahead

☐ A variable speed limit ahead

☐ A mandatory speed-limit change ahead

In the interests of road safety, temporary mandatory speed limits are imposed at all major roadworks. Signs like this, giving advance warning of the speed limit, are normally placed about three-quarters of a mile ahead of where the speed limit comes into force.

11.91   What does this traffic sign mean?

☐ Compulsory maximum speed limit

☐ Advisory maximum speed limit

☐ Compulsory minimum speed limit

☐ Advised separation distance

The sign gives you an early warning of a speed restriction. If you're travelling at a higher speed, slow down in good time. You could come across queuing traffic due to roadworks or a temporary obstruction.

11.92   What should you do when you see this sign at a crossroads?

☐ Maintain the same speed

☐ Carry on with great care

☐ Find another route

☐ Telephone the police

When traffic lights are out of order, treat the junction as an unmarked crossroads. Be very careful and be prepared to stop; no-one has priority.

11.93   You're signalling to turn right in busy traffic. How would you confirm your intention safely?

☐ Sound the horn

☐ Give an arm signal

☐ Flash your headlights

☐ Position over the centre line

In some situations, you may feel your indicators can't be seen by other road users. If you think you need to make your intention more obvious, give the arm signal shown in The Highway Code.

11.94 What does this sign mean?

☐ Motorcycles only

☐ No cars

☐ Cars only

☐ No motorcycles

You must comply with all traffic signs and be especially aware of those signs that apply specifically to the type of vehicle you're using.

11.95 You're on a motorway. A lorry has stopped in the right-hand lane. What should you do when you see this sign on the lorry?

☐ Move into the right-hand lane

☐ Stop behind the flashing lights

☐ Pass the lorry on the left

☐ Leave the motorway at the next exit

Sometimes work is carried out on the motorway without closing the lanes. When this happens, signs are mounted on the back of lorries to warn other road users of the roadworks ahead.

11.96 You're on a motorway. Red flashing lights appear above your lane only. What should you do?

☐ Continue in that lane and look for further information

☐ Move into another lane in good time

☐ Pull onto the hard shoulder

☐ Stop and wait for an instruction to proceed

Flashing red lights above your lane show that your lane is closed. You should move into another lane as soon as you can do so safely.

11.97 When may you sound the horn?

☐ To give you right of way

☐ To attract a friend's attention

☐ To warn others of your presence

☐ To make slower drivers move over

Never sound the horn aggressively. You mustn't sound it when driving in a built-up area between 11.30 pm and 7.00 am, or when you're stationary, unless another road user poses a danger. Don't scare animals by sounding your horn.

11.98 Your vehicle is stationary. When may you use its horn?

☐ When another road user poses a danger

☐ When the road is blocked by queuing traffic

☐ When it's used only briefly

☐ When signalling that you've just arrived

When your vehicle is stationary, only sound the horn if you think there's a risk of danger from another road user. Don't use it just to attract someone's attention. This causes unnecessary noise and could be misleading.

11.99 What does this sign mean?

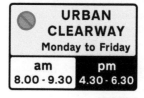

☐ You can park on the days and times shown

☐ No parking on the days and times shown

☐ No parking at all from Monday to Friday

☐ End of the urban clearway restrictions

Urban clearways are provided to keep traffic flowing at busy times. You may stop only briefly to set down or pick up passengers. Times of operation will vary from place to place, so always check the signs.

11.100 What does this sign mean?

☐ Quayside or river bank

☐ Steep hill downwards

☐ Uneven road surface

☐ Road liable to flooding

You should be careful in these locations, as the road surface is likely to be wet and slippery. There may be a steep drop to the water, and there may not be a barrier along the edge of the road.

11.101 What does this white line along the centre of the road mean?

☐ Bus lane marking   ☐ Hazard warning

☐ Give way warning   ☐ Lane marking

The centre of the road is usually marked by a broken white line, with lines that are shorter than the gaps. When the lines become longer than the gaps, this is a hazard warning line. Look well ahead for these, especially when you're planning to overtake or turn off.

11.102 What's the reason for the yellow crisscross lines painted on the road here?

☐ To mark out an area for trams only

☐ To prevent queuing traffic from blocking the junction on the left

☐ To mark the entrance lane to a car park

☐ To warn you of the tram lines crossing the road

Yellow 'box junctions' like this are often used where it's busy. Their purpose is to keep the junction clear for crossing traffic. Don't enter the painted area unless your exit is clear. The one exception is when you're turning right and are only prevented from doing so by oncoming traffic or by other vehicles waiting to turn right.

11.103 What's the reason for the hatched area along the centre of this road?

☐ It separates traffic flowing in opposite directions

☐ It marks an area to be used by overtaking motorcyclists

☐ It's a temporary marking to warn of the roadworks

☐ It separates the two sides of the dual carriageway

Areas of 'hatched markings' such as these separate traffic streams that could be a danger to each other. They're often seen on bends or where the road becomes narrow. If the area is bordered by a solid white line, you mustn't enter it except in an emergency.

11.104 Other drivers may sometimes flash their headlights at you. In which situation are they allowed to do this?

☐ To warn of a radar speed trap ahead

☐ To show that they're giving way to you

☐ To warn you of their presence

☐ To let you know there's a fault with your vehicle

If other drivers flash their headlights, this isn't a signal to show priority. The flashing of headlights has the same meaning as sounding the horn: it's a warning of their presence.

11.105 What speed limit is often found in narrow residential streets?

☐ 20 mph ☐ 25 mph ☐ 35 mph ☐ 40 mph

In some built-up areas, you may find the speed limit reduced to 20 mph. Driving at a slower speed will help give you the time and space to see and deal safely with hazards such as pedestrians and other vulnerable road users.

11.106 What does this signal mean?

☐ Cars must stop

☐ Trams must stop

☐ Both trams and cars must stop

☐ Both trams and cars can continue

The white light shows that trams must stop. The green light shows that other vehicles can go if the way is clear. Trams are being introduced into more cities, so you're likely to come across them and you should learn which signs apply to them.

11.107 Where would you find these road markings?

☐ At a railway crossing

☐ At a mini-roundabout

☐ On a motorway

☐ On a pedestrian crossing

These markings show the direction in which the traffic should go at a mini-roundabout.

11.108 A police car is following you. The police officer flashes the headlights and points to the left. What should you do?

☐ Turn left at the next junction

☐ Pull up on the left

☐ Stop immediately

☐ Move over to the left

You must pull up on the left as soon as it's safe to do so and switch off your engine.

11.109 You see this amber traffic light ahead. Which light, or lights, will come on next?

☐ Red alone

☐ Red and amber together

☐ Green and amber together

☐ Green alone

At junctions controlled by traffic lights, you must stop behind the white line until the lights change to green. A red light, an amber light, and red and amber lights showing together all mean stop.

You may proceed when the light is green unless your exit road is blocked or pedestrians are crossing in front of you.

If you're approaching traffic lights that are visible from a distance and the light has been green for some time, be ready to slow down and stop, because the lights are likely to change.

11.110 You see this signal overhead on the motorway. What does it mean?

☐ Leave the motorway at the next exit

☐ All vehicles use the hard shoulder

☐ Sharp bend to the left ahead

☐ Stop: all lanes ahead closed

You'll see this sign if there has been an incident ahead and the motorway is closed. You must obey the sign. Make sure that you prepare to leave in good time.

Don't cause drivers to take avoiding action by cutting in at the last moment.

11.111 What must you do when you see this sign?

☐ Stop only if traffic is approaching

☐ Stop even if the road is clear

☐ Stop only if children are waiting to cross

☐ Stop only if a red light is showing

'Stop' signs are situated at junctions where visibility is restricted or where there's heavy traffic. They must be obeyed: you must stop.

Take good all-round observation before moving off.

11.112 Which shape is used for a 'give way' sign?

☐

☐

☐

☐

Other warning signs are the same shape and colour, but the 'give way' triangle points downwards. When you see this sign, you must give way to traffic on the road that you're about to enter.

11.113 What does this sign mean?

☐ Buses turning

☐ Ring road

☐ Mini-roundabout

☐ Keep right

When you see this sign, look out for any direction signs and judge whether you need to signal your intentions. Do this in good time so that other road users approaching the roundabout know what you're planning to do.

11.114 What does this sign mean?

☐ Two-way traffic straight ahead

☐ Two-way traffic crosses a one-way road

☐ Two-way traffic over a bridge

☐ Two-way traffic crosses a two-way road

Be prepared for traffic approaching from junctions on either side of you. Try to avoid unnecessary changing of lanes just before the junction.

11.115 What does this sign mean?

☐ Two-way traffic crosses a one-way road

☐ Traffic approaching you has priority

☐ Two-way traffic straight ahead

☐ Motorway contraflow system ahead

This sign may be at the end of a dual carriageway or a one-way street. It's there to warn you of oncoming traffic.

11.116 What does this sign mean?

☐ Hump bridge

☐ Traffic-calming hump

☐ Low bridge

☐ Uneven road

You'll need to slow down. At hump bridges, your view ahead will be restricted and the road will often be narrow. If the bridge is very steep, sound your horn to warn others of your approach. Going over the bridge too fast is highly dangerous to other road users and could even cause your wheels to leave the road, with a resulting loss of control.

11.117 What does this sign mean?

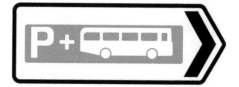

☐ Direction to park-and-ride car park

☐ No parking for buses or coaches

☐ Direction to bus and coach park

☐ Parking area for cars and coaches

To ease the congestion in town centres, some cities and towns provide park-and-ride schemes. These allow you to park in a designated area and ride by bus into the centre.

Park-and-ride schemes are usually cheaper and easier than car parking in the town centre.

11.118 What should you do when approaching traffic lights where red and amber are showing together?

☐ Pass the lights if the road is clear

☐ Take care because there's a fault with the lights

☐ Wait for the green light

☐ Stop because the lights are changing to red

Be aware that other traffic might still be clearing the junction as you approach. A green light means you may go on, but only if the way is clear.

11.119   Where does this marking normally appear on a road?

□ Just before a 'no entry' sign

□ Just before a 'give way' sign

□ Just before a 'stop' sign

□ Just before a 'no through road' sign

This road marking means you should give way to traffic on the main road. It might not be used at junctions where there isn't much traffic. However, if there's a double broken line across the junction, the 'give way' rules still apply.

11.120   At a railway level crossing, the red lights continue to flash after a train has gone by. What should you do?

□ Phone the signal operator

□ Alert drivers behind you

□ Wait

□ Proceed with caution

You must always obey red flashing stop lights. If a train passes but the lights continue to flash, another train will be passing soon. Cross only when the lights go off and the barriers open.

11.121   You're in a tunnel and you see this sign. What does it mean?

□ Direction to emergency pedestrian exit

□ Beware of pedestrians: no footpath ahead

□ No access for pedestrians

□ Beware of pedestrians crossing ahead

If you have to leave your vehicle and get out of a tunnel by an emergency exit, do so as quickly as you can. Follow the signs directing you to the nearest exit point. If there are several people using the exit, don't panic but try to leave in a calm and orderly manner.

11.122   Which of these signs shows that you're entering a one-way system?

□   □

□   □

If the road has two lanes, you can use either lane and overtake on either side. Use the lane that's more convenient for your destination unless signs or road markings indicate otherwise.

11.123   What does this sign mean?

□ With-flow bus and cycle lane

□ Contraflow bus and cycle lane

□ No buses and cycles allowed

□ No waiting for buses and cycles

Buses and cycles can travel in this lane. In this example, they'll flow in the same direction as other traffic. If it's busy, they may be passing you on the left, so watch out for them. Times on the sign will show the lane's hours of operation; if no times are shown, or there's no sign at all, this means the lane is in operation 24 hours a day. In some areas, other vehicles, such as taxis and motorcycles, are allowed to use bus lanes. The sign will show if this is the case.

11.124 What does this sign mean?

- ☐ School crossing patrol
- ☐ No pedestrians allowed
- ☐ Pedestrian zone – no vehicles
- ☐ Zebra crossing ahead

Look well ahead and be ready to stop for any pedestrians crossing, or about to cross, the road. Also check the pavements for anyone who looks like they might step or run into the road.

11.125 Which arm signal tells you that the car you're following is going to pull up?

There may be occasions when drivers need to give an arm signal to confirm their intentions. This could include in bright sunshine, at a complex road layout, when stopping at a pedestrian crossing or when turning right just after passing a parked vehicle. You should understand what each arm signal means. If you give arm signals, make them clear, correct and decisive.

11.126 Which of these signs means turn left ahead?

Blue circles tell you what you must do and this sign gives a clear instruction to turn left ahead. You should be looking out for signs at all times and know what they mean.

11.127 You're approaching a red traffic light. What will the signal show next?

- ☐ Red and amber
- ☐ Green alone
- ☐ Amber alone
- ☐ Green and amber

If you know which light is going to show next, you can plan your approach accordingly. This can help prevent excessive braking or hesitation at the junction.

11.128 What does this sign mean?

- ☐ Low bridge ahead
- ☐ Tunnel ahead
- ☐ Ancient monument ahead
- ☐ Traffic danger spot ahead

When approaching a tunnel, switch on your dipped headlights. Be aware that your eyes might need to adjust to the sudden darkness. You may need to reduce your speed.

11.129   What does the white line along the side of the road indicate?

☐ The edge of the carriageway

☐ The approach to a hazard

☐ No parking

☐ No overtaking

A continuous white line is used on many roads to indicate the edge of the carriageway. This can be useful when visibility is restricted. The line is discontinued at junctions, lay-bys, and entrances to or exits from private drives.

11.130   What does this white arrow on the road ahead mean?

☐ Entrance on the left

☐ All vehicles turn left

☐ Keep left of the hatched markings

☐ Road bends to the left

Don't attempt to overtake here, as there might be unseen hazards over the brow of the hill. Keep to the left.

11.131   How should you give an arm signal to turn left?

☐

☐

☐

☐

There may be occasions when other road users are unable to see your indicator, such as in bright sunlight or at a busy, complicated junction. In these cases, an arm signal will help others to understand your intentions.

11.132   You're waiting at a T-junction. A vehicle is coming from the right, with its left indicator flashing. What should you do?

☐ Move out and accelerate hard

☐ Wait until the vehicle starts to turn in

☐ Pull out before the vehicle reaches the junction

☐ Move out slowly

Other road users may give misleading signals. When you're waiting at a junction, don't emerge until you're sure of their intentions.

11.133   When may you use hazard warning lights while you're driving?

☐ Instead of sounding the horn in a built-up area between 11.30 pm and 7.00 am

☐ On a motorway or unrestricted dual carriageway, to warn of a hazard ahead

☐ On rural routes, after a sign warning of animals

☐ On the approach to toucan crossings where cyclists are waiting to cross

When there's queuing traffic ahead and you have to slow down or even stop, briefly showing your hazard warning lights will help alert following traffic to the hazard.

11.134   When can you park on these markings outside a school?

IΛ-SCHOOL KEEP CLEAR-ΛI

☐ When you're picking up children

☐ Not under any circumstances

☐ When there's nowhere else available

☐ When you're dropping off children

You shouldn't stop on yellow zigzag lines outside schools, not even to set down or pick up children or other passengers. This is to make sure passing drivers and pedestrians have an unobstructed view.

11.135   Why should you make sure that your indicators are cancelled after turning?

☐ To avoid flattening the battery

☐ To avoid misleading other road users

☐ To avoid dazzling other road users

☐ To avoid damage to the indicator relay

Leaving your indicators on could confuse other road users and may even lead to a crash. Be aware that if you haven't taken a sharp turn, your indicators may not self-cancel and you'll need to turn them off manually.

11.136   You're driving in busy traffic. You want to pull up on the left just after a junction on the left. When should you signal?

☐ As you're passing or just after the junction

☐ Just before you reach the junction

☐ Well before you reach the junction

☐ It would be better not to signal at all

You need to signal to let other drivers know your intentions. However, if you indicate too early, they may think you're turning left into the junction. Correct timing of the signal is very important to avoid misleading others.

Section 12 Essential Documents

12.1 For how long is an MOT certificate normally valid?

☐ Three years after the date it was issued

☐ 10,000 miles

☐ One year after the date it was issued

☐ 30,000 miles

Some garages will remind you that your vehicle is due for its annual MOT test, but not all do. To ensure continuous cover, you may take your vehicle for its MOT up to one month before its existing MOT certificate runs out. The expiry date on the new certificate will be 12 months after the expiry date on the old certificate.

12.2 What is a cover note?

☐ A document issued before you receive your driving licence

☐ A document issued before you receive your insurance certificate

☐ A document issued before you receive your registration document

☐ A document issued before you receive your MOT certificate

Sometimes an insurance company will issue a temporary insurance certificate called a cover note. It gives you the same insurance cover as your certificate but lasts for a limited period, usually one month.

12.3 You've just passed your practical test. You don't hold a full licence in another category. Within two years you get six penalty points on your licence. What will you have to do?

☐ Retake only your theory test

☐ Retake your theory and practical tests

☐ Retake only your practical test

☐ Reapply for your full licence immediately

If you accumulate six or more penalty points within two years of gaining your first full licence, it will be revoked. The six or more points include any gained due to offences you committed before passing your test. If this happens, you may only drive as a learner until you pass both the theory and practical tests again.

12.4 For how long is a Statutory Off-Road Notification (SORN) valid?

☐ Until the vehicle is taxed, sold or scrapped

☐ Until the vehicle is insured and MOT'd

☐ Until the vehicle is repaired or modified

☐ Until the vehicle is used on the road

A SORN allows you to keep a vehicle off-road and untaxed. SORN will end when the vehicle is taxed, sold or scrapped.

12.5 What is a Statutory Off-Road Notification (SORN)?

☐ A notification to tell DVSA that a vehicle doesn't have a current MOT

☐ Information kept by the police about the owner of a vehicle

☐ A notification to tell DVLA that a vehicle isn't being used on the road

☐ Information held by insurance companies to check a vehicle is insured

If you want to keep a vehicle untaxed and off the public road, you must make a SORN. It's an offence not to do so. Your SORN is valid until your vehicle is taxed, sold or scrapped.

12.6 What's the maximum fine for driving without insurance?

☐ Unlimited ☐ £500 ☐ £1000 ☐ £5000

Driving without insurance is a serious offence. As well as an unlimited fine, you may be disqualified or incur penalty points.

12.7 Who's legally responsible for ensuring that a vehicle registration certificate (V5C) is updated?

☐ The registered vehicle keeper

☐ The vehicle manufacturer

☐ Your insurance company

☐ The licensing authority

It's your legal responsibility to keep the details on your vehicle registration certificate (V5C) up to date. You should tell the licensing authority about any changes. These include your name, address or vehicle details. If you don't do this, you may have problems when you try to sell your vehicle.

12.8 In which of these circumstances must you show your insurance certificate?

☐ When making a SORN

☐ When buying or selling a vehicle

☐ When a police officer asks you for it

☐ When having an MOT inspection

You must produce a valid insurance certificate when requested by a police officer. If you can't do this immediately, you may be asked to take it to a police station. Other documents you may be asked to produce are your driving licence and the vehicle's MOT certificate.

12.9 Which of these is needed before you can legally use a vehicle on the road?

☐ A valid driving licence

☐ Breakdown cover

☐ Proof of your identity

☐ A vehicle handbook

Using a vehicle on the road illegally carries a heavy fine and can lead to penalty points on your driving licence. You must have

• a valid driving licence
• paid the appropriate vehicle tax
• proper insurance cover.

12.10 What must you have when you apply to renew your vehicle tax?

☐ Valid insurance

☐ The vehicle's chassis number

☐ The handbook

☐ A valid driving licence

You can renew your vehicle tax online, at post offices and vehicle registration offices, or by phone. When applying, make sure you have all the relevant valid documents, including a valid MOT test certificate where applicable.

12.11 A police officer asks to see your documents. You don't have them with you. Within what time must you produce them at a police station?

☐ 5 days ☐ 7 days ☐ 14 days ☐ 21 days

You don't have to carry around your vehicle's documents wherever you go. If a police officer asks to see them and you don't have them with you, you may be asked to produce them at a police station within 7 days.

12.12 What must you make sure of before you drive someone else's vehicle?

☐ That the vehicle owner has third-party insurance cover

☐ That your own vehicle has insurance cover

☐ That the vehicle is insured for your use

☐ That the insurance documents are in the vehicle

Driving a vehicle without insurance cover is illegal, so be sure that, whoever's car you drive, you're insured – whether on their policy or on your own. If you need to take out insurance, it's worth comparing several quotes before you decide which insurance provider best meets your needs.

12.13 Your car needs to pass an MOT test. What may be invalidated if you drive the car without a current MOT certificate?

☐ The vehicle service record

☐ Your insurance

☐ The vehicle tax

☐ Your vehicle registration document

If your vehicle requires an MOT certificate, it's illegal to drive it without one and your insurance may be invalid if you do so. The only exceptions are that you may drive to a pre-arranged MOT test appointment, or to a garage for repairs required for the test.

12.14 What must a newly qualified driver do?

☐ Display green L plates

☐ Keep under 40 mph for 12 months

☐ Be accompanied on a motorway

☐ Have valid motor insurance

It's your responsibility to make sure you're properly insured for the vehicle you're driving. This is the case regardless of whether you're a newly qualified driver or one with more experience.

12.15 You have third-party insurance. What does this cover?

☐ Damage to your vehicle

☐ Fire damage to your vehicle

☐ Flood damage to your vehicle

☐ Damage to other vehicles

Third-party insurance doesn't cover damage to your own vehicle or injury to yourself. If you have a crash and your vehicle is damaged, you might have to carry out the repairs at your own expense.

12.16 Who's responsible for paying the vehicle tax?

☐ The driver of the vehicle

☐ The registered keeper of the vehicle

☐ The car dealer

☐ The Driver and Vehicle Licensing Agency (DVLA)

The registered keeper of the vehicle is responsible for paying the vehicle tax or making a Statutory Off-Road Notification (SORN) if the vehicle is to be kept untaxed and off the road.

12.17 What information is found on a vehicle registration document?

☐ The registered keeper

☐ The type of insurance cover

☐ The service history details

☐ The date of the MOT

Every vehicle used on the road has a registration document. This shows the vehicle's details, including date of first registration, registration number, registered keeper, previous keeper, make of vehicle, engine size, chassis number, year of manufacture and colour.

12.18   When must you contact the vehicle licensing authority?

☐ When you take your vehicle abroad on holiday

☐ When you change your vehicle

☐ When you use your vehicle for work

☐ When your vehicle's insurance is due

The licensing authority needs to keep its records up to date. It sends out a reminder when a vehicle's tax is due for renewal. To do this, it needs to know the name and address of the registered keeper. Every vehicle in the country is registered, so it's possible to trace its history.

12.19   When must you notify the licensing authority?

☐ When your health affects your driving

☐ When you have to work abroad

☐ When you lend your vehicle to someone

☐ When your vehicle needs an MOT certificate

The licensing authorities hold the records of all vehicles, drivers and riders in Great Britain and Northern Ireland. They need to know if you have a medical condition that might affect your ability to drive safely. You must tell them if your health deteriorates and you become unfit to drive.

12.20   When may the cost of your insurance come down?

☐ When you're under 25 years old

☐ When you don't wear glasses

☐ When you pass the driving test first time

☐ When you complete the Pass Plus scheme

The cost of insurance varies with your age and how long you've been driving. Usually, the younger you are, the more expensive it is, especially if you're under 25.

Pass Plus provides additional training to newly qualified drivers. The scheme is recognised by many insurance companies, and taking this extra training could give you reduced insurance premiums, as well as improving your skills and experience.

12.21   Which of these is a requirement before you can supervise a learner driver?

☐ You must have held a licence for at least a year

☐ You must be at least 21 years old

☐ You must be an approved driving instructor

☐ You must hold an advanced driving certificate

Learner drivers benefit by combining professional driving lessons with private practice. However, you need to be at least 21 years old and have held your driving licence for at least 3 years before you can supervise a learner driver.

12.22   Your car requires an MOT certificate. When is it legal to drive it without an MOT certificate?

☐ Up to seven days after the old certificate has run out

☐ When driving to an MOT centre to arrange an appointment

☐ When driving the car with the owner's permission

☐ When driving to an appointment at an MOT centre

When a car is three years old (four years old in Northern Ireland), it must pass an MOT test and have a valid MOT certificate before it can be used on the road. Exceptionally, you may

• drive to a pre-arranged test appointment or to a garage for repairs required for the test

• drive vehicles made before 1960 without an MOT test, but they must be in a roadworthy condition before being used on the road.

12.23   A new car will need its first MOT test when it's how old?

☐ One year   ☐ Three years

☐ Five years   ☐ Seven years

The vehicle you drive must be roadworthy and in good condition. If it's over three years old, it must pass an MOT test to remain in use on the road (unless it's exempt from the MOT test – see GOV.UK).

12.24 The Pass Plus scheme has been created for new drivers. What's its main purpose?

☐ To allow you to drive faster

☐ To allow you to carry passengers

☐ To improve your basic skills

☐ To let you drive on motorways

New drivers are far more vulnerable on the road and more likely to be involved in incidents. The Pass Plus scheme has been designed to improve new drivers' basic skills and help widen their driving experience.

12.25 Your vehicle is insured third-party only. What does this cover?

☐ Damage to your vehicle

☐ Damage to other vehicles

☐ Injury to yourself

☐ All damage and injury

Third-party insurance cover is usually cheaper than comprehensive cover. However, it doesn't cover any damage caused to your own vehicle or property. It only covers damage and injury you cause to others.

12.26 What's the legal minimum insurance cover you must have to drive on public roads?

☐ Third party, fire and theft

☐ Comprehensive

☐ Third party only

☐ Personal injury cover

The minimum insurance required by law is third-party cover. This covers your liability to others involved in a collision but not damage to your vehicle. Basic third-party insurance also won't cover theft or fire damage. Ask your insurance company for advice on the best cover for you and make sure that you read the policy carefully.

12.27 You claim on your insurance to have your car repaired. Your policy has an excess of £100. What does this mean?

☐ The insurance company will pay the first £100 of any claim

☐ You'll be paid £100 if you don't claim within one year

☐ Your vehicle is insured for a value of £100 if it's stolen

☐ You'll have to pay the first £100 of the cost of repairs to your car

Having an excess on your policy will help to keep the premium down. However, if you make a claim, you'll have to pay the excess yourself – in this case, £100.

12.28 What's the purpose of the Pass Plus scheme?

☐ To give you a discount on your MOT

☐ To improve your basic driving skills

☐ To increase your mechanical knowledge

☐ To allow you to drive anyone else's vehicle

After passing your practical driving test, you can take further training. One option is known as the Pass Plus scheme. It's designed to improve your basic driving skills and involves a series of modules, including night-time and motorway driving.

12.29 What does the Pass Plus scheme enable newly qualified drivers to do?

☐ Widen their driving experience

☐ Supervise a learner driver

☐ Increase their insurance premiums

☐ Avoid mechanical breakdowns

The Pass Plus scheme was created for newly qualified drivers. It aims to widen their driving experience and improve basic skills. After passing the practical driving test, additional professional training can be taken with an approved driving instructor (ADI). Some insurance companies also offer discounts to holders of a Pass Plus certificate.

Section 13 Incidents, Accidents and Emergencies

13.1   You see a car on the hard shoulder of a motorway with a 'help' pennant displayed. What does this mean?

☐ The driver is likely to be a disabled person

☐ The driver is first-aid trained

☐ The driver is a foreign visitor

☐ The driver is a rescue patrol officer

If a disabled driver's vehicle breaks down and they're unable to walk to an emergency phone, they're advised to stay in their car and switch on the hazard warning lights. They may also display a 'help' pennant in their vehicle.

13.2   When should you use hazard warning lights?

☐ When you slow down quickly on a motorway because of a hazard ahead

☐ When you leave your car at the roadside to visit a shop

☐ When you wish to stop on double yellow lines

☐ When you need to park on the pavement

Hazard warning lights are fitted to all modern cars and some motorcycles. They should be used to warn

• other road users when your vehicle is causing a temporary obstruction; for example, after a collision or when it's broken down

• following drivers on a motorway of a hazard or obstruction ahead.

They shouldn't be used as an excuse for dangerous or illegal parking.

13.3   When are you allowed to use hazard warning lights?

☐ When stopped and temporarily obstructing traffic

☐ When travelling during darkness without headlights

☐ When parked on double yellow lines to visit a shop

☐ When travelling slowly because you're lost

You mustn't use hazard warning lights while moving, except to warn traffic behind when you slow suddenly on a motorway or unrestricted dual carriageway.

Never use hazard warning lights to excuse dangerous or illegal parking.

13.4   You're going through a congested tunnel and have to stop. What should you do?

☐ Pull up very close to the vehicle in front to save space

☐ Ignore any message signs, as they're never up to date

☐ Keep a safe distance from the vehicle in front

☐ Make a U-turn and find another route

It's important to keep a safe distance from the vehicle in front at all times. This still applies in congested tunnels, even if you're moving very slowly or have stopped. If the vehicle in front breaks down, you may need room to manoeuvre past it.

13.5   On a motorway, when should the hard shoulder be used?

☐ When answering a mobile phone

☐ When an emergency arises

☐ When taking a short rest

☐ When checking a road map

The hard shoulder should only be used in a genuine emergency. If possible, and if it's safe, use a roadside telephone to call for help. This will give your exact location to the operator. Never cross the carriageway or a slip road to use a telephone on the other side of the road.

13.6   You arrive at the scene of a crash where someone is bleeding heavily from a wound in their arm. Nothing is embedded in the wound. What could you do to help?

☐ Walk them around and keep them talking

☐ Dab the wound

☐ Get them a drink

☐ Apply pressure over the wound

If possible, lay the casualty down. Protect yourself from exposure to blood and, when you're sure there's nothing in the wound, apply firm pressure to it using clean material.

13.7   You're at an incident. What could you do to help a casualty who's unconscious?

☐ Take photographs of the scene

☐ Check that they're breathing normally

☐ Move them to somewhere more comfortable

☐ Splash their face with cool water

If a casualty is unconscious, you need to check that they're breathing normally. Look for chest movements, look and listen for breathing, and feel for breath on your cheek.

13.8   Following a collision, someone has suffered a burn. The burn needs to be cooled. What's the shortest time it should be cooled for?

☐ 5 minutes   ☐ 10 minutes

☐ 15 minutes   ☐ 20 minutes

Check the casualty for shock and, if possible, try to cool the burn for at least 10 minutes using clean, cool water.

13.9   A casualty isn't breathing normally and needs CPR. At what rate should you press down and release on the centre of their chest?

☐ 10 times per minute

☐ 120 times per minute

☐ 60 times per minute

☐ 240 times per minute

If a casualty isn't breathing normally, cardiopulmonary resuscitation (CPR) may be needed to maintain circulation. Place two hands on the centre of the chest and press down hard and fast – around 5–6 centimetres and about twice a second.

13.10   A person has been injured. They may be suffering from shock. What are the warning signs to look for?

☐ Flushed complexion

☐ Warm dry skin

☐ Slow pulse

☐ Pale grey skin

The effects of shock may not be immediately obvious. Warning signs are rapid pulse, sweating, pale grey skin and rapid shallow breathing.

13.11 An injured person has been placed in the recovery position. They're unconscious but breathing normally. What else should be done?

☐ Press firmly between their shoulders

☐ Place their arms by their side

☐ Give them a hot sweet drink

☐ Check their airway remains open

After a casualty has been placed in the recovery position, make sure their airway remains open and monitor their condition until medical help arrives. Where possible, don't move a casualty unless there's further danger.

13.12 An injured motorcyclist is lying unconscious in the road. The traffic has stopped and there's no further danger. What should you do to help?

☐ Remove their safety helmet

☐ Seek medical assistance

☐ Move the person off the road

☐ Remove their leather jacket

If someone has been injured, the sooner proper medical attention is given the better. Ask someone to phone for help or do it yourself. An injured person should only be moved if they're in further danger. An injured motorcyclist's helmet shouldn't be removed unless it's essential.

13.13 What should you do if you see a large box fall from a lorry onto the motorway?

☐ Go to the next emergency telephone and report the hazard

☐ Catch up with the lorry and try to get the driver's attention

☐ Stop close to the box until the police arrive

☐ Pull over to the hard shoulder, then remove the box

Lorry drivers can be unaware of objects falling from their vehicles. If you see something fall onto a motorway, look to see if the driver pulls over. If they don't stop, don't attempt to retrieve the object yourself. Pull onto the hard shoulder near an emergency telephone and report the hazard.

13.14 You're going through a long tunnel. What will warn you of congestion or an incident ahead?

☐ Hazard warning lines

☐ Other drivers flashing their lights

☐ Variable message signs

☐ Areas with hatch markings

Follow the instructions given by the signs or by tunnel officials. In congested tunnels, a minor incident can soon turn into a major one, with serious or even fatal results.

13.15 An adult casualty isn't breathing. To maintain circulation, CPR should be given. What's the correct depth to press down on their chest?

☐ 1 to 2 centimetres

☐ 5 to 6 centimetres

☐ 10 to 15 centimetres

☐ 15 to 20 centimetres

An adult casualty isn't breathing normally. To maintain circulation, place two hands on the centre of the chest. Then press down hard and fast – around 5–6 centimetres and about twice a second.

13.16 You're the first to arrive at the scene of a crash. What should you do?

☐ Leave as soon as another motorist arrives

☐ Flag down other motorists to help you

☐ Drag all casualties away from the vehicles

☐ Call the emergency services promptly

At a crash scene you can help in practical ways, even if you aren't trained in first aid. Call the emergency services and make sure you don't put yourself or anyone else in danger. The safest way to warn other traffic is by switching on your hazard warning lights.

13.17 You're the first person to arrive at an incident where people are badly injured. You've switched on your hazard warning lights and checked all engines are stopped. What else should you do?

☐ Make sure that an ambulance is called for

☐ Stop other cars and ask the drivers for help

☐ Try and get people who are injured to drink something

☐ Move the people who are injured clear of their vehicles

If you're the first to arrive at a crash scene, the first concerns are the risk of further collision and fire. Ensuring that vehicle engines are switched off will reduce the risk of fire. Use hazard warning lights so that other traffic knows there's a need for caution. Make sure the emergency services are contacted; don't assume this has already been done.

13.18 You arrive at the scene of a motorcycle crash. The rider is injured. When should their helmet be removed?

☐ Only when it's essential

☐ Always straight away

☐ Only when the motorcyclist asks

☐ Always, unless they're in shock

Don't remove a motorcyclist's helmet unless it's essential. Remember they may be suffering from shock. Don't give them anything to eat or drink, but do reassure them confidently.

13.19 You arrive at an incident. There's no danger from fire or further collisions. What's your first priority when attending to an unconscious motorcyclist?

☐ Check whether they're breathing normally

☐ Check whether they're bleeding

☐ Check whether they have any broken bones

☐ Check whether they have any bruising

At the scene of an incident, always be aware of danger from further collisions or fire. The first priority when dealing with an unconscious person is to ensure they're breathing normally. If they're having difficulty breathing, follow the DR ABC code.

13.20 At an incident, someone is unconscious. What would your priority be?

☐ Find out their name

☐ Wake them up

☐ Make them comfortable

☐ Check their airway is open

Remember this procedure by saying DR ABC. This stands for Danger, Response, Airway, Breathing, Circulation. Give whatever first aid you can and stay with the injured person until the emergency services arrive.

13.21 You've stopped at an incident to give help. What should you do?

☐ Keep injured people warm and comfortable

☐ Give injured people something to eat

☐ Keep injured people on the move by walking them around

☐ Give injured people a warm drink

There are a number of things you can do to help, even without expert training. Be aware of further danger from other traffic and fire; make sure the area is safe. People may be in shock. Don't give them anything to eat or drink. Keep them warm and comfortable and reassure them. Don't move injured people unless there's a risk of further danger.

13.22 There's been a collision. A driver is suffering from shock. What should you do?

☐ Give them a drink

☐ Reassure them

☐ Ask who caused the incident

☐ Offer them a cigarette

A casualty suffering from shock may have injuries that aren't immediately obvious. Call the emergency services, then stay with the person in shock, offering reassurance until the experts arrive.

13.23 You arrive at the scene of a motorcycle crash. No other vehicle is involved. The rider is unconscious and lying in the middle of the road. What's the first thing you should do at the scene?

□ Move the rider out of the road

□ Warn other traffic

□ Clear the road of debris

□ Give the rider reassurance

The motorcyclist is in an extremely vulnerable position, exposed to further danger from traffic. Approaching vehicles need advance warning in order to slow down and safely take avoiding action or stop. Don't put yourself or anyone else at risk. Use the hazard warning lights on your vehicle to alert other road users to the danger.

13.24 At an incident, a small child isn't breathing. What should you do to try and help?

□ Find their parents and get permission to help

□ Open their airway and begin CPR

□ Put them in the recovery position and slap their back

□ Talk to them confidently until an ambulance arrives

If a young child has stopped breathing, first check that their airway is open and then begin CPR. With a young child, you may only need to use one hand and you shouldn't press down as far as you would with an adult. Continue the procedure until the child is breathing again or until a medical professional takes over.

13.25 At an incident, a casualty isn't breathing. What should you do while helping them to start breathing again?

□ Put their arms across their chest

□ Shake them firmly

□ Roll them onto their side

□ Tilt their head back gently

It's important to ensure that the airway is open before you start CPR. To open the casualty's airway, place your fingers under their chin and lift it forward.

13.26 At an incident, someone is suffering from severe burns. What should you do to help them?

□ Apply lotions to the injury

□ Burst any blisters

□ Remove anything sticking to the burns

□ Douse the burns with clean, cool water

Your priority is to cool the burns with clean, cool water. Its coolness will help take the heat out of the burns and relieve the pain. Keep the wound doused for at least 10 minutes. If blisters appear, don't attempt to burst them, as this could lead to infection.

13.27 You arrive at an incident. A pedestrian is bleeding heavily from a leg wound. The leg isn't broken and there's nothing in the wound. How could you help?

□ Dab the wound to stop the bleeding

□ Keep the casualty's legs flat on the ground

□ Fetch them a warm drink

□ Apply firm pressure over the wound

If there's nothing in the wound, applying firm pressure using a pad of clean cloth or bandage will help stem the bleeding. Don't tie anything tightly round the leg, as this will restrict circulation and could result in long-term injury.

13.28 At an incident, a casualty is unconscious but breathing. When should you move them?

□ When an ambulance is on its way

□ When bystanders advise you to

□ When there's further danger

□ When bystanders will help you

Don't move a casualty unless there's further danger; for example, from other traffic or fire. They may have unseen or internal injuries. Moving them unnecessarily could cause further injury. Don't remove a motorcyclist's helmet unless it's essential.

13.29 At an incident, it's important to look after any casualties. What should you do with them when the area is safe?

☐ Move them away from the vehicles

☐ Ask them how it happened

☐ Give them something to eat

☐ Keep them where they are

When the area is safe and there's no danger from other traffic or fire, it's better not to move casualties. Moving them may cause further injury.

13.30 A tanker is involved in a collision. Which sign shows that it's carrying dangerous goods?

☐

☐

☐

☐

There will be an orange label on the side and rear of the tanker. Look at this carefully and report what it says when you phone the emergency services. Details of hazard warning plates are given in The Highway Code.

13.31 You're involved in a collision. Afterwards, which document may the police ask you to produce?

☐ Vehicle registration document

☐ Driving licence

☐ Theory test certificate

☐ Vehicle service record

You must stop if you've been involved in a collision which results in injury or damage. The police may ask to see your driving licence and insurance details at the time or later at a police station.

13.32 After a collision, someone is unconscious in their vehicle. When should you call the emergency services?

☐ Only as a last resort

☐ As soon as possible

☐ After you've woken them up

☐ After checking for broken bones

It's important to make sure that the emergency services arrive as soon as possible. When a person is unconscious, they could have serious injuries that aren't immediately obvious.

13.33 A collision has just happened. An injured person is lying in a busy road. What's the first thing you should do to help?

☐ Treat the person for shock

☐ Warn other traffic

☐ Place them in the recovery position

☐ Make sure the injured person is kept warm

The most immediate danger is further collisions and fire. You could warn other traffic by switching on hazard warning lights, displaying an advance warning triangle or sign (but not on a motorway), or by any other means that doesn't put you or others at risk.

13.34 At an incident, what should you do with a casualty who has stopped breathing?

☐ Keep their head tilted forwards as far as possible

☐ Follow the DR ABC code

☐ Raise their legs to help with circulation

☐ Try to give them something to drink

The DR ABC code has been devised by medical experts to give the best outcome until the emergency services arrive and take care of casualties.

13.35 You're at the scene of an incident. Someone is suffering from shock. How should you treat them?

□ Reassure them confidently

□ Offer them a cigarette

□ Give them a warm drink

□ Offer them some food

If someone is suffering from shock, try to keep them warm and as comfortable as you can. Don't give them anything to eat or drink but reassure them confidently and try not to leave them alone.

13.36 There's been a collision. A motorcyclist is lying injured and unconscious. Unless it's essential, why should you not usually attempt to remove their helmet?

□ They might not want you to

□ This could result in more serious injury

□ They'll get too cold if you do this

□ You could scratch the helmet

When someone is injured, any movement that isn't absolutely necessary should be avoided, since it could make the injuries worse. Unless it's essential to remove a motorcyclist's helmet, it's generally safer to leave it in place.

13.37 You've broken down on a two-way road. You have a warning triangle. At least how far from your vehicle should you place the warning triangle?

□ 5 metres (16 feet)

□ 25 metres (82 feet)

□ 45 metres (147 feet)

□ 100 metres (328 feet)

Advance warning triangles fold flat and don't take up much room. Use one to warn other road users if your vehicle has broken down or if there has been an incident. Place it at least 45 metres (147 feet) behind your vehicle (or the incident), on the same side of the road or verge. Place it further back if the scene is hidden by, for example, a bend, hill or dip in the road. Don't use warning triangles on motorways.

13.38 You break down on a level crossing. The lights haven't yet begun to flash. What's the first thing you should do?

□ Tell drivers behind what has happened

□ Leave your vehicle and get everyone clear

□ Walk down the track and signal the next train

□ Stay in your car until you're told to move

If your vehicle breaks down on a level crossing, your first priority is to get everyone out of the vehicle and clear of the crossing. Then use the railway telephone, if there is one, to tell the signal operator. If you have time before the train arrives, move the vehicle clear of the crossing, but only do this if alarm signals are not on.

13.39 Your tyre bursts while you're driving. What should you do?

□ Pull on the handbrake

□ Brake as quickly as possible

□ Pull up slowly at the side of the road

□ Continue on at a normal speed

A tyre bursting can lead to a loss of control, especially if you're travelling at high speed. Using the correct procedure should help you to stop the vehicle safely.

13.40   Your vehicle has a puncture on a motorway. What should you do?

☐ Drive slowly to the next service area to get assistance

☐ Pull up on the hard shoulder. Change the wheel as quickly as possible

☐ Pull up on the hard shoulder. Use the emergency phone to get assistance

☐ Switch on your hazard warning lights. Stop in your lane

"Pull up on the hard shoulder and make your way to the nearest emergency telephone to call for assistance.

Don't attempt to repair your vehicle while it's on the hard shoulder, because of the risk posed by traffic passing at high speeds."

13.41   You've stalled in the middle of a level crossing and can't restart the engine. The warning bells start to ring. What should you do?

☐ Get out of the car and clear of the crossing

☐ Run down the track to warn the signal operator

☐ Carry on trying to restart the engine

☐ Push the vehicle clear of the crossing

Try to stay calm, especially if you have passengers with you. If you can't restart your engine before the warning bells ring, leave the vehicle and get yourself and any passengers well clear of the crossing.

13.42   You're driving on a motorway. When can you use hazard warning lights?

☐ When a vehicle is following too closely

☐ When you slow down quickly because of danger ahead

☐ When you're towing another vehicle

☐ When you're driving on the hard shoulder

Briefly using your hazard warning lights will warn the traffic travelling behind you that there's a hazard ahead. This can reduce the chance of vehicles crashing into the back of each other.

13.43   You've broken down on a motorway. When you use the emergency telephone, what will you be asked for?

☐ Details about your vehicle

☐ Your driving licence details

☐ The name of your vehicle's insurance company

☐ Your employer's details

Have the correct details ready before you use the emergency telephone. The operator will need to know the details of your vehicle and its fault. For your own safety, always face the traffic when you speak on a roadside telephone.

13.44   Before driving through a tunnel, what should you do?

☐ Switch off your radio

☐ Remove any sunglasses

☐ Close your sunroof

☐ Switch on your windscreen wipers

If you're wearing sunglasses, you should remove them before driving into a tunnel. If you don't, your vision will be restricted, even in tunnels that appear to be well lit.

13.45   You're driving through a tunnel and the traffic is flowing normally. What should you do?

☐ Use parking lights

☐ Use front spotlights

☐ Use dipped headlights

☐ Use rear fog lights

Before entering a tunnel, you should switch on your dipped headlights, as this will allow you to see and be seen. In many tunnels, it's a legal requirement.

Don't wear sunglasses while driving in a tunnel. You may wish to tune your radio to a local channel for traffic information.

13.46 What safeguard could you take against fire risk to your vehicle?

☐ Keep water levels above maximum

☐ Check out any strong smell of fuel

☐ Avoid driving with a full tank of fuel

☐ Use fuel additives

The fuel in your vehicle can be a dangerous fire hazard. If you smell fuel, check out where it's coming from. Never

• use a naked flame near the vehicle if you can smell fuel

• smoke when refuelling your vehicle.

13.47 You're on the motorway. Luggage falls from your vehicle. What should you do?

☐ Stop at the next emergency telephone and contact the police

☐ Stop on the motorway and switch on hazard warning lights while you pick it up

☐ Walk back up the motorway to pick it up

☐ Pull up on the hard shoulder and wave traffic down

If any object falls onto the motorway carriageway from your vehicle, pull onto the hard shoulder near an emergency telephone and call for assistance. Don't stop on the carriageway or attempt to retrieve anything.

13.48 While you're driving, a warning light on your vehicle's instrument panel comes on. What should you do?

☐ Continue if the engine sounds all right

☐ Hope that it's just a temporary electrical fault

☐ Deal with the problem when there's more time

☐ Check out the problem quickly and safely

Make sure you know what the different warning lights mean. An illuminated warning light could mean that your car is unsafe to drive. If you aren't sure about the problem, get a qualified mechanic to check it.

13.49 Your vehicle breaks down in a tunnel. What should you do?

☐ Stay in your vehicle and wait for the police

☐ Stand in the lane behind your vehicle to warn others

☐ Stand in front of your vehicle to warn oncoming drivers

☐ Switch on hazard warning lights, then go and call for help

A broken-down vehicle in a tunnel can cause serious congestion and danger to other road users. If your vehicle breaks down, get help without delay. Switch on your hazard warning lights, then go to an emergency telephone to call for help.

13.50 Your vehicle catches fire while driving through a tunnel. It's still driveable. What should you do?

☐ Leave it where it is, with the engine running

☐ Pull up, then walk to an emergency telephone

☐ Park it away from the carriageway

☐ Drive it out of the tunnel if you can do so

If it's possible, and you can do so without causing further danger, it may be safer to drive a vehicle that's on fire out of a tunnel. The greatest danger in a tunnel fire is smoke and suffocation.

13.51 You're in a tunnel. Your vehicle is on fire and you can't drive it. What should you do?

☐ Stay in the vehicle and close the windows

☐ Switch on hazard warning lights

☐ Leave the engine running

☐ Switch off all of your lights

It's usually better to drive a burning vehicle out of a tunnel. If you can't do this, pull over and stop at an emergency point if possible. Switch off the engine, use hazard warning lights, and leave the vehicle immediately. Call for help from the nearest emergency point. If you have an extinguisher it may help to put out a small fire, but don't try to tackle a large one.

13.52 What should you do as you approach a long road tunnel?

□ Put on your sunglasses and use the sun visor

□ Turn your headlights on to main beam

□ Change down to a lower gear

□ Make sure your radio is tuned to the frequency shown

On the approach to tunnels, a sign will usually show a local radio channel. This should give a warning of any incidents or congestion in the tunnel ahead. Many radios can be set to automatically pick up traffic announcements and local frequencies. If you have to tune the radio manually, don't be distracted while doing so. Incidents in tunnels can lead to serious casualties. The greatest hazard is fire. Getting an advance warning of problems could save your life and others.

13.53 Your vehicle has broken down on an automatic railway level crossing. What should you do first?

□ Get everyone out of the vehicle and clear of the crossing

□ Telephone your vehicle recovery service to move it

□ Walk along the track to give warning to any approaching trains

□ Try to push the vehicle clear of the crossing as soon as possible

First, get yourself and anyone else well away from the crossing. If there's a railway telephone, use that to get instructions from the signal operator. Then, if there's time, move the vehicle clear of the crossing.

13.54 What should you carry for use in the event of a collision?

□ Road map   □ Can of petrol

□ Jump leads   □ Fire extinguisher

Various items – such as a first aid kit and a fire extinguisher – can provide invaluable help in the event of a collision or breakdown. They could even save a life.

13.55 You have a collision while your car is moving. What's the first thing you must do?

□ Stop only if someone waves at you

□ Call the emergency services

□ Stop at the scene of the incident

□ Call your insurance company

If you're in a collision that causes damage or injury to any other person, vehicle, animal or property, by law you must stop. Give your name, the vehicle owner's name and address, and the vehicle's registration number to anyone who has reasonable grounds for requesting them.

13.56 You're in collision with another moving vehicle. Someone is injured and your vehicle is damaged. What information should you find out?

□ Whether the other driver is licensed to drive

□ The other driver's name, address and telephone number

□ The destination of the other driver

□ The occupation of the other driver

Try to keep calm and don't rush. Make sure that you've shared all the relevant details with the other driver before you leave the scene. If possible, take pictures and note the positions of all the vehicles involved.

13.57 You lose control of your car and damage a garden wall. No-one is around. What must you do?

□ Report the incident to the police within 24 hours

□ Go back to tell the house owner the next day

□ Report the incident to your insurance company when you get home

□ Find someone in the area to tell them about it immediately

If the property owner isn't available at the time, you must inform the police about the incident. This should be done as soon as possible, and in any case within 24 hours.

Section 14 Vehicle Loading

14.1   You're towing a small trailer on a busy three-lane motorway. What must you do if all the lanes are open?

☐ Not exceed 50 mph

☐ Not overtake

☐ Have a stabiliser fitted

☐ Use only the left-hand and centre lanes

The motorway regulations for towing a trailer state that you mustn't

• use the right-hand lane of a three-lane motorway unless directed to do so (for example, at roadworks or due to a lane closure)

• exceed 60 mph.

14.2   What should you do if a trailer starts to swing from side to side while you're towing it?

☐ Ease off the accelerator to reduce your speed

☐ Let go of the steering wheel and let it correct itself

☐ Brake hard and hold the pedal down

☐ Accelerate until it stabilises

Strong winds or buffeting from large vehicles can cause a trailer or caravan to swing from side to side ('snake'). If this happens, ease off the accelerator. Don't brake harshly, steer sharply or increase your speed.

14.3   On which occasion should you inflate your tyres to more than their normal pressure?

☐ When the roads are slippery

☐ When the vehicle is fitted with anti-lock brakes

☐ When the tyre tread is worn below 2 mm

☐ When carrying a heavy load

Check the vehicle handbook. This should give you guidance on the correct tyre pressures for your vehicle and when you may need to adjust them. If you're carrying a heavy load, you may need to adjust the headlights as well. Most cars have a switch on the dashboard to do this.

14.4   How will a heavy load on your roof rack affect your vehicle's handling?

☐ It will improve the road holding

☐ It will reduce the stopping distance

☐ It will make the steering lighter

☐ It will reduce stability

A heavy load on your roof rack will reduce the stability of the vehicle because it moves the centre of gravity away from that designed by the manufacturer. Be aware of this when you drive round bends and corners. If you change direction at speed, your vehicle and/or load could become unstable and you could lose control.

14.5   What can be badly affected when you overload your vehicle?

☐ The vehicle's gearbox

☐ The vehicle's ventilation

☐ The vehicle's handling

☐ The vehicle's battery

Any load will have an effect on the handling of your vehicle, and this becomes worse as you increase the load. You need to be aware of this when carrying passengers or heavy loads, fitting a roof rack or towing a trailer.

14.6   Who's responsible for making sure that a vehicle isn't overloaded?

☐ The driver of the vehicle

☐ The owner of the items being carried

☐ The person who loaded the vehicle

☐ The licensing authority

Carrying heavy loads will affect control and the vehicle's handling characteristics. If the vehicle you're driving is overloaded, you'll be held responsible.

14.7 You're planning to tow a caravan. Which of these will be the biggest aid to the vehicle handling?

☐ A jockey wheel fitted to the towbar

☐ Power steering fitted to the towing vehicle

☐ Anti-lock brakes fitted to the towing vehicle

☐ A stabiliser fitted to the towbar

Towing a caravan or trailer affects the way the towing vehicle handles. A stabiliser device is not designed to overcome instability caused by incorrect loading but it can give added security in side winds and from buffeting caused by large vehicles.

14.8 Are passengers allowed to ride in a caravan that's being towed?

☐ Yes, if they're over 14

☐ No, not at any time

☐ Only if all the seats in the towing vehicle are full

☐ Only if a stabiliser is fitted

Riding in a towed caravan is highly dangerous. The safety of the entire unit is dependent on the stability of the trailer. Moving passengers would make the caravan unstable and could cause loss of control.

14.9 A trailer must stay securely hitched to the towing vehicle. What additional safety device must be fitted to a trailer braking system?

☐ Stabiliser

☐ Jockey wheel

☐ Corner steadies

☐ Breakaway cable

In the event that the trailer becomes detached from the towing vehicle, the breakaway cable activates the trailer brakes before snapping. This allows the towing vehicle to get free of the trailer and out of danger.

14.10 You wish to tow a trailer. Where would you find the maximum noseweight allowed on your vehicle's tow hitch?

☐ In the vehicle handbook

☐ In The Highway Code

☐ In your vehicle registration certificate

☐ In your licence documents

You must know how to load your trailer or caravan so that the hitch exerts an appropriate downward force on the tow ball. Information about the maximum permitted noseweight can be found in your vehicle handbook or obtained from your vehicle manufacturer's agent.

14.11 How should a load be carried on your roof rack?

☐ Securely fastened with suitable restraints

☐ Loaded towards the rear of the vehicle

☐ Visible in your exterior mirror

☐ Covered with plastic sheeting

Any load must be securely fastened to the vehicle. The safest way to carry items on the roof is in a specially designed roof box. This will help to keep your luggage secure and dry, and it also has less wind resistance than loads carried exposed on a roof rack.

14.12 You're carrying a child in your car. They're under three years old. Which of these is a suitable restraint?

☐ A child seat

☐ An adult holding a child

☐ An adult seat belt

☐ An adult lap belt

It's your responsibility to ensure that all children in your car are secure. Suitable restraints include a child seat, baby seat, booster seat or booster cushion. It's essential that any restraint used is suitable for the child's size and weight, and fitted according to the manufacturer's instructions.

Section 15 Case Sudy Practice

Some of the questions within the test will be presented as a case study.

You'll be presented with a scenario – the case study – which will appear on the left-hand side of the screen. The scenario will be presented in a text format and may be accompanied by a supporting picture or diagram. As you move within the case study, the questions will appear, one by one, on the right-hand side of the screen, and you'll be asked to respond. You can re-read the scenario throughout the case study should you wish to do so.

A case study example is shown below and on the following pages.

In this section, you'll also find five mixed-topic, practice case studies similar to the ones in the actual test. Use these to help you prepare for the real thing.

Answers to all the case studies in this book are in section 16, Answers.

CASE STUDY

You decide to visit your friend who lives about 20 miles away.

The journey will take you on various roads including country lanes and A-roads.

You've been before so you think you know the way. You also have a mobile phone with you, so you will be able to ring for directions if you get lost.

During the journey you may go the wrong way and need to turn round. Later on, you decide to ring your friend to make sure you are still travelling in the right direction.

Mark one answer

To turn round after going the wrong way, you decide to make a U-turn in the road. Before doing this, what should you do?

☐ Give an arm signal as well as using indications

☐ Signal so that other road users can slow down for you

☐ Look over your shoulder for a final check

☐ Select a higher gear than normal

CASE STUDY

You decide to visit your friend who lives about 20 miles away.

The journey will take you on various roads including country lanes and A-roads.

You've been before so you think you know the way. You also have a mobile phone with you, so you will be able to ring for directions if you get lost.

During the journey you go the wrong way and need to turn round. Later on, you decide to ring your friend to make sure you are still travelling in the right direction.

Mark three answers

What should you do as you approach this bridge on your journey?

☐ Move into the middle of the road to get a better view

☐ slow down

☐ consider using the horn

☐ Find another route

☐ Beware of the pedestrians

CASE STUDY

You decide to visit your friend who lives about 20 miles away.

The journey will take you on various roads including country lanes and A-roads.

You've been before so you think you know the way. You also have a mobile phone with you, so you will be able to ring for directions if you get lost.

During the journey you go the wrong way and need to turn round. Later on, you decide to ring your friend to make sure you are still travelling in the right direction.

Mark oneanswers

During your journey, you ring your friend. What is the safest way for you to use your mobile phone?

☐ Use hands-free equipment

☐ Find a suitable place to stop

☐ Travel slowly on a quiet road

☐ Direct your call through the operator

CASE STUDY

You decide to visit your friend who lives about 20 miles away

The journey will take you on various roads including country lanes and A-roads.

You've been before so you think you know the way. You also have a mobile phone with you, so you will be able to ring for directions if you get lost.

During the journey you go the wrong way and need to turn round. Later on, you decide to ring your friend to make sure you are still travelling in the right direction.

Mark two answers

You are travelling along a country road. A horse and rider are approaching. What should you do?

☐ Increase your speed

☐ Sound your horn

☐ Flash your headlights

☐ Go slowly past

☐ Give plenty of room

☐ Rev your engine

CASE STUDY

You decide to visit your friend who lives about 20 miles away

The journey will take you on various roads including country lanes and A-roads.

You've been before so you think you know the way. You also have a mobile phone with you, so you will be able to ring for directions if you get lost.

During the journey you go the wrong way and need to turn round. Later on, you decide to ring your friend to make sure you are still travelling in the right direction.

Mark one answer

Near the end of your journey, you come to a pedestraian crossing, with pedestrians who are hesitating to cross. Why should you never wave people across at pedestrian crossings?

☐ There may be another vehicle coming

☐ They may not be looking

☐ It is safer for you to carry on

☐ They may not be ready to cross

CASE STUDY PRACTICE – A

You plan to visit a friend who lives in a town a full day's drive away. You'll be away for a week.

Two weeks before the journey, you realise that your vehicle tax will expire while you're away.

At the beginning of your journey, you reach a roundabout. Another car cuts in front of you, causing you to do an emergency stop.

Later, you join the motorway, where a red X is flashing above the outside lane.

While travelling along the motorway, you start to feel tired and stop at a service station.

It's just after 11 pm when you park outside your friend's house.

Mark one answer

1 What should you do two weeks before you leave?

☐ Tell your insurance company when the vehicle tax expires

☐ Notify DVLA that the vehicle is off the road

☐ Make a note to renew the vehicle tax on your return

☐ Renew your vehicle tax immediately

2 What should you do at the service station?

☐ Drink two cups of coffee and rest for 15 minutes

☐ Drink a bottle of mineral water and leave immediatley

☐ Drink two cups of coffee and leave immediately

☐ Drink a bottle of mineral water and rest for 5 minutes

3 What should you do at the roundabout?

☐ Flash your lights and change lanes

☐ Sound your horn at the other car

☐ Stay calm and continue when it's safe

☐ Continue on your journey immediately

4 What must you do on the motorway?

☐ Drive down the outside lane

☐ Overtake in the outside lane

☐ Pull over in the outside lane

☐ Stay out of the outside lane

5 Why must you avoid using your horn when parked outside your friend's house?

☐ Because they have children

☐ Because it's before midnight

☐ Because it's after 10.30 pm

☐ Because you're stationary

CASE STUDY PRACTICE – B

You're taking your 14-year-old nephew on a day trip.

You drive through town and reach a zebra crossing. A man carrying a white cane with a red band is waiting to cross.

You join a dual carriageway and see a sign which has a white circle with a diagonal black stripe.

As you drive across a roundabout, you're involved in a collision with a cyclist. You and your nephew aren't injured. The cyclist is conscious but is lying at the side of the road and their leg is bleeding heavily.

Mark one answer

1 Who's responsible for your nephew wearing a seat belt?

☐ He is

☐ You are

☐ His parents

☐ The police

2 What do the markings on the man's cane mean?

☐ He's blind

☐ He's deaf and blind

☐ He's deaf

☐ He has mobility problems

3 What does the sign mean?

☐ Pedestrian zone ends

☐ End of goods-vehicle restriction

☐ End of minimum speed requirement

☐ National speed limit applies

4 What should you do at the roundabout?

☐ Take your nephew to the hospital

☐ Drive to the nearest police station

☐ Put on your hazard warning lights

☐ Flag down passing drivers for help

5 What should you do about the cyclist?

☐ Leave them for the emergency services

☐ Restrict the blood flow from their leg

☐ Help them back onto their bike

☐ Give them a drink of water

CASE STUDY PRACTICE – C

You're driving into the town centre. The weather is cold and wet.

There are several cars parked down either side of the main road.

It's market day and there are many pedestrians around.

Ahead of you, a large van is being unloaded on your side of the road and there's oncoming traffic.

Later, you reach a junction with some traffic lights that aren't working. There are several other vehicles in the area.

On your way home, your steering begins to feel a little heavy. You stop at a nearby filling station.

Mark one answer

1 What's the recommended time gap that should be left between vehicles in these weather conditions?

☐ Two seconds

☐ Four seconds

☐ Six seconds

☐ Eight seconds

2 What should you watch out for in this area?

☐ Sales posters going up in any of the shop windows

☐ The next available free parking space on the road

☐ Pedestrians stepping out from between vehicles

☐ Traffic wardens who may be working in the area

3 How should you react to the van?

☐ Stop and wait until the way ahead is clear

☐ Move out and pass as quickly as possible

☐ Find another route to your destination

☐ Wait until the van is unloaded and moved

4 What has right of way at the lights?

☐ No-one

☐ Oncoming drivers

☐ Drivers in large vehicles

☐ Drivers in fast vehicles

5 What might cause the steering to feel this way?

☐ Being very low on fuel

☐ Engine oil level is low

☐ Driving at a show speed

☐ Tyre pressure is too low

CASE STUDY PRACTICE – D

You're driving to work on a single carriageway road.

It's early morning and there's patchy fog, which is very thick in places.

A sports car is travelling too closely behind you.

Later, you reach a roundabout where you need to turn right. The approach road is still a single carriageway. There's only one line of traffic.

When you get to work, you find that the car park is full. You have to park on the main road, facing downhill.

You need to leave some camera equipment in your vehicle until later.

Mark one answer

1 What lights would you use under these weather conditions?

☐ Headlights with fog lights as necessary

☐ Full-beam headlights at all times on the journey.

☐ No lights at all during the whole journey

☐ Sidelights and hazard warning lights

2 What should you do about the sports car?

☐ Brake sharply and allow the other vehicle past

☐ Pull over to the side of the road and then stop

☐ Increase speed and pull away from the vehicle

☐ Slowly drop back to allow more room in front

3 How should you position your vehicle when approaching the roundabout?

☐ Move closer to the centre line but give no signal at all

☐ Stay close to the left-hand kerb and signal to go right

☐ Move nearer to the centre line and signal to go right

☐ Stay in the middle of the lane but don't signal to go right

4 How should you position your front wheels when parking here?

☐ Turned in towards the kerb

☐ Aligned alongside the kerb

☐ Turned away from the kerb

☐ Mounted up onto the kerb

5 What should you do with the equipment?

☐ Put it on the back seat in a bag

☐ Lock it away securely out of sight

☐ Cover it with a blanket or jacket

☐ Put it in the passenger footwell

CASE STUDY PRACTICE – E

You're taking a friend and their two children to the coast. The children are aged two and six.

With fuel and tyre pressures done, you make other final checks.

After helping the children into the vehicle, you set off.

It rained heavily overnight and the roads are still wet in places. However, the sun is now shining and the day is very warm and bright.

Once on the motorway, the traffic is very heavy. A large goods vehicle is travelling in front of you.

Further on, you see an overhead gantry with the number 40 in a red circle showing above all lanes, including the hard shoulder.

Mark one answer

1 What else should you check before your journey?

□ Oil and water levels

□ The ashtray is empty

□ The central locking is working

□ Interior temperature

2 How must you seat the younger child?

□ On a cushion with a lap belt

□ In a normal adult sent belt

□ On a booster cushion only

□ In a suitable child restraint

3 What hazards would you expect to encounter in these weather conditions?

□ Puddles making the tyres muddy

□ Glare from the sun on wet roads

□ Road surface drying out too fast

□ Mud on the roads

4 What positions should you take behind the goods vehicle?

□ Well back, so you can see ahead and be seen

□ Close enough to stay out of the sun's glare

□ Just far enough back to stay in its slipstream

□ Close enough to prevent another vehicle pulling into the gap

5 What does the sign on the overhead gantry mean?

□ There's an obstruction on the hard shoulder 40 yards ahead

□ Only 40 vehicles can use the hard shoulder until further notice

□ This lane can be used as a running lane at a speed of 40 mph

□ Traffic must merge in turn back onto the motorway in 40 minutes

Section 16 Answers

Section 1 Alertness

1.1 ☐ Look over your shoulder for a final check

1.2 ☐ Slow down

1.3 ☐ Approaching a dip in the road

1.4 ☐ Overtaking traffic should move back to the left

1.5 ☐ Ignore it

1.6 ☐ To make you aware of your speed

1.7 ☐ Be ready to stop

1.8 ☐ Use the mirrors

1.9 ☐ You'll allow the driver to see you in their mirrors

1.10 ☐ To assess how your actions will affect following traffic

1.11 ☐ Stop and then move forward slowly and carefully for a clear view

1.12 ☐ Your view could be obstructed

1.13 ☐ Leave the motorway and stop in a safe place

1.14 ☐ So others can see you more easily

1.15 ☐ Keeep both hands on the steering wheel

1.16 ☐ When suitably parked

1.17 ☐ Using a mobile phone

1.18 ☐ Check both interior and exterior mirrors

1.19 ☐ Leave them plenty of room as you pass

1.20 ☐ Find a safe place to stop

1.21 ☐ Turn into a side road, stop and check a map

1.22 ☐ When you're approaching bends and junctions

1.23 ☐ Ask someone to guide you

1.24 ☐ An area not covered mirrors

1.25 ☐ It will divert your attention

1.26 ☐ Check that the central reservation is wide enough for your vehicle

1.27 ☐ Motorcyclists

1.28 ☐ Stop in a safe place before programming the system

Section 2 Attitude

2.1 ☐ Give way to pedestrians already on the crossing

2.2 ☐ Another vehicle may be coming

2.3 ☐ Following another vehicle too closely

2.4 ☐ Your view ahead will be reduced

2.5 ☐ Four seconds

2.6 ☐ Slow down

2.7 ☐ Bomb disposa

2.8 ☐ Pull over as soon as it's safe to do so

2.9 ☐ Doctor's car

2.10 ☐ Tram drivers

2.11 ☐ Cycles

2.12 ☐ To alert others to your presence

2.13 ☐ In the right-hand lane

2.14 ☐ To help other road users know what you intend to do

2.15 ☐ Toucan

2.16 ☐ Allow the vehicle to overtake

2.17 ☐ When letting them know that you're there

2.18 ☐ Slow down and look both ways

2.19 ☐ When checking your gap from the vehicle in front

2.20 ☐ Steady amber

2.21 ☐ Slow down, gradually increasing the gap between you and the vehicle in front

2.22	☐ Dipped headlights	3.8	☐ When its tyres are under-inflated
2.23	☐ Slow down and let the vehicle turn	3.9	☐ Take it to a local-authority site
2.24	☐ Drop back to leave the correct separation distance	3.10	☐ Harsh braking and accelerating
		3.11	☐ Distilled water
2.25	☐ Use the parking brake only	3.12	☐ Where the speed limit exceeds 30 mph
2.26	☐ Keep a steady course and allow the driver behind to overtake		
		3.13	☐ Keep engine revs low
2.27	☐ The lane is in operation 24 hours a day	3.14	☐ A faulty braking system
		3.15	☐ Just above the cell plates
2.28	☐ Stop and switch off your engine	3.16	☐ Look at a map
2.29	☐ Go past slowly and carefully	3.17	☐ You'll have an easier journey
2.30	☐ Slow down and prepare to stop	3.18	☐ You're less likely to be delayed
2.31	☐ Slow down and be ready to stop	3.19	☐ Your original route may be blocked
2.32	☐ When the pedestrians have cleared the crossing	3.20	☐ Allow plenty of time for the trip
		3.21	☐ Increased fuel consumption
		3.22	☐ Brake fluid level
2.33	☐	3.23	☐ Faults in the suspension
		3.24	☐ The brakes overheating
2.34	☐ Dry	3.25	☐ Have the brakes checked immediately
2.35	☐ Use dipped headlights	3.26	☐ A fault in the braking system
2.36	☐ Pull in when you can, to let following vehicles overtake	3.27	☐ To maintain control of the pedals
		3.28	☐ A properly adjusted head restrain
2.37	☐ It can make the roads slippery for other road users	3.29	☐ Worn shock absorbers
		3.30	☐ Fuel consumption will increase
2.38	☐ Check that your filler cap is securely fastened	3.31	☐ They have a large, deep cut in the side wall
		3.32	☐ 1.6 mm
2.39	☐ Competitive	3.33	☐ You, the driver
		3.34	☐ By accelerating gently

Section 3 Safety and Your Vehicle

3.1	☐ Braking	3.35	☐ By having your vehicle serviced regularly
3.2	☐ Between 11.30 pm and 7.00 am in a built-up area	3.36	☐ Walk or cycle on short journeys
		3.37	☐ Under-inflated tyres
3.3	☐ It's powered by electricity	3.38	☐ Seat belts
3.4	☐ To help the traffic flow	3.39	☐ 30%
3.5	☐ To reduce traffic speed	3.40	☐ Have the brakes checked as soon as possible
3.6	☐ To reduce harmful exhaust gases		
3.7	☐ When tyres are cold		

3.41 ☐ The steering will vibrate

3.42 ☐ Tyres

3.43 ☐ Lock them out of sight

3.44 ☐ Etching the registration number on the windows

3.45 ☐ The vehicle registration document

3.46 ☐ Lock it and remove the key

3.47 ☐ Reducing your speed

3.48 ☐ Take it to a local-authority site

3.49 ☐ To help protect the environment against pollution

3.50 ☐ Anticipate well ahead

3.51 ☐ Better fuel economy

3.52 ☐ Maintain a reduced speed throughout

3.53 ☐ Before a long journey

3.54 ☐ No, not under any circumstances

3.55 ☐ Lock it and remove the key

3.56 ☐ In a secure car park

3.57 ☐ In front of a property entrance

3.58 ☐ To help you avoid neck injury

3.59 ☐ Making a lot of short journeys

3.60 ☐ Walk or cycle

3.61 ☐ Take all valuables with you

3.62 ☐ Install a security-coded radio

3.63 ☐ Leave it in a well-lit area

3.64 ☐ Vehicle watch scheme

3.65 ☐ On the exhaust system

3.66 ☐ Reduction in fuel consumption by about 15%

3.67 ☐ Missing out some gears

3.68 ☐ By reducing exhaust emissions

3.69 ☐ Improved road safety

3.70 ☐ 1.6 mm

3.71 ☐ Accelerating

3.72 ☐ When they're exempt for medical reasons

3.73 ☐ You, the driver

3.74 ☐ Oil leaks

3.75 ☐ Using an adult seat belt

3.76 ☐ That a suitable child restraint is available

3.77 ☐ Switch off the engine

3.78 ☐ Deactivate the airbag

3.79 ☐ Never if you're away from the vehicle

Section 4 Safey Margins

4.1 ☐ Ten times

4.2 ☐ Passing pedal cyclists

4.3 ☐ To improve your view of the road

4.4 ☐ Go slowly while gently applying the brakes

4.5 ☐ The tyre grip

4.6 ☐ On an open stretch of road

4.7 ☐ 96 metres (315 feet)

4.8 ☐ 73 metres (240 feet)

4.9 ☐ Drop back to regain a safe distance

4.10 ☐ 53 metres (175 feet)

4.11 ☐ 36 metres (118 feet)

4.12 ☐ Pass wide

4.13 ☐ 38 metres (125 feet)

4.14 ☐ Increase your distance from the vehicle in front

4.15 ☐ Reduce your speed and increase the gap in front

4.16 ☐ Choose an appropriate lane in good time

4.17 ☐ Drive at a slow speed in as high a gear as possible

4.18 ☐ The driver

4.19 ☐ Slow down before you reach the bend

4.20 ☐ Steer carefully to the right

4.21 ☐ The window

4.22 ☐ Use a higher gear than normal

4.23 ☐ Brake gently in plenty of time

4.24	☐ Improved grip on the road		5.10	☐ Lorry
4.25	☐ Select a low gear and use the brakes carefully		5.11	☐ Stop behind the line, then edge forward to see clearly
4.26	☐ Turn the steering wheel towards the kerb		5.12	☐ Ignore the error and stay calm
			5.13	☐ They'll take longer to react to hazards
4.27	☐ Check your mirror and slow down		5.14	☐ A school crossing patrol
4.28	☐ When you're braking in an emergency		5.15	☐ Yes, regular stops help concentration
4.29	☐ Loose		5.16	☐ Stop before the barrier
4.30	☐ When you're braking harshly		5.17	☐ Be prepared to stop for any traffic
4.31	☐ Steer and brake harshly at the same time		5.18	☐ Wait for the pedestrian in the road to cross
4.32	☐ Rapidly and firmly		5.19	☐ Only consider overtaking when you're past the junction
4.33	☐ On loose road surfaces		5.20	☐ Be prepared to give way to large vehicles in the middle of the road
4.34	☐ Test your brakes			
4.35	☐ There's less tyre noise		5.21	☐ They give a wider field of vision
4.36	☐ The steering will feel very light		5.22	☐ Approach with care and pass on the left of the lorry
4.37	☐ In the rain		5.23	☐ Stay behind and don't overtake
4.38	☐ A two-second time gap		5.24	☐ The bus may move out into the road
4.39	☐ By changing to a lower gear		5.25	☐ A school bus
4.40	☐ When you brake promptly and firmly until you've stopped		5.26	☐ Children running out between vehicles
			5.27	☐ The cyclist may swerve into the road
4.41	☐ When the wheels are about to lock		5.28	☐ Stop and take a break
4.42	☐ Dipped headlights		5.29	☐ At a reduced speed
4.43	☐ Reduction in control		5.30	☐ Because of the level crossing
4.44	☐ Allow more time for your journey		5.31	☐ To enable you to change lanes early
			5.32	☐ Traffic in both directions can use the middle lane to overtake

Section 5 Hazard Awareness

5.1	☐ On a large goods vehicle		5.33	☐ A disabled person's vehicle
5.2	☐ The cyclist crossing the road		5.34	☐ Stop
5.3	☐ The parked car (arrowed A)		5.35	☐ People may cross the road in front of it
5.4	☐ Slow down and get ready to stop			
5.5	☐ Doors opening on parked cars		5.36	☐ Approaching a junction
5.6	☐ The road will bend sharply to the left		5.37	☐ Poor judgement of speed
5.7	☐ Slow down and allow the cyclist to turn		5.38	☐ Edge of the carriageway
			5.39	☐ A steady amber light
5.8	☐ The view is restricted		5.40	☐ Allow the cyclist time and room
5.9	☐ Buses			

5.41 □ Wait for the cyclist to pull away

5.42 □ Check for bicycles on your left

5.43 □ A staggered junction is ahead

5.44 □ Traffic will move into the left-hand lane

5.45 □ The two left lanes are open

5.46 □ Don't drink any alcohol at all

5.47 □ Insurance premiums

5.48 □ Go home by public transport

5.49 □ Avoid driving and check with your doctor

5.50 □ Get someone else to driver

5.51 □ Make sure you're medically fit to driver

5.52 □ Stop and rest as soon as possible

5.53 □ Leave the motorway at the next exit and rest

5.54 □ Wait until you're fit and well before driving

5.55 □ Take regular refreshment breaks

5.56 □ Check the label to see if the medicine will affect your driving

5.57 □ Continue to the end of the road

5.58 □ Looking at road maps

5.59 □ Sound your horn and be prepared to stop

5.60 □ Calm down

5.61 □ There are roadworks ahead of you

5.62 □ Keep a safe gap

5.63 □ Find a way of getting home without driving

5.64 □ Increased confidence

5.65 □ Some types of medicine can cause your reactions to slow down

5.66 □ At all times when driving

5.67 □ Tinted

5.68 □ Drugs

5.69 □ The driver licensing authority

5.70 □ When your vehicle has broken down and is causing an obstruction

5.71 □ Approach slowly and edge out until you can see more clearly

5.72 □ Quick acceleration

5.73 □ Be aware of spray reducing your vision

5.74 □ Pedestrians walking towards you

5.75 □ Slow down, keeping a safe separation distance

5.76 □ When driving on a motorway to warn traffic behind of a hazard ahead

5.77 □ Reflections of traffic in shop windows

5.78 □ Inform the licensing authority

5.79 □ To allow vehicles to enter and emerge

5.80 □ Open a window and stop as soon as it's safe and legal

Section 6 Vulnerable Road Users

6.1 □

6.2 □ Give way to them

6.3 □ Pedestrians

6.4 □ They may be overtaking on your right

6.5 □ Cyclists can use it

6.6 □ By displaying a 'stop' sign

6.7 □ On the rear of a school bus or coach

6.8 □ A route for pedestrians and cyclists

6.9 □ They're deaf and blind

6.10 □ Be patient and allow them to cross in their own time

6.11 □ Be careful; they may misjudge your speed

6.12 □ Give the cyclist plenty of room

6.13 □ Bicycle

6.14 □ They're harder to see

6.15 □ Motorcycles can easily be hidden behind obstructions

6.16	☐ So that the rider can be seen more easily	6.44	☐ The cyclist is slower and more vulnerable
6.17	☐ Drivers often do not see them	6.45	☐ Prepare to slow down and stop
6.18	☐ Stay behind	6.46	☐ The pedestrian is deaf
6.19	☐ To check for traffic in their blind area	6.47	☐ Cyclists and pedestrians
6.20	☐ Motorcyclist	6.48	☐ To allow cyclists to position in front of other traffic
6.21	☐ Give them plenty of room	6.49	☐ The cyclist might swerve
6.22	☐ Wait patiently because they'll probably take longer to cross	6.50	☐ Go very slowly
6.23	☐ Reduce speed until you're clear of the area	6.51	☐ You're approaching an organised walk
6.24	☐ To allow a clear view of the crossing area	6.52	☐ By taking further training
6.25	☐ On a school bus	6.53	☐ Get out and check
6.26	☐ Any direction	6.54	☐ Give way to the pedestrian
6.27	☐ Stay behind until the moped has passed the junction	6.55	☐ Children
6.28	☐ Stay well back	6.56	☐ Stop, then move forward slowly until you have a clear view
6.29	☐ Be patient and prepare for them to react more slowly	6.57	☐ To check for overtaking vehicles
6.30	☐ Be patient, as you expect them to make mistakes	6.58	☐ Give way to any pedestrians on the crossing
6.31	☐ Pedestrians	6.59	☐ Wait for them to finish crossing
6.32	☐ Be aware that their reactions may be slower than yours	6.60	☐ Slow down and be prepared to stop for children
6.33	☐ Hold back until the cyclist has passed the junction	6.61	☐ Check for traffic overtaking on your right
6.34	☐ In any direction	6.62	☐ Look for motorcyclists filtering through the traffic
6.35	☐ They'll have a flashing amber light	6.63	☐ Pedestrians might come from behind the bus
6.36	☐ Just before you turn left	6.64	☐ Drive slowly and leave plenty of room
6.37	☐ The vehicle is slow moving	6.65	☐ The rider may be blown across in front of you
6.38	☐ With-flow cycle lane	6.66	☐ At junctions
6.39	☐ Slow down and be ready to stop	6.67	☐ You mustn't wait or park your vehicle here at all
6.40	☐ To ensure children can see and be seen when crossing the road	6.68	☐ Slow down and be prepared to stop for a cyclist
6.41	☐ Watch out for pedestrians walking in the road	6.69	☐ Set your mirror to the anti-dazzle position
6.42	☐ Allow extra room in case they swerve to avoid potholes	6.70	☐ Be prepared to stop
6.43	☐ Cycle route ahead		

Section 7 Other Types of Vehicle

7.1 ☐

7.2 ☐ The large vehicle can easily hide an overtaking vehicle

7.3 ☐ Stay well back and give it room

7.4 ☐ Wait behind the long vehicle

7.5 ☐ keep well back

7.6 ☐ To get the best view of the road ahead

7.7 ☐ Watch carefully for pedestrians

7.8 ☐ Drop back until you can see better

7.9 ☐ Drop back further

7.10 ☐ Allow it to pull away, if it's safe to do so

7.11 ☐ Keep well back until you can see that it's clear

7.12 ☐ Cars

7.13 ☐ Slow down and be prepared to wait

7.14 ☐ Don't overtake as you approach or at the junction

7.15 ☐ 8 mph

7.16 ☐ It will take longer to pass one

7.17 ☐ Keep well back

7.18 ☐ Watch carefully for the sudden appearance of pedestrians

7.19 ☐ Slow down and give way

7.20 ☐ Because they can't steer to avoid you

7.21 ☐ Extended-arm side mirrors

7.22 ☐ Dipped headlights

7.23 ☐ Allow extra room

Section 8 Vehicle Handling

8.1 ☐ When you're in a one-way street

8.2 ☐ It will be doubled

8.3 ☐ Beware of bends in the road ahead

8.4 ☐ When oncoming traffic prevents you turning right

8.5 ☐ **Humps for ½ mile**

8.6 ☐ Slow traffic down

8.7 ☐ Red

8.8 ☐ Alert you to a hazard

8.9 ☐ Leave plenty of time for your journey

8.10 ☐ Make sure you don't dazzle other road users

8.11 ☐ Slow down and stay behind

8.12 ☐ To make you aware of your speed

8.13 ☐ There would be a different surface texture

8.14 ☐ Stop at a passing place

8.15 ☐ To prevent the motorcycle sliding on the metal drain covers

8.16 ☐ Your brakes will be soaking wet

8.17 ☐ It's more difficult to see what's ahead

8.18 ☐ The engine will work harder

8.19 ☐ Be wary of a sudden gust

8.20 ☐ Steer into it

8.21 ☐ In case it stops suddenly

8.22 ☐ Leave sidelights switched on

8.23 ☐ Slow down or stop

8.24 ☐ When visibility is seriously reduced

8.25 ☐ Switch them off as long as visibility remains good

8.26 ☐ To prevent dazzling following drivers

8.27 ☐ They'll dazzle other drivers

8.28 ☐ Skidding in deep snow

8.29 ☐ By changing to a lower gear

8.30 ☐ You'll have less steering and braking control

8.31 ☐ Ten times the normal distance

8.32 ☐ Use your headlights

8.33 ☐ Dipped headlights

8.34 ☐ The condition of the tyres

8.35 ☐ When your vehicle is broken down on the hard shoulder

8.36 ☐ When you change to a lower gear

8.37 ☐ Dipped headlights

8.38 ☐ To make them more visible in thick fog

8.39 ☐ Switch them off when visibility improves

8.40 ☐ Don't drive unless it's essential

8.41 ☐ The brakes overheating

8.42 ☐ Make sure that the windows are clean

8.43 ☐ Switch off your fog lights

8.44 ☐ They may be confused with brake lights

8.45 ☐ It will reduce your control

8.46 ☐ Your vehicle will pick up speed

8.47 ☐ The vehicle will gain speed

8.48 ☐ Use a low gear and drive slowly

8.49 ☐ There won't be any engine braking

8.50 ☐ In poor visibility

8.51 ☐ Release the footbrake

Section 9 Motorway Rules

9.1 ☐ Give way to traffic already on the motorway

9.2 ☐ 70 mph

9.3 ☐ Any vehicle

9.4 ☐ A vehicle towing a trailer

9.5 ☐ It allows easy location by the emergency services

9.6 ☐ Gain speed on the hard shoulder before moving out onto the carriageway

9.7 ☐ On a steep gradient

9.8 ☐ They're countdown markers to the next exit

9.9 ☐ Between the central reservation and the carriageway

9.10 ☐ White

9.11 ☐ Green

9.12 ☐ In the direction shown on the marker posts

9.13 ☐ To build up a speed similar to traffic on the motorway

9.14 ☐ Face the oncoming traffic

9.15 ☐ Red

9.16 ☐ Left

9.17 ☐ Keep a good distance from the vehicle ahead

9.18 ☐ In the left-hand lane

9.19 ☐ Obey all speed limits

9.20 ☐ Powered mobility scooters

9.21 ☐ Look much further ahead than you would on other roads

9.22 ☐ Keep in the left-hand lane

9.23 ☐ Overtaking

9.24 ☐ Stopping in an emergency

9.25 ☐ Move to the left and reduce your speed to 50 mph

9.26 ☐ When you're signalled to do so by flashing red lights

9.27 ☐ Move to another lane

9.28 ☐ Keep to the left-hand lane unless overtaking

9.29 ☐ When in queues and traffic to your right is moving more slowly than you are

9.30 ☐ In cases of emergency or breakdown

9.31 ☐ Stop and direct anyone on a motorway

9.32 ☐ You shouldn't travel in this lane

9.33 ☐ The hard shoulder can be used as a running lane

9.34 ☐ To reduce congestion

9.35 ☐ You must obey the speed limits shown

9.36 ☐ Your overall journey time will normally improve

9.37 ☐ When signs direct you to

9.38 ☐ Variable speed limits

9.39 ☐ In an emergency or breakdown

9.40 ☐ 70 mph

9.41 ☐ Stop and wait

9.42 ☐ The hard shoulder is for emergency or breakdown use only

9.43 ☐ Use all the lanes, including the hard shoulder

9.44 ☐ At the nearest service area

9.45 ☐ 60 mph

9.46 ☐ Normal driving

9.47 ☐ Switch on your hazard warning lights

9.48 ☐ Use an emergency telephone and call for help

9.49 ☐ Carry on to the next exit

9.50 ☐ Switch on your hazard warning lights

9.51 ☐ Continuous high speeds increase the risk of your vehicle breaking down

9.52 ☐ Traffic ahead is slowing or stopping suddenly

9.53 ☐ In the left-hand lane

9.54 ☐ They can't drive unaccompanied

9.55 ☐ Check your location from the marker posts on the left

9.56 ☐ When there are lane closures

9.57 ☐ Lower speed limits

9.58 ☐ In an emergency

Section 10 Rules of the Road

10.1 ☐ National speed limit applies

10.2 ☐ 70 mph

10.3 ☐ By street lighting

10.4 ☐ 30 mph

10.5 ☐ End of minimum speed

10.6 ☐ Stay behind the tractor if you're in any doubt

10.7 ☐ Long lorry

10.8 ☐ At any time

10.9 ☐ Waiting restrictions

10.10 ☐ When you're in a one-way street

10.11 ☐ Overtaking or turning right

10.12 ☐ Continue in that lane

10.13 ☐ On either the right or the left

10.14 ☐ Indicate left before leaving the roundabout

10.15 ☐ Long vehicle

10.16 ☐ When your exit road is clear

10.17 ☐ When oncoming traffic prevents you from turning right

10.18 ☐ A police officer

10.19 ☐ Stop to let them cross and wait patiently

10.20 ☐ Cyclists and pedestrians

10.21 ☐ Wait for pedestrians on the crossing to clear

10.22 ☐ To pick up or set down passengers

10.23 ☐ You'll have a clearer view of any approaching traffic

10.24 ☐ Children may run out from between the vehicles

10.25 ☐ Give way to oncoming traffic

10.26 ☐ To overtake slower traffic

10.27 ☐ No-one has priority

10.28 ☐ 10 metres (32 feet)

10.29 ☐ At or near a bus stop

10.30 ☐ Carry on waiting

10.31 ☐ No-waiting zone ends

10.32 ☐ Obey the speed limit

10.33 ☐ You can be easily seen by others

10.34 ☐ Wait until the road is clear in both directions

10.35 ☐ 60 mph

10.36 ☐ Park with parking lights on

10.37 ☐ Approaching a concealed level crossing

10.38 ☐ A traffic officer

10.39 ☐ Signal left just after you pass the exit before the one you're going to take

10.40 ☐ To get onto a property

10.41 ☐ 50 mph

10.42 ☐ 60 mph

10.43 ☐ Park in a bay and pay

10.44 ☐ You mustn't drive in that lane

10.45 ☐ Keep well to the left of the road

10.46 ☐ Continue to wait

10.47 ☐ Keep going and clear the crossing

10.48 ☐ Turn around in a side road

10.49 ☐ Reversing

10.50 ☐ No further than is necessary

10.51 ☐ Get out and check

10.52 ☐ Not at any time

10.53 ☐ Wait in the box junction if your exit is clear

10.54 ☐ When the front of your vehicle swings out

10.55 ☐ In a garage

10.56 ☐ To set down and pick up passengers

10.57 ☐ You can't park there, unless you're permitted to do so

10.58 ☐ Pull into a passing place on your left

10.59 ☐ As soon as the vehicle passes you

10.60 ☐ Outside its hours of operation

10.61 ☐ By using brake lights

10.62 ☐ Find a quiet side road to turn around in

10.63 ☐ In a well-lit area

10.64 ☐ Move to the left in good time

10.65 ☐ You shouldn't drive in the lane unless it's unavoidable

10.66 ☐ A Blue Badge

10.67 ☐ If you're involved in an incident that causes damage or injury

Section 11 Road and Traffic Signs

11.1 ☐ They're circular with a red border

11.2 ☐

11.3 ☐

11.4 ☐ Maximum speed limit with traffic calming

11.5 ☐

11.6 ☐ End of 20 mph zone

11.7 ☐ No motor vehicles

11.8 ☐ No entry

11.9 ☐ No right turn

11.10 ☐

11.11 ☐ Route for trams only

11.12 ☐ High vehicles

11.13 ☐

11.14 ☐ No overtaking

11.15 ☐ Waiting restrictions apply

11.16 ☐ End of restricted parking area

11.17 ☐

11.18 ☐ No stopping

11.19 ☐ Distance to parking place ahead

11.20 ☐ Vehicles may park fully on the verge or footway

11.21 ☐ Give priority to oncoming traffic

11.22 □ You have priority over vehicles coming towards you

11.23 □

11.24 □ Stop

11.25 □ Minimum speed 30 mph

11.26 □ Pass either side to get to the same destination

11.27 □ Route for trams

11.28 □ Give an instruction

11.29 □ On a one way street

11.30 □ Contraflow bus lane

11.31 □ Tourist directions

11.32 □ Tourist attraction

11.33 □ To give warnings

11.34 □ T-junction

11.35 □ Risk of ice

11.36 □ Crossroads

11.37 □ Roundabout

11.38 □ Road narrows

11.39 □ Cycle route ahead

11.40 □

11.41 □

11.42 □ Give way to trams

11.43 □ Humps in the road

11.44 □

11.45 □ End of dual carriageway

11.46 □ Side winds

11.47 □ Danger ahead

11.48 □ Hold back until you can see clearly ahead

11.49 □ Level crossing with gate or barrier

11.50 □ Trams crossing ahead

11.51 □ Steep hill downwards

11.52 □ Water across the road

11.53 □ No through road on the left

11.54 □ No through road

11.55 □

11.56 □ The right-hand lane is closed

11.57 □ Contraflow system

11.58 □ Lane for heavy and slow vehicles

11.59 □ You must stop and wait behind the stop line

11.60 □ Stop at the stop line

11.61 □ When your exit from the junction is blocked

11.62 □

11.63 □ Traffic lights out of order

11.64 □ Nobody

11.65 □ Level crossings

11.66 □ No parking at any time

11.67 □ To pass a road maintenance vehicle travelling at 10 mph or less

11.68 □ You're approaching a hazard

11.69 □ On road humps

11.70 □

11.71 □ Visibility along the major road is restricted

11.72 □ Give way to traffic from the right

11.73 □ Flash the headlights, indicate left and point to the left

11.74 □ Stop at the stop line

11.75 □ The driver intends to turn left

11.76 □ On a motorway slip road

11.77 □ Change to the lane on your left

11.78 ☐ Temporary maximum speed 50 mph	11.109 ☐ Red alone
11.79 ☐ Right-hand lane closed ahead	11.110 ☐ Leave the motorway at the next exit
11.80 ☐ The number of the next junction	11.111 ☐ Stop even if the road is clear
11.81 ☐ As an overtaking lane	11.112 ☐
11.82 ☐ On the right-hand edge of the road	
11.83 ☐ At slip-road entrances and exits	11.113 ☐ Mini-roundabout
11.84 ☐ Leave the motorway at the next exit	11.114 ☐ Two-way traffic crosses a one-way road
11.85 ☐ End of motorway	11.115 ☐ Two-way traffic straight ahead
11.86 ☐	11.116 ☐ Hump bridge
	11.117 ☐ Direction to park-and-ride car park
11.87 ☐ 60 mph	11.118 ☐ Wait for the green light
11.88 ☐ End of restriction	11.119 ☐ Just before a 'give way' sign
11.89 ☐ A diversion route	11.120 ☐ Wait
11.90 ☐ A mandatory speed-limit change ahead	11.121 ☐ Direction to emergency pedestrian exit
11.91 ☐ Compulsory maximum speed limit	11.122 ☐
11.92 ☐ Carry on with great care	
11.93 ☐ Give an arm signal	
11.94 ☐ No motorcycles	11.123 ☐ With-flow bus and cycle lane
11.95 ☐ Pass the lorry on the left	11.124 ☐ Zebra crossing ahead
11.96 ☐ Move into another lane in good time	11.125 ☐
11.97 ☐ To warn others of your presence	
11.98 ☐ When another road user poses a danger	11.126 ☐
11.99 ☐ No parking on the days and times shown	
11.100 ☐ Quayside or river bank	11.127 ☐ Red and amber
11.101 ☐ Hazard warning	11.128 ☐ Tunnel ahead
11.102 ☐ To prevent queuing traffic from blocking the junction on the left	11.129 ☐ The edge of the carriageway
	11.130 ☐ Keep left of the hatched markings
11.103 ☐ It separates traffic flowing in opposite directions	11.131 ☐
11.104 ☐ To warn you of their presence	
11.105 ☐ 20 mph	11.132 ☐ Wait until the vehicle starts to turn in
11.106 ☐ Trams must stop	11.133 ☐ On a motorway or unrestricted dual carriageway, to warn of a hazard ahead
11.107 ☐ At a mini-roundabout	
11.108 ☐ Pull up on the left	11.134 ☐ Not under any circumstances

11.135 ☐ To avoid misleading other road users

11.136 ☐ As you're passing or just after the junction

Section 12 Essential Documents

12.1 ☐ One year after the date it was issued

12.2 ☐ A document issued before you receive your insurance certificate

12.3 ☐ Retake your theory and practical tests

12.4 ☐ Until the vehicle is taxed, sold or scrapped

12.5 ☐ A notification to tell DVLA that a vehicle isn't being used on the road

12.6 ☐ Unlimited

12.7 ☐ The registered vehicle keeper

12.8 ☐ When a police officer asks you for it

12.9 ☐ A valid driving licence

12.10 ☐ Valid insurance

12.11 ☐ 7 days

12.12 ☐ That the vehicle is insured for your use

12.13 ☐ Your insurance

12.14 ☐ Have valid motor insurance

12.15 ☐ Damage to other vehicles

12.16 ☐ The registered keeper of the vehicle

12.17 ☐ The registered keeper

12.18 ☐ When you change your vehicle

12.19 ☐ When your health affects your driving

12.20 ☐ When you complete the Pass Plus scheme

12.21 ☐ You must be at least 21 years old

12.22 ☐ When driving to an appointment at an MOT centre

12.23 ☐ Three years

12.24 ☐ To improve your basic skills

12.25 ☐ Damage to other vehicles

12.26 ☐ Third party only

12.27 ☐ You'll have to pay the first £100 of the cost of repairs to your car

12.28 ☐ To improve your basic driving skills

12.29 ☐ Widen their driving experience

Section 13 Incidents, Accidents and Emergencies

13.1 ☐ The driver is likely to be a disabled person

13.2 ☐ When you slow down quickly on a motorway because of a hazard ahead

13.3 ☐ When stopped and temporarily obstructing traffic

13.4 ☐ Keep a safe distance from the vehicle in front

13.5 ☐ When an emergency arises

13.6 ☐ Apply pressure over the wound

13.7 ☐ Check that they're breathing normally

13.8 ☐ 10 minutes

13.9 ☐ 120 times per minute

13.10 ☐ Pale grey skin

13.11 ☐ Check their airway remains open

13.12 ☐ Seek medical assistance

13.13 ☐ Go to the next emergency telephone and report the hazard

13.14 ☐ Variable message signs

13.15 ☐ 5 to 6 centimetres

13.16 ☐ Call the emergency services promptly

13.17 ☐ Make sure that an ambulance is called for

13.18 ☐ Only when it's essential

13.19 ☐ Check whether they're breathing normally

13.20 ☐ Check their airway is open

13.21 ☐ Keep injured people warm and comfortable

13.22 ☐ Reassure them

13.23 ☐ Warn other traffic

13.24 ☐ Open their airway and begin CPR

13.25 ☐ Tilt their head back gently

13.26 ☐ Douse the burns with clean, cool water

13.27 ☐ Apply firm pressure over the wound

13.28 ☐ When there's further danger

13.29 ☐ Keep them where they are

13.30 ☐ 2YE 1089

13.31 ☐ Driving licence

13.32 ☐ As soon as possible

13.33 ☐ Warn other traffic

13.34 ☐ Keep their head tilted forwards as far as possible

13.35 ☐ Reassure them confidently

13.36 ☐ This could result in more serious injury

13.37 ☐ 45 metres (147 feet)

13.38 ☐ Leave your vehicle and get everyone clear

13.39 ☐ Pull up slowly at the side of the road

13.40 ☐ Pull up on the hard shoulder. Use the emergency phone to get assistance

13.41 ☐ Get out of the car and clear of the crossing

13.42 ☐ When you slow down quickly because of danger ahead

13.43 ☐ Details about your vehicle

13.44 ☐ REmove any sunglasses

13.45 ☐ Use dipped headlights

13.46 ☐ Check out any strong smell of fuel

13.47 ☐ Stop at the next emergency telephone and contact the police

13.48 ☐ Check out the problem quickly and safely

13.49 ☐ Switch on hazard warning lights, then go and call for help

13.50 ☐ Drive it out of the tunnel if you can do so

13.51 ☐ Switch on hazard warning lights

13.52 ☐ Make sure your radio is tuned to the frequency shown

13.53 ☐ Get everyone out of the vehicle and clear of the crossing

13.54 ☐ Fire extinguisher

13.55 ☐ Stop at the scene of the incident

13.56 ☐ The other driver's name, address and telephone number

13.57 ☐ Report the incident to the police within 24 hours

Section 14 Vehicle Loading

14.1 ☐ Use only the left-hand and centre lanes

14.2 ☐ Ease off the accelerator to reduce your speed

14.3 ☐ When carrying a heavy load

14.4 ☐ It will reduce stability

14.5 ☐ The vehicle's handling

14.6 ☐ The driver of the vehicle

14.7 ☐ A stabiliser fitted to the towbar

14.8 ☐ No, not at any time

14.9 ☐ Breakaway cable

14.10 ☐ In the vehicle handbook

14.11 ☐ Securely fastened with suitable restraints

14.12 ☐ A child seat

Section 15 Case Study Practice

Case study on pages 151–152

1 Look over your shoulder for a final check

2 Slow down
Consider using the horn
Beware of pedestrians

3 Find a suitable place to stop

4 Go slowly past
Give plenty of room

5 There may be another vehicle coming

Case study practice A

1 Renew your vehicle tax immediately

2 Drink two cups of coffee and rest for 15 minutes

3 Stay calm and continue when it's safe

4 Stay out of the outside lane

5 Because you're stationary

Case study practice B

1 He is

2 He's deaf and blind

3 National speed limit applies

4 Put on your hazard warning lights

5 Restrict the blood flow from their leg

Case study practice C

1 Four seconds

2 Pedestrians stepping out from between vehicles

3 Stop and wait until the way ahead is clear

4 No-one

5 Tyre pressure is too low

Case study practice D

1 Headlights with fog lights as necessary

2 Slowly drop back to allow more room in front

3 Move nearer to the centre line and signal to go right

4 Turned in towards the kerb

5 Lock it away securely out of sight

Case study practice E

1 Oil and water levels

2 In a suitable child restraint

3 Glare from the sun on wet roads

4 Well back, so you can see ahead and be seen

5 This lane can be used as a running lane at a speed of 40 mph

Part 2

Guide to Passing the Driving Test

Choosing a Training School

Training School's Reputation

Check them out thoroughly, do your research and try to find some genuine reviews before making a booking.

Gaining a driving licence is an expensive undertaking – choosing the wrong school could be a costly mistake.

Questions to Keep in Mind

Can you take an assessment drive? (This puts you and them to the test).

Do the instructors have the ADI qualification (approved driving instructor?)

Are they reasonably priced? Or does it seem much too cheap? Be careful paying peanuts, because this can sometimes result in attracting monkeys.

What is their average pass rate?

Can you visit the school?

Are the vehicles in good condition?

Why Do You Need a Driving Instructor?

It's really important to learn to drive safely and correctly right from the beginning, thus avoiding picking up bad habits which are hard to break! Instructors are specially trained to teach you everything that you need to know to drive correctly, be safe on the road and ultimately pass your test. They have lots of experience and knowledge which they can pass on to you to help you become a proficient, confident and safe driver.

If you choose to have a member of your family or friends teach you to drive they need to meet certain requirements. They have to have held a driving licence for at least three years and be qualified to drive the particular vehicle you're learning in, i.e. manual or automatic.

If your friends or family know someone who has recently passed their test, it might be worth asking if they can recommend an instructor?

It is important to find an instructor that fits with you. Try to pick an instructor who has a good reputation, has a car that suits your needs and is friendly and reliable. If during the beginning of your lessons you find it difficult to get on with your instructor then find someone else. It's important that you get on well with whoever is teaching you!

How Much Does it Cost on Average to Learn to Drive?

An average driving lesson costs between £20 and £30: the recommended time period of lessons prior to taking a test is 45 hours. Estimated costs including a mock test and the driving test are £1000.

Five-Day Intensive Courses

Intensive courses allow trainees to distance themselves from other life distractions and become fully immersed in the training. On an intensive course it is possible to lose concentration and to start making mistakes during one of the five consecutive days. This may or may not happen. If it does, do not lose confidence, it is perfectly natural, the mind will only focus intensely for a certain amount of time before wandering. Concentration will and always does return.

Block Booking

Some driving schools have special deals for block booking lessons or reduced rates for two hour lessons. It is worth asking what possible deals are available before booking.

To get the most out of your lessons it's a good idea to make a plan with your instructor and record your progress. Reviewing your plan and progress will help to give you an idea of how ready you are to book your test.

Practice is a very important. The more you practice driving the easier it will become and the better you will get. With practice comes experience. There are no short cuts . . .

What to Expect on Your Driving Test

You must bring your photocard driving licence. If you don't have your photocard driving licence then your paper licence and a valid passport will suffice.

Your test will be **cancelled** and you will lose your fee if you don't bring these items on the day.

Ideally take a 45 minute pre-test lesson, then arrive at the test centre around 10 to 15 minutes prior to your test, so that you're not hurried or waiting for too long.

Remember to **switch off** your mobile phone and any other personal distractions.

What Happens During the Test

There are five parts to the UK driving test:

1. Eyesight check
2. 'Show me, tell me' vehicle safety questions
3. General driving ability
4. Reversing your vehicle
5. Independent driving

The test criteria is the same for both manual and automatic cars.

How Long Does the Test Last?

You will drive for around 40 minutes (previously banned drivers will take a 70 minute test).

Eye Sight Check

You will have to read a number plate from a distance of 20 metres for vehicles with a new style number-plate and 20.5 metres for vehicles with an old-style number plate.

New style number plates start with two letters followed by two numbers such as AB 51 ABC.

You automatically fail your driving test if you fail the eyesight check. The test will end abruptly.

Show Me, Tell Me Questions

You will be asked two vehicle safety questions, known as the 'show me, tell me' questions.

'Tell me' questions at the start of your test, before you start driving and 'show me' questions while you're driving.

Your General Driving Ability

You will drive in various road and traffic conditions, but not on motorways.

The examiner will give you directions that you should follow.

Pulling Over at the Side of the Road

- You will be asked to pull over and pull away during your test

- Normal stops at the side of the road

- Pulling out from behind a parked vehicle

- A hill start

- You might also be asked to carry out an emergency stop

Reversing Your Vehicle

The examiner will ask you to do one of the following exercises:

1. Parallel park at the side of the road.
2. Park in a parking bay-either by driving in and reversing out, or reversing in and driving out (the examiner will tell you which you have to do).

Independent Driving

You have to drive for about 20 minutes by following either:

1. directions from a satnav.

2. traffic signs.

The examiner will tell you which you have to follow. They will set the satnav up for you. You are not allowed to use your own Sat Nav.

If You Can't See Traffic Signs

If you can't see a traffic sign (for example, because it's covered by trees), the examiner will give you directions to follow until you can see the next one.

The examiner won't give you a fault for taking a wrong turning.

If You Make Mistakes During Your Test

You can carry on if you make a mistake. It might not affect your test result if it's not serious.

The examiner will only stop your test if they think you're driving is a danger to other road users.

You can still pass your practical test with up to 15 minor faults. In the event of a mistake, simply move on and do not dwell on it. After you've taken the practical test your examiner will tell you if you passed and explain how you did. You pass your test if you make:

1. 15 or less minor faults.

2. No serious or dangerous faults.

If you fail you can book another driving test straight away, but you can't take it for another 10 days.

Useful Contacts for Learners

Booking your the theory test
(https://www.gov.uk/book-theory-test)

Booking a driving test(https://www.gov.uk/book-driving-test)

Note: Check your spam periodically for a possible cancellation …

In the case of your test being cancelled by the DVSA at short notice you can then apply for a refund of expenses here:
(https://www.gov.uk/government/publications/application-for-refunding-out-of-pocket-expenses)

For more information on learning to drive go to
(https://www.gov.uk/browse/driving)

Using Your Own Car for the Test

You can take your driving test in your own car rather than your driving instructor's as long as it meets certain criteria.

Your test will be cancelled and you'll have to pay again if your car doesn't meet the criteria.

Your car must:

- be taxed

- be insured for a driving test (check with your insurance company)

- be roadworthy and have a current MOT (if it's over 3 years old)

- have no warning lights showing, for example, the airbag warning light

- have no tyre damage and the legal tread depth on each tyre – you can't have a space-saver spare tyre fitted

- be smoke-free – this means you can't smoke in it just before or during the test

- be able to reach at least 62mph and have an mph speedometer

- have 4 wheels and a maximum authorised mass (MAM) of no more than 3,500 kg

The MAM is the limit on how much the car can weigh when it's loaded. It'll be in the car's handbook.

Things that must be fitted

The car must have:

- an extra interior rear-view mirror for the examiner

- L-plates ('L' or 'D' plates in Wales) on the front and rear

- a passenger seatbelt for the examiner and a proper passenger head restraint (not a slip-on type)

Dashcams and Other Cameras

You can use a camera fitted for insurance purposes, as long as it:

- faces outside of the car and doesn't film the inside

- doesn't record audio from inside the car

Manual and Automatic Cars

You can take the test in a:

- manual car – these have 3 pedals

- automatic or semi-automatic car – these have 2 pedals

If you take your test in a semi-automatic car you'll only be able to drive automatic and semi-automatic cars once you've passed your test.

Hire Cars

You can take your test in a hire car if it's fitted with dual controls and meets all the other rules.

Vehicle Features

You can use a car with:

- an electronic parking brake

- hill-start assist

Cars You Can't Use

Some cars can't be used in the test because they don't give the examiner all-round vision.

You can't use any of the following:

- BMW Mini convertible

- Ford Ka convertible

- Toyota iQ

- VW Beetle convertible

Check with the Driver and Vehicle Standards Agency (DVSA) before you book your test if you want to use a:

- convertible car

- panel van

Cars With Known Safety Faults

You can't use one of the cars shown in the table unless you have proof that it's safe. This is because these cars have been recalled for a safety reason.

You must bring the proof that it's safe with you when you take your test.

Model	Reason for recall	Vehicles affected	Recall issue date
Citroen C1	Steering failure	Vehicles built between 9 Sep 2014 and 15 Oct 2014, with vehicle identification numbers (VINs) between wF7xxxxxxER516105 and VF7xxxxxxER523367	28 Jun 2016
Peugeot 108	Steering failure	Vehicles built between 9 Jun 2014 and 15 Oct 2014, with VINs between VF3xxxxxxER256527 and F3xxxxxxER017078	28 Jun 2016
Toyota Aygo	Steering failure	Vehicles built between 9 Jun 2014 and 15 Oct 2014, with VINs between JTDJGNEC#0N022080 and 0N026438, JTDJPNEC#0N002099 and 0N002100, JTDKGNEC#0N022186 and 0N031372, and JTDKPNEC#0N002083 and 0N002102	28 Jun 2016
Toyota Yaris	Potentially defective seat rail track and / or steering column mounting	Some models built between Jun 2005 and May 2010 ('05' to '10' registration plates)	9 Apr 2014
Vauxhall ADAM	Potential steering problem	VINs with last 8 digits between E6077301 to E6113446, and F6000001 to F6006544	29 Sep 2014
Vauxhall Corsa D	Potential steering problem	VINs with last 8 digits between E6071016 and E6118738, and E4181031 and E4308122	29 Sep 2014

Proof You Need to Bring to Your Test

You must bring proof that says one of the following:

- the car was recalled and the recall work has been done

- the car was recalled but didn't need any work to be done

- the car wasn't part of the recall

The proof must be either:

- the recall letter or safety notice, stamped by the manufacturer or dealer

- on official or headed notepaper from the manufacturer or a dealer

Your test will be cancelled and you could lose your fee if you don't bring the right proof !!!

"Show Me" and "Tell Me" Vehicle Safety Questions

About The Questions

The examiner will ask you one: 'Tell me' question (where you explain how you'd carry out a safety task) at the start of your test, before you start driving.

TELL ME ABOUT IT

'Show me questions' (where you show how you'd carry out a safety task) will be asked whilst you're driving.

"Tell Me" Questions

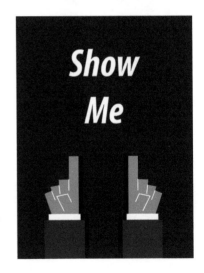

Show Me

1. Tell me how you'd check that the brakes are working before starting the journey?

   Brakes should not feel spongy or slack, brakes should be tested as you set off. Vehicle should not pull to one side.

2. Tell me where you'd find the information for the recommended tyre pressures for this car and how pressures should be checked?

Manufacturers guide, use a reliable pressure gauge, check and adjust pressures when tyres are cold, don't forget spare tyre, remember to refit valve caps.

3. Tell me how you make sure your head restraint is correctly adjusted and so provides the best protection in the event of a crash?

The head restraint should be adjusted so the rigid part of the head restraint is at least as high as the eye or the top of the ears, and is close to the back of the head as is comfortable. Note: some restraints might not be adjustable.

4. Tell me how you'd check the tyres to ensure that they have sufficient tread depth and that their general condition is safe to use on the road?

No cuts and bulges,1.6mm of tread depth across the central three-quarters of the breadth of the tyre, and around the entire outer circumference of the tyre.

5. Tell me how you check that the headlights and tail lights are working? (You don't need to exit the vehicle.)

Explain that you'd operate the switch (turn on ignition if necessary), then walk round vehicle (as this is a 'tell me' question, you don't need to physically check the lights).

6. Tell me how you'd know if there was a problem with your anti-lock braking system?

Warning lights should illuminate if there is a fault with the anti-lock braking system.

7. Tell me how you check the direction indicators are working? (You don't need to exit the vehicle).

Explain that you'd operate switch (turn on ignition if necessary), and then walk round vehicle (as this is a' tell me' question, you don't need to physically check the lights).

8. Tell me how you'd check the brake lights are working on this car?

Explain you'd operate the brake pedal, make use of reflections in windows or doors, or ask someone to help.

9. Tell me how you'd check the power-assisted steering is working before starting the journey?

If the steering becomes heavy, the system may not be working properly. Before starting the journey, two simple checks can be made:

Gentle pressure on the steering wheel, maintained while the engine is started, should result in a slight but noticeable movement as system begins to operate. Alternatively turning the steering wheel just after moving off will give you an immediate indication that the power assistance is functioning.

10. Tell me how you'd switch on the rear fog light(s) and explain when you'd use it/them? (You don't need to exit the vehicle)

Operate switch (turn on dipped headlights and ignition if necessary) check warning light is on. Explain use.

11. Tell me how you switch your headlights from dipped to main beam and explain how you'd know the main beam is on.

Operate switch (with ignition or engine on if necessary), check with main beam warning light.

12. Open the bonnet and tell me how you'd check that the engine has sufficient oil?

Identify dipstick/oil level indicator, describe check oil level against the minimum and maximum markers.

13. Open the bonnet and tell me how you'd check that the engine has sufficient engine coolant?

Identify high and low-level markings on header tank where fitted or radiator filler cap, and describe how to top up to correct level.

14. Open the bonnet and tell me how you'd check that you have a safe level of hydraulic brake fluid.

Identify a reservoir, check level against high and low markings.

Note (you need to open the bonnet and tell the examiner how you'd do the check if you're asked question 12, 13, 14).

'Show Me' Questions

1. When it's safe to do so, can you show me how you wash and clean the front windscreen?

2. When it's safe to do so, can you show me how you wash and clean the rear windscreen?

3. When it's safe to do so, can you show me how you'd switch on your dipped headlights?

4. When it's safe to do so, can you show me how you set the rear demister?

5. When it's safe to do so, can you show me how you'd operate the horn?

6. When it's safe to do so, can you show me how you de-mist the front windscreen?

7. When it's safe to do so, can you show me how you'd open and close the side window?

Examiner's Test Criteria

There are three main types of fault recorded. Minor, serious and dangerous.

Minor Faults. examples:
Undue hesitancy, gear crunching, insufficient use of mirrors, insufficient road progress etc.

When a driver makes a mistake a fault is noted down on the examiners test report in the relevant section. If the driver makes the same mistake again it will be noted again in the same section. If the same mistake is made a third time the examiner can and probably will change the fault from minor to serious.

To Summarise.
If a driver has 15 points to play with and they make a few small errors which are noted in various sections of the test sheet, they will probably pass. If they make three of the same errors they could well fail.

Serious Faults.

Examples: Pulling out in front of another vehicle causing it to alter course. Mounting the curb, going through a red light at a crossing, etc.

The likelihood of a driver failing their test after committing one or more serious faults is extremely high.

Dangerous Faults.

Examples include: going the wrong way down a one-way road, almost hitting a pedestrian, colliding with another vehicle etc. A dangerous fault is an immediate fail.

Psychology – The examiner and you

The examiners take potentially dangerous vehicles and their personal role in public safety very seriously. To gain their confidence, a demonstration of the following is necessary:

- Competence, ability to keep the vehicle fully under control at all times.

- Anticipation, forward thinking, awareness of all road users, road signs and hazards.

- Road safey, the driver and public.

Correcting Bad Habits

To pass the test you will have to drive in a certain way adhering to all the rules. Demonstrate a high ability to concentrate, attention to detail, a high level of control over the vehicle and good road sense and road manners.

Bad habits built up over time can easily be your undoing on the test day. They don't just disappear overnight. Either get rid of them or be aware of which ones prevail and could effectively be your achilles heel on the day.

Usual culprits that scupper people are:

Incorrect mirror signal manoeuvre
Using crossed hands instead of shuffling the wheel
Poor choice of gears
Tailgating other vehicles
Poor road positioning
Erratic steering and braking
Incorrect road speed
Forgetting to signal on entering and exiting a roundabout,(Resulting in pulling out in front of other vehicles leaving them insufficient room)
Pulling away from the curb without checking the blind spot/looking over their shoulder
Lack of anticipation
Improper handbrake use
Poor reversing skills

The Solution: make a concerted effort to practice away the old habits. During the few weeks leading up to the test, drive your car or van as if it's examination day. Make driving to the rules become second nature. Not having to worry about making mistakes due to bad habits will free up more headspace and make concentration on all of the other necessary details of the test easier.

Most Common Test Mistakes, Faults and Fails

Response to Signs and Road Markings

- Driving unnecessarily over central dividing line.

- Not correctly following lane directional arrows

- Stopping inside a yellow box junction when the exit is not clear

- Not coming to a dead stop at a stop sign (stop means stop!)

Not Moving Off Under Control

- Rolling back on an uphill start

- Moving off with handbrake on

- Trying to move off in neutral

- Moving off in wrong gear

- Repeated stalling

Mistakes at Junctions or When Turning

- Improper mirror signal manoeuvre

- Unnecessarily cutting corners

- Mounting the kerb

Road Positioning/Normal Driving

- Driving too far from / too close to kerb

- Not driving in a bus lane when allowed and safe to do so

- On a roundabout creeping forward beyond the white line, whilst waiting for an opportunity to enter (deemed as being in a position likely to cause another vehicle to alter course: Serious Fault)

- Straying across lanes on a roundabout

- Not increasing or decreasing speed according to road signs

Not Maintaining Control/Steering

- Erratic / jerky

- Crossing hands

- Striking a kerb

- Not having both hands on the wheel where possible (two hands)

Not Responding

- Not moving off on a green filter arrow when safe to do so

- Not going on a green light when safe to do so

- Driving through a red light

- Not reducing speed on approach to traffic lights (failure to show caution)

Use of Mirrors

- Not checking prior to signal, manoeuvring

- Not being fully aware of cyclists and overtaking motorcyclists

- Not checking mirrors often enough

- Not being seen to check!!! (move your head)

Moving Off Safely

- Not checking mirrors, blind spot and road ahead

- Incorrect indicating

Reversing Exercise

- Lack of observation

- Poor positioning

- Hitting cones

Driving Test Tips and Scenarios

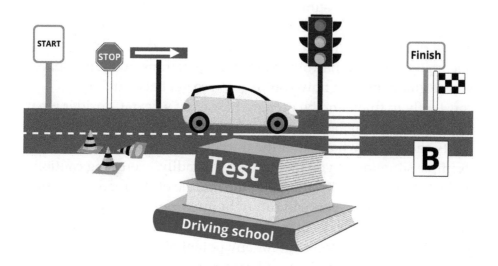

Anticipation/Observation/Assumptions

Anticipate what will and might happen next and keep planning ahead. Traffic conditions are unpredictable .You never know what's going to happen next or what's around the next corner, roundabout or junction. During the test there will be certain situations that you can expect and shouldn't be surprised by. Examples are people walking into the road from a bus at a busy bus stop, or traffic light sequence at road junctions-if the light's been green for a while it's a safe bet that it's going to change. Another is pedestrians waiting at a crossing, if there's a crowd of people someone will have pressed the button, it's just a matter of time. Show caution on approaching zebra crossings. It's important to take extra care and be observant, particularly when the zebra crossing is close to an awkward junction or partially obscured by a large vehicle. Keep **scanning** the area for possible adults in a hurry on their phone, or young children stepping straight out oblivious in to the road.

Be **prepared** and fully aware of all other traffic.. If you can't see round a corner then approach it slowly ready for the worst. At a junction where you can't see very well, emerge carefully, **observe** properly and don't assume the roads clear. Its better in fact to always expect the worst. Effective observations are very important in avoiding potential incidents and accidents. When meeting oncoming traffic on narrow roads, don't just think about the space you're going into but how you're going to get back out. Try constantly to think and be prepared for what's next. Consider what parked lorries may be hiding from your view and also the traffic lights ahead and what's after the traffic lights. In a narrow road example situation, if you do not take it steadily, exercising caution and instead keep on heading into the middle of the road **expecting** the road to be clear, you will run right into trouble and probably have to reverse. Always plan ahead and expect the worst. Keep up your awareness and look out for any potentially unexpected situations. Remember, signs and road markings are all there to help you.

Always concentrate and plan ahead for what might happen next and try to be ready for the unexpected. Take in all the information around you including what you see in your mirrors and keep **planning** and **scanning**. Be aware of buses, cyclists passing on the (nearside) inside and motorcycles and emergency vehicles speeding by.

Look well ahead and try to spot road signs early so you have time to think and react. Be aware of dual carriageways ending and traffic merging or bus lanes, cycle lanes ending and traffic merging. All it takes is to miss signs and road markings and you could end up going the wrong way up a one way street or driving over the speed limit, or even driving too slowly. If the speed limit raises and it's safe to drive faster you need to take notice. If you're unsure what the speed limit is then look for smaller repeater signs.

It is vital to anticipate and plan ahead. Also don't forget to keep checking the mirrors and being seen to check them and also checking the blind spot when pulling out or changing lanes.

In various situations such as these; try asking yourself; can I enter and exit the box junction before the lights change? Have any of the people at the pedestrian crossing pressed the button? Is it safe to go around the stopped bus or are there people starting to cross? Plan for what might and will happen next, it is very important to keep anticipating and planning. If you fail to keep doing this it is more than likely that mistakes will start to happen.

Assumptions. Don't assume the speed limits on the road your on are not going to alter, or that to go straight on at a roundabout you always have to use the left hand lane (mostly you do, sometimes you don't), or you can never drive in bus lanes or two in one lanes.

Never assume you have failed your test. If you make a mistake that totally puts you off, such as stalling when moving off. Don't continue on the test dwelling on what has just happened. If you do you will not be concentrating in the moment and may start to make more and more mistakes. Just let go of the past situation, recover from it and focus on what's next. Keep going. Be positive ...

Try not to be distracted by what the examiner is writing or if and when they speak . You don't know what it is they've written, and can't do anything about it anyway. Don't be distracted from the task in hand. Drive safely and within the law.

Note: Pre Test
Get to know the roads immediately in the vicinity of the test centre. This makes the start and end of the test easier. Practice lots, learn from mistakes. Build up your experience. A pre-test mock test is recommended.

Take the test when you're ready and confident. Believe in yourself .

Nerves

Day of the Test

Most people get nervous. On the day of the test, try to keep to your normal routine . Eat breakfast .If you find your feeling butterflies in your stomach, still try to eat something. This will help to keep your energy levels up as nervousness tends to burn up a lot of energy. Ideally you don't want to be stressed by feeling hungry.

Prepare your day. No rushing around , have a calm day but stay occupied …

It can be helpful to ease nerves by drawing confidence from experience. Remember all the preparation you've put in leading up to now.

All the effort, the hours spent behind the wheel and the on road experience you have.

Another good thing is to take a 45 minute pre test lesson. Talk to the instructor, re familiarise yourself with the vehicle, get into the driving zone.

If possible arrive at the test centre in plenty of time. Take 10 minutes to relax in the car. Listen to calming music and take 5 or 10 good long deep breaths. This will help circulation and help get oxygen to the brain.

If you still find yourself with an over active chattering mind, answer it with positivity using the knowledge you've gained up to now as an edge. "I'm used to focussing, I've put plenty of practise time in, I've got experience, I can do this etc".

Switch off your phone, then head into the test centre, ideally 5 to 10 minutes prior to test. Show proof of identity etc.

Walk out and ease yourself into the car. Ease into the test.

Start steadily. Once you get going focus will concentrate the mind and help to ease nerves.

Note
In case your throat gets dry having a bottle of water with you is a good idea. Some of the smaller test centres do not have toilets. Your instructor should know if they do.

Stacking the Odds in Your Favour

By Doing The Following:

- Lots of practising

- Choosing the best driving school

- Mock tests

- Assessing test centre entrance and exit

- Driving the roads close to the test centre

- Learning most of the route

- Showing caution on blind bends, traffic lights etc

- Driving the route

- Knowing the difficult junctions

- Knowing the speed limits

- Keeping the same vehicle

- Overcoming bad habits

- Anticipating, forward thinking on the road

- Anticipating other motorists intentions

- Avoiding lack of road progress

- Avoiding hesitancy, where appropriate keep the wheels rolling

- Knowing the highway code

- Focus, focus, focus

- Confident calm and concentrated

Conclusion

I fully understand how time-consuming and expensive it is to gain a driving licence. I also understand that everyone is different. What works for one person may not work for another. I recommend you cherry pick from the information provided for whatever works best for you. I hope this chapter helps with the challenge of passing your test!

Part 3

The Essential New Driver's Handbook

Road Safety

Please take note of the following, potentially dangerous scenarios that you may run into on the road:

Temporary Road Works

Be aware that some temporary road work sites do not have signs placed far enough back to give you enough, or even any, warning. During busy times, such as rush hour, cars may be queuing way back beyond sight of the signs. Therefore, always ensure that you slow down when approaching a blind bend. This is not an uncommon situation; you will come across it.

Cresting a Hill

When cresting a hill you should also ensure that you reduce your speed. As with the previous scenario, you never know what awaits you on the other side. There could potentially be a queue of traffic, a broken-down vehicle or somebody waiting to turn.

Turning off the Motorway

If, when you are planning to turn off onto a slip road and your vision is obscured whilst following a truck or coach, ensure you slow down in order to create space to see. There could potentially be a queue of stationary traffic that you are not aware of.

Tyre Scrub Build Up

Summer

During the hotter period of the year scrub builds up on the road surface. In itself not a real problem until the first heavy rain shower which turns it back into oil. Be ready for this hazard. The road can very suddenly turn into a skating ring.

Autumn

Same scenario, but add a covering of wet leaves and the road becomes even slippier. Hit the brakes and vehicle just slides.

Wasps, Bees and Spiders

These can be an instantaneous hazard. There are numerous accidents every year due to driver's attention being diverted away from the road for a second or two. I've personally heard of at least one fatality. A passing car driver saw an oncoming truck driver doing battle with a bee. The truck veered off the road and hit a farm wall head on.

Slamming Into Reverse

Avoid stopping quickly and then instantly beginning to reverse. Give time for a possible motorcyclist/cyclist to take evasive action (they do not have a reverse gear and you may not hear them). I have seen a motorcyclist back pedalling a bike for all he was worth, trying to get out the way of a quickly reversing van.

Blind Spots/Cyclists Listening to Music

Considerations When Driving a Van or Truck: Cyclists and motorcyclists have a nasty habit of creeping up the nearside of trucks undetected or stopping directly in front, below windscreen level at a set of traffic lights/junction. Be mindful of them getting part of their clothing or bag caught up on the side of the van/truck and being dragged underneath. In the past there have been several very serious incidents of cyclists/motorcyclists sitting in the blind spots of truck mirrors. In a rush the truck driver suddenly changed his/her mind about which route to take. With or without indicating the driver turned suddenly, thus leaving no time for the person to react (you can guess the rest).

Winter Driving

Use screen wash to avoid windscreen washers becoming frozen. Salt and slush picked up on motorways and A roads will make it impossible to see in no time at all!

Black Ice

This is an unseen danger, especially found on untreated roads and shady areas after the temperature drops below freezing. I spoke to an articulated truck driver who hit a stretch of black ice whilst driving at speed in the middle lane of a motorway. The trailer started sliding sideward pulling the tractor unit out of line (pre-jack knife). He managed to gently ease off the accelerator and slowly, as the speed decreased, it all came back under control and into line. He was fortunate.

Blinding Low Winter Sun

A real hazard, especially when travelling towards the sun whilst cresting a hill. I know of a truck driver who crested a hill and was sun blinded and completely unable to see anything for a few seconds. At the last moment, still partially blinded, he saw a queue of traffic. He swerved to the left to avoid it and by doing so accidentally hit a lady walking her dog. The driver, subsequently traumatised, then faced manslaughter charges for over two years until the case was finally dropped. This same situation applies to all vehicles.

Where safe to do so, if you can't see- slow down. Drive defensively to anticipate the sun's level.

Mobile Phone

Using one whilst driving is a major distraction to concentration, and a big risk to your license. A much bigger problem occurs in the event of an accident involving a fatality. The driver can then possibly be charged with manslaughter. I have heard tell of a driver being involved in an accident. The police seized his phone and inserted a code. By doing this they were able to see all phone use prior to the accident.

Horses

Horses are very easily spooked when they come into close proximity with a moving vehicle-ideally pull over to the side of the road, switch off your engine then let them pass. If it's a tight space then very slowly crawl past them whilst looking for any possible signals from the rider to advance, or stop and switch off the engine.

Driver Fatigue

Driver Fatigue and Falling Asleep at the Wheel

How to know when you are suffering from serious driver fatigue – example scenario:

Your eyelids become heavy and constantly try to close, your head starts to nod. You can't stop yawning and you find it hard to focus.

Suddenly you become aware of the rumble strips; you blink hard and realise that you have veered onto the hard shoulder for a moment and quickly straighten the wheel. You were asleep; this time you were lucky ...

Serious fatigue symptoms

- Frequent blinking, difficulty focusing and droopy eyelids.

- Daydreaming/scrambled thoughts.

- Missing exits and street signs, an inability to remember last few miles driven.

- Constant yawning/sore eyes.

- Head feels heavy.

- Drifting across lanes, hitting the rumble strip of hard shoulder and tailgating.

- Suddenly being aware of getting too close to another vehicle.

- Feeling restless, irritable and confused.

Temporary cures

- Open both windows and turn up the radio loud.

- Sugary foods and caffeine-containing drinks.

- Pinch yourself to feel slight pain, and keep pinching until parked.

- Say something aloud or sing. If absolutely exhausted, you will have no prior warning or control over falling asleep, it will just happen. Pull over and stop! Take a 20-minute sleep break, get up, take a brisk walk. If you are still exhausted, sleep for another hour or two. Sometimes you have to just give in to the situation, rather than endanger yourself or an innocent person/family. There are other people's lives in your hands, not just your own!

Winter Driving Tips

Winter weather can have an effect on a car's reliability, increasing the chances of a breakdown and leaving you in trouble. Here are some ideas for preparing for winter and dealing with emergencies.

Prior to Making a Journey

- Check the weather forecast for your area and your destination (especially if rural).

- Check travel reports for blocked roads and accidents.

- If you have to take a long journey, let others know your route, destination and estimated time of arrival be alert. avoid driving when tired.

- Check your phone is fully charged.

- Never warm up a vehicle in an enclosed area, such as a garage (the fumes are toxic).

- It's not advisable to use cruise control when driving on snow, ice or wet roads. (It's not designed for slippery conditions) check vehicle manual for any possible driver aids.

- If the vehicle is fitted with a dif lock only use it at slow speed and in a straight line. The lock engages all drive wheels to rotate at the same speed, thus making turning difficult.

- Keep the fuel tank at least half full to avoid moisture in the system freezing-up.

- Make sure all tyres are evenly inflated, never mix tyres. Radials with cross plies etc. (doing so dramatically reduces the handling of the vehicle).

- Check you have plenty of fuel. Carry a spare gallon can in the boot.

- Check all lights and wipers are working before travel.

- Check wind screen washer bottle is full of screen wash and water mix .(If it's a long journey carry a spare gallon in the boot).

- If the windscreen wipers become frozen to the screen, release them by using warm water, de-icer or warming the screen gently with the interior heater. Warning: pouring hot water onto a screen or using high heater air temperatures can crack a frozen screen! Trying to use frozen wipers often results in blowing the fuse. To save time, a useful tip is to place a little piece of cardboard under the wipers upon parking up.

- Release a frozen handbrake by either repeatedly pulling it on and off, gently rocking the vehicle back and forth, hitting the wheels or all three.

Advice for Driving in the Snow

- Accelerate and decelerate gently. Let the tyres gain and keep traction.

- Plan ahead. Take time to slow down for traffic lights, junctions etc. Remember: It takes longer to slow down when driving on compacted snow and ice.

- In these conditions at least double the normal stopping distances apply.

- Know your brakes. Whether you have antilock brakes or not, get a feel for the conditions. Try to avoid braking. Slow the vehicle by down shifting through the gears instead.

- In order to avoid getting stuck, do not stop unless absolutely necessary. Anticipate, plan ahead and try to keep the wheels rolling if at all possible.

- Prior to steep hills, try to build up momentum. Let that inertia carry you up to the top and at the crest of the hill, reduce your speed, select a low gear and proceed downhill slowly avoiding braking.

- Drive cautiously. Steer, accelerate, decelerate and brake gently. Make no sudden movements. If you start to skid, gently ease your foot off the break and avoid over correcting.

- In a built up area. If you do lose control into a slide or spin, let other people know, especially make pedestrians aware, sound the horn repeatedly to alert them to the danger coming their way.

- If you get stuck and become stranded there are two very useful tricks to help to get going again. Let at least half the air out of all the drive tyres. This creates a much larger foot print and helps tyres to dig in and grip much better. Also, remove loose snow then place the foot mats under the drive tyres, ideally rubber side up.

- If stranded and you're keeping the engine running for warmth, periodically check exhaust is free of snow and ice. A blocked exhaust can cause deadly carbon monoxide gas to leak up inside the vehicle. In the event of being broken down or running out of fuel, to stay warm use anything inside the vehicle to insulate your body. News papers, maps, floor mats, seat covers etc.

- Ideally stay with the car. Use it as a refuge. Beware of leaving the vehicle and becoming disorientated and lost in blizzard conditions.

Emergency Kit

Ice Scraper and De-Icer

These are winter must-haves.

It is a legal requirement to keep your front and rear windscreen clear of snow and ice before driving.

An ice scraper is effective but a can or spray bottle of de-icer speeds up the process. If you don't have these a plastic CD case will work.

In wintry conditions you will need to do this before setting off but both items need to be kept in the car ahead of the return journey.

First Aid Kit

Carry a small first aid kit in your vehicle. It should include wash proof plasters in various sizes, scissors, dressings, sterile gloves, bandages, pain killers and sterile cleansing wipes.

High-visibility Jacket or Vest

High-visibility reflective clothing is important. If you break down or get stranded it can help when being tied on to vehicle or waved to get the attention of other motorists. Because of its perceived importance, keeping a high vis jacket in your vehicle is law in some European countries.

Sturdy Boots With Good Grip

If you get stuck and have to abandon the vehicle, you could have to walk for a long distance in freezing and wet conditions. Comfortable warm and dry boots are important! Avoid a long walk with painful freezing feet.

Sat Nav and Road Map

An increasing number of drivers are only using Sat Navs to find their way. They can be a very good tool but being electrical they can break. A back up map is always a useful item and if stranded gives you a very good over view of the area.

Torch and Spare Batteries

A powerful torch with extra batteries is definitely a very necessary item in a break down kit. Torches are a must. If you have a breakdown on an unlit country road at night, you may need to use one to find a fault, change a tyre or find your way to safety on pitch dark unlit country roads. If you live in a town or city it's very easy to forget just how total darkness is without any light source.

Warm Clothes and Blankets

A breakdown could mean a long freezing cold wait. Make sure that you have a warm coat, hat, scarf and a good blanket to keep you warm.

Jump Start Cables

Extreme weather increases the possibility of getting a flat battery. Keep a good quality set of jump leads with you (not a cheap set). If you have a flat battery then getting a jump start is the best way of getting going again. Attaching the leads the sequence is: red (live) goes to the positive terminal (plus + sign marked on battery casing). Black (negative) goes to the negative terminal (marked with a minus sign –).

Fuel Can

It can't be stressed enough: when journeying in bad weather keep the fuel tank full and a spare gallon in the boot. Remember that if the weather's been bad for a while there's a high possibility the fuel tankers may not have been able to get through. Relying on filling up with fuel at a services is a high risk!

Screen Wash

Very important! Keep your washer bottle topped up with a mix of screenwash and water and keep a spare mixed gallon in the boot. On a fast A road or motorway, due to all the slush, dirt and salt being thrown up from other vehicles it is usual to have to clear the screen every 100 yards or so, and this uses up a lot of wash. You don't want to find yourself speeding down the road in freezing conditions, suddenly unable to see anything and with no way to pull over and top up. In sub zero conditions water alone will just freeze on the screen!

Shovel

A necessary tool. It's no fun trying to dig a vehicle out buried in deep snow with just frozen hands.

Carpet

TOP TIP: Carry two pieces of carpet, the thicker the better. In very slippy conditions lay them end to end starting under the drive wheels, and then drive from one piece to the next, replacing as you go.

Food and Drink

Getting stranded at the side of the side of the road is unpleasant at best. Being in this situation without food for a long time can make things much worse. Carry water, hot drinks and something filling and energy providing, such as protein bars, peanuts or chocolate.

Two Reflective Warning Signs

Having two reflective warning signs in the vehicle is a legal requirement in many countries. These signs are generally triangular and they are used to let other motorists know that you have broken down. Place them a fair distance away, front and rear, at least 7 metres.

In-Car Phone Charger

If you break down or become stranded you want to be able to use your phone in order to liaise with breakdown services or emergency services. Keep an in-car charger with you and keep the phone's battery topped up. Note/Motorways have emergency phones located at the side of the carriageway roughly every mile and a half.

Sunglasses

Low winter sun can affect driver visibility and strain eyes. Sunglasses are useful.

Smart Motorways

Smart motorways are increasingly common throughout U.K., so it's well worth learning what they are and how to use them.

How Smart Motorways Work

A smart motorway is a section of a motorway that uses traffic management systems to increase capacity and reduce congestion in busy areas. These systems include using the hard shoulder as a live lane and varying speed limits to control the flow of traffic.

Types of Smart Motorway

The three different types of smart motorway are controlled motorways, all lane running and dynamic hard shoulder running.

Controlled Motorway

These feature variable speed limits without hard shoulder running, but keep a hard shoulder for genuine emergencies.

All Lane Running Schemes

Just as you might have guessed, all lane running means the hard shoulder is permanently used as a running lane.

Under all lane running schemes, what was the hard shoulder becomes lane one. This lane is always open to traffic unless there is an incident. In this case the lane will be closed temporarily. Overhead gantry and verge signs will illuminate to state this. On these road sections broken white lines between all lanes indicates that each lane has the same status.

Overhead gantry signs display the mandatory speed limit which varies depending on the traffic flow etc. and speed cameras are used to enforce these limits. Where necessary the signs are also used to close lanes.

A red cross will be displayed on an overhead gantry sign if the lane is closed. Driving in this lane is thus illegal and could lead to a prosecution.

Traffic flow is constantly monitored by CCTV. In an emergency refuge lay bys are located every one and a half miles.

Dynamic Hard Shoulder Running Schemes

Dynamic hard shoulder running means the hard shoulder is only used as a live lane at busy congested times in order to create more effective traffic flow and ease over congestion. Gantry signs indicate mandatory speed limits and also an unbroken white line separates the hard shoulder from the main carriageway.

All smart motorways are monitored constantly by CCTV for any incidents. If a driver breaks down or is involved in a collision, the emergency refuge areas are there for them to utilise.

INPORTANT ADVICE!!!

It is highly recommended that if you are involved in an accident or break down on a running lane to switch the hazard warning lights on and then vacate the vehicle and get to safety as quickly as possible, ideally from the passenger side (near side), then immediately call the emergency services.

Useful Tips For Motorway Driving

Threat to Licence

It is very easy, when tired or distracted by things, to forget to look up and check the ever changing gantry speed limit signs on entering a smart motorway zone. It's also easy to find that you check the 1st speed limit sign, then assume wrongly, this is the limit for the whole section of road. It is important to be extra vigilant when travelling through these zones!, due to the signs being slightly above and out of normal eye line. It may be worth considering having some quiet in the vehicle on these sections of road.

Personal Safety

On all motorways it's important to take care when overtaking large vehicles travelling along the slow lane, especially if they are close together or are left hand drive. Large vehicles have mirror blind spots. Due to driver fatigue or rash impatience they can move into your lane, so it's advisable that you keep your finger poised ready over the horn and also check what space around you is available to move into. If you think that you've not been seen or feel under threat, give a few short sharp bursts on the horn to let them know you're there. If there is space to move into, be ready to move.

Maintaining Safe Tyre Pressures

It is important to adhere to the tyre manufacture's recommended pressure. These can be found written on the tyre wall or in the vehicle handbook. Tyres running at lower than designed pressures get very hot on a long drive, making them susceptible to blowing out. This risk doubles in the summer when the road surface is hot.

Driving with overly inflated tyres makes the vehicle unstable and harder to handle. It also reduces the surface area / footprint.

Space Saving Tyres

Most have a recommended top speed of 55 mph and a lifespan of between 50–70 miles. They are designed as a temporary fix.

The Law: Driving Offences/Endorsements

COURT
HEARING

UK driving licences may be endorsed by order of the courts if the driver has been convicted of an offence concerned with driving or operating a vehicle. An endorsement may also be accompanied by a number of points which can remain on the licence for up to 11 years. If the total of points on a licence equals or exceeds 12, the courts may decide to ban a driver for a period of time. The list below does not apply to Northern Ireland. However, 'Mutual recognition' (MR) codes have been included as these are added to the driving record if one is disqualified whilst driving in Northern Ireland, the Isle of Man or the Republic of Ireland. The disqualification period will also be valid in GB and will stay on the record for 4 years from the date of conviction.

Code	Description	Penalty points	Period endorsements remain on licence (years)
AC10	Failing to stop after an accident	5 – 10	4
AC20	Failing to give particulars or to report an accident within 24 hours	5 – 10	4
AC30	Undefined accident offences	4 – 9	4
BA10	Driving while disqualified by order of Court	6	4
BA30	Attempting to drive while disqualified by order of Court	6	4
BA40	Causing death by driving while disqualified	3 – 11	4
BA60	Causing serious injury by driving while disqualified	3 – 11	4
CD10	Driving without due care and attention	3 – 9	4
CD20	Driving without reasonable consideration for other road users	3 – 9	4
CD30	Driving without due care and attention/reasonable consideration	3 – 9	4
CD40	Causing death through careless driving when unfit through drink	3 – 11	11
CD50	Causing death by careless driving when unfit through drugs	3 – 11	11
CD60	Causing death by careless driving when alcohol level above limit	3 – 11	11
CD70	Causing death by careless driving then failing to supply a specimen for alcohol analysis	3 – 11	11
CD80	Causing death by careless, or inconsiderate, driving	3 – 11	4
CD90	Causing death by driving: unlicensed, disqualified or uninsured drivers	3 – 11	4
CU10	Using a vehicle with defective brakes	3	4

Code	Description	Penalty points	Period endorsements remain on licence (years)
CU20	Causing or likely to cause danger by reason of use of unsuitable vehicle or using a vehicle with parts or accessories (excluding brakes, steering or tyres) in a dangerous condition	3	4
CU30	Using a vehicle with defective tyre(s)	3	4
CU40	Using a vehicle with defective steering	3	4
CU50	Causing or likely to cause danger by reason of load or passengers	3	4
CU80	Breach of requirements as to control of the vehicle, mobile telephone etc.	3	4
DD10	Causing serious injury by dangerous driving	3 – 11	4
DD40	Dangerous Driving	3 – 11	4
DD60	Manslaughter or culpable homicide while driving a vehicle	3 – 11	4
DD80	Causing death by dangerous driving	3 – 11	4
DD90	Furious driving	3 – 9	4
DR10	Driving or attempting to drive with alcohol concentration above limit	3 – 11	11
DR20	Driving or attempting to drive when unfit through drink	3 – 11	11
DR30	Driving or attempting to drive then refusing to provide a specimen	3 – 11	11
DR31	Driving or attempting to drive then refusing to give permission for analysis of a blood sample that was taken without consent due to incapacity	3 – 11	11
DR40	In charge of a vehicle while alcohol level above limit	10	4
DR50	In charge of a vehicle while unfit through drink	10	4

Code	Description	Penalty points	Period endorsements remain on licence (years)
DR60	Failure to provide a specimen for analysis in circumstances other than driving or attempting to drive	10	4
DR61	Refusing to give permission for analysis of a blood sample that was taken without consent due to incapacity in circumstances other than driving or attempting to drive	10	11
DR70	Failing to provide specimen for breath test	4	4
DG10	Driving or attempting to drive with drug level above the specified limit	3 – 11	11
DG40	In charge of a vehicle while drug level above specified limit	10	4
DG60	Causing death by careless driving with drug level above the limit	3 – 11	11
DR80	Driving or attempting to drive when unfit through drugs	3 – 11	11
DR90	In charge of a vehicle when unfit through drugs	10	4
IN10	Using a vehicle uninsured against third party risks	6 – 8	4
LC20	Driving otherwise than in accordance with a licence	3 – 6	4
LC30	Driving after making a false declaration about fitness when applying for a licence	3 – 6	4
LC40	Driving a vehicle having failed to notify a disability	3 – 6	4
LC50	Driving after a licence has been revoked or refused on medical grounds	3 – 6	4
MS10	Leaving a vehicle in a dangerous position	3	4
MS20	Unlawful pillion riding	3	4
MS30	Playstreet Offence	2	4
MS50	Motor racing on the highway	3 – 11	4

Code	Description	Penalty points	Period endorsements remain on licence (years)
MS60	Offences not covered by other codes (including offences relating to breach of requirements as to control of vehicle)	3	4
MS70	Driving with uncorrected defective eyesight	3	4
MS80	Refusing to submit to an eyesight test	3	4
MS90	Failing to give information as to identity of driver etc.	6	4
MW10	Contravention of Special Roads Regulations (excluding speed limits)	3	4
PC10	Undefined contravention of Pedestrian Crossing Regulations	3	4
PC20	Contravention of Pedestrian Crossing Regulations with moving vehicle	3	4
PC30	Contravention of Pedestrian Crossing Regulations Stationary vehicle	3	4
SP10	Exceeding goods vehicle speed limit	3 – 6	4
SP20	Exceeding speed limit for type of vehicle (excluding goods or passenger vehicles)	3 – 6	4
SP30	Exceeding statutory speed limit on a public road	3 – 6	4
SP40	Exceeding passenger vehicle speed limit	3 – 6	4
SP50	Exceeding speed limit on a motorway	3 – 6	4
TS10	Failing to comply with traffic light signals	3	4
TS20	Failing to comply with double white lines	3	4
TS30	Failing to comply with a 'Stop' sign	3	4
TS40	Failing to comply with directions of a constable / traffic warden	3	4
TS50	Failing to comply with traffic sign (excluding 'stop' signs, traffic lights or double white lines)	3	4

Code	Description	Penalty points	Period endorsements remain on licence (years)
TS60	Failing to comply with a school crossing patrol sign	3	4
TS70	Undefined failure to comply with a traffic direction sign	3	4
TT99	Disqualified for having more than 12 points in the "totting up" process	N/A	4
UT50	Aggravated taking of a vehicle	3 – 11	4
MR09	Reckless or dangerous driving (whether or not resulting in death, injury or serious risk)	N/A	4
MR19	Wilful failure to carry out the obligation placed on driver after being involved in a road accident (hit and run)	N/A	4
MR29	Driving a vehicle while under the influence of alcohol or other substance affecting or diminishing the mental and physical abilities of a driver	N/A	4
MR39	Driving a vehicle faster than the permitted speed	N/A	4
MR49	Driving a vehicle whilst disqualified	N/A	4
MR59	Other conduct constituting an offence for which a driving disqualification has been imposed by the State of Offence	N/A	4

Insurance Advice

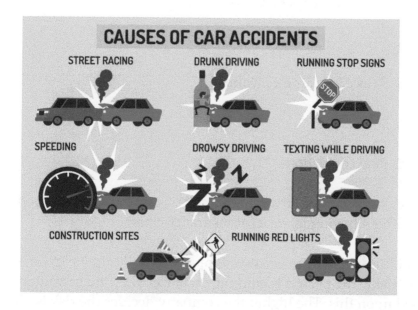

CAUSES OF CAR ACCIDENTS

STREET RACING · DRUNK DRIVING · RUNNING STOP SIGNS

SPEEDING · DROWSY DRIVING · TEXTING WHILE DRIVING

CONSTRUCTION SITES · RUNNING RED LIGHTS

Getting insured as a young driver is usually very expensive because you are an unknown risk and statistically young drivers tend to have more accidents. This chapter will look at what you need to know about new drivers' car insurance and how to go about getting a good deal and keeping your premiums to a minimum.

Young Driver Insurance Tips

The amount you pay for your car insurance is called a premium. Insurance companies will use lots of different information about you and your vehicle to decide how much this should be. They consider:

- personal details, such as age, occupation and postcode

- model of car

- engine size

- how much cover is required

- the estimated annual mileage

- previous car insurance claims

- purpose of use

- criminal convictions

- no claims bonus – the number of years a person's been driving without having made a car insurance claim.

All of this helps the insurance company to build up a picture of how 'risky' the person is, and they will calculate the premium based upon this. The higher the company decides the risk is, the higher the premium will be.

Levels of Car Insurance Cover

When choosing your insurance, one of the first things you will need to think about is what kind of cover you require. There are three levels of cover to choose from – third party, third party, fire and theft and fully comprehensive.

If the car is expensive and would be financially difficult to replace if it was written off in an accident, it's best to go for the highest level of cover – fully comprehensive. Third party cover might be the best option if your car is not worth a lot of money.

However, in some instances fully comprehensive cover can cost less than third party, so check the price of both.

Best Way to Insure Young Drivers

Here are some ways to reduce your premiums.

Your choice of car is important. Each car is assigned an insurance group number from one to fifty, with one being the cheapest to insure and fifty the most expensive. Driving a car in a low insurance group is the easiest way to reduce your premium costs.

Adding a second, low-risk driver can also lower the costs of insurance. Parents are a good bet, but they can't pretend to be the main driver – this is called 'fronting' and is illegal.

The lower the mileage you drive annually, the lower your insurance premium. When applying for insurance you will be asked about how often the vehicle will be used and what distances you expect to cover. Less miles and less frequent use can lower premiums. the best deals usually depend on an annual 5000 miles or less. Ask what mileage deals are on offer.

Other Ways to Reduce Car Insurance

A good way to get cheaper car insurance is to shop around for the best deal. Comparison sites are worth a try and social media or money saving forums can be helpful.

Once you've found a couple of good quotes, call a insurance broker and ask them to see if they can beat them. Then let them do the searching and they'll get back to you. If you have the funds it also works out as a cheaper option to buy 12 months of insurance as a block rather than paying in monthly direct debit instalments.

Paying a higher voluntary excess on top of your compulsory excess will lower the cost of car insurance. The down side is you will end up paying more yourself if you need to make a claim.

Avoid getting caught out by unnecessary insurance bolt-ons.For example extra breakdown cover etc, it can often be purchased cheaper elsewhere.

Black Box Car Insurance

These policies involve fitting a gadget to your car to monitor acceleration, braking, cornering, miles covered and what time of day you are driving.

The price of your insurance then goes down if you prove you are a good, safe driver.

However, there is a downside because bad driving can see your premiums go up and under certain circumstances your insurance could even be cancelled.

Note: Don't get scammed. Fake insurers sometimes target young drivers. Your insurer (and your broker, if you're using one) must be authorised and regulated by the Financial Conduct Authority (FCA). Check that your insurer is FCA registered. You are also advised to read your policy before you buy it. This doesn't tend to be an exciting read but it's the only way to know that you are totally covered.

Parking Guide

Places you are Allowed to Park

A car park, at the side of an unrestricted road or a designated bay. These will be marked by a large white 'P' on a blue background, usually found alongside the parking area and also on directional signage.

Some parking bays will be free, others will need to be paid for and some might have restrictions for non permit holders and also what types of vehicles are allowed to park there.

None permit holders may have to adhere to the indicated restrictions of use. Always check by reading the accompanying signs.

Added list of locations you are not allowed to stop or park and are punishable by the full weight of the law ...

- On a bus or tram stop, or a taxi rank

- On the approach to a level crossing

- Near the brow of a hill or humpback bridge

- Near a school entrance

- Anywhere that would prevent access for emergency vehicles

- Where the kerb has been lowered to help wheelchair and mobility vehicle users

- Where you would force another vehicle to enter a tram lane

- On a bend

- Opposite or within 32 feet of a junction, except in an authorised parking bay

- A pedestrian crossing, including the area marked by the zig-zag lines

- Where you would obstruct a cycle lane

- Also do not park facing against the traffic flow

- Stop as close as possible to the roadside

- Passengers should exit the vehicle on the side next to the kerb

- Do not park too close to a vehicle displaying a Blue Badge

- The handbrake must be applied before exiting the car

- The engine, headlights and fog lights must be switched off

- You must look out for other road users when you open your door

- Valuables should be stored out of sight and the car locked

- Parking lights must be used on a road or lay-by on a highway with a speed limit higher than 30 mph

Parking Variables

Named vehicle parking

- Parking reserved for a specific type of vehicle or user, the bay will be indicated by a dotted line and the name of the user painted on the road. This might be for a doctor, ambulance, a disabled person etc. Parking for electric vehicles will be marked as 'Electric Vehicles Only' or a car and plug icon.

Single yellow lines

- A painted single yellow line – either on the road or on the kerb – means no waiting, parking, loading or unloading at the times shown on the signs provided.

- The restrictions are often lifted during evenings and weekends, but always check the signs before parking.

- The same as on double yellow lines, Blue Badge holders can park on single lines for up to three hours, providing there isn't signage to say otherwise, it is safe to do so and is not causing an obstruction.

Double Yellow Lines

- Painted double yellow lines featured either on the road or on the kerb – means parking and waiting are not allowed at any time.

- In some areas, there might be seasonal restrictions, which are highlighted by the signs provided.

- Loading and unloading may be allowed, providing you can be seen doing so continuously – unless there are specific restrictions against it, indicated either by yellow 'kerb dashes' or signs.

- Blue Badge holders are allowed to park on single or double yellow lines for up to three hours, providing there isn't signage to the country, it is safe to do so and it is not causing an obstruction.

Parking on Double Yellow Lines Fine

- A double yellow line average parking fine is £70 and is reduced by 50% if paid within 14 days. The costs can vary depending on the local council.

Red Routes

- In some locations, red lines are used instead of yellow lines. In London, the single and double red lines used on Red Routes indicate that stopping to park, load, unload, or to board and alight from a vehicle is prohibited, except for licensed taxis and Blue Badge holders.

- The times that the red line restrictions apply will be indicated on nearby signs, a double red line means no stopping at any time.

- One some Red Routes, it is allowed to stop to park, load or unload in specially marked boxes at times and for purposes specified by nearby signs. For example, a Red Route might allow parking between the hours of 7am and 7pm, for one hour, with no return within two hours.

- Due to the variation. Always check the signage before parking.

Loading Bays

- A loading bay is indicated by a dotted white line surround, along with the words 'Loading Only' painted on the road.

- Various restrictions will apply. See signs.

White Zig-Zag Lines

- Are found just before and after pedestrian crossings. Drivers are not allowed to park or overtake in these areas.

- There is a risk of a fine and penalty points by parking on either yellow or white zig-zag lines

Yellow Zig-Zag Lines

- Yellow zig-zag lines found outside schools, fire, police or ambulance stations mark the length of road where stopping or waiting is strictly prohibited.

Parking Outside Someone's House

- It is legal to park outside someone's house, unless the vehicle is blocking a driveway, has a wheel over a kerb or it is residents parking only.

Clearways signs

- A red cross over a blue background indicates a clearway, which means no stopping at any time – not even to pick up or set down passengers. The sign is used to indicate a 24-hour clearway and might be incorporated into other signs with the words 'No Stopping'.

- There will be a sign at the start of the clearway indicating its length, i.e. 'For 4 miles'. there are no special road markings on a clearway, but there should be smaller, repeater signs at intervals.

Parking Zones

The British Parking Association (BPA) outlines four different types of parking zones in the UK, namely.

Pedestrian Zones

- Controlled Parking Zone (CPZ)

- Restricted Parking Zone (RPZ)*

- Permit Parking Area (PPA)

- Zones can be described differently, for example, Pay & Display Zone or metre zone

- Note, Seasonal variations to zones can apply

Parking on the Pavement

- This is a bit of a grey area.

- Some council's allow it, others in force penalty fines for obstruction etc.

- The Highway Code states that you must not park partially or wholly on the pavement in London, and should not do elsewhere unless signs permit it.

- Parking on a pavement can obstruct and inconvenience people with visual impairments, people with pushchairs and people in wheel chairs.

- If parking on the pavement is permitted, it will be marked by a blue and white sign.

Note: Restricted Parking Zone (RPZ)*

In this zone, residential only parking and pay and display are often mixed. One side or end of the road can be residents parking only and the other side/end can be pay and display. It is very easy to be caught out by this. Always read the sign where the vehicle is actually being parked. A few metres either way could be the difference between a fine or no fine.

Buying a Used Car

Useful Places to Search

- Auto Trader

- eBay

- Gumtree

- Loot

- Classified Local Papers

Here you will find mainly Private Sellers, but there are also some trade who will state this fact on the adverts.

Note Having a wide sweeping search helps to open opportunities up, making it far more likely to find the vehicle you're looking for. Around a hundred miles search is a useful setting.

First Things First

If you find a vehicle your interested in, the first thing to do is get an insurance quote The very last thing you want is to travel a long way, pay for a car and then find for some reason it's impossible to insure it or that the premium is so high that it's unaffordable. Just imagine what you would do if you've just paid for a car you can't move.

Insurance companies have clamped down heavily on vehicles that have been altered even slightly. They classed these vehicles as modified and usually won't touch them with a barge pole.

It is a good idea to arrange temporary insurance in order to test drive the vehicle. Not test driving the vehicle is taking a very big gamble.

Trade Vs Private

Advantages of buying from a motor trader's lot:

- Finding a local dealer saves the hassle of travelling

- More time to contemplate your decision

- No need to make a snap decision

- Time to get the car checked by the AA, RAC or a trusted mechanic.

- The vehicle should have had some sort of HPI check

- Time to take a lengthy test drive

- Time to negotiate a better warranty

- The possibility of buying on finance

Disadvantages

- Possibility of high pressure selling.

- Price: Usually more expensive than Private Sellers due to overheads

It is important to take a good test drive before buying. Check whether the owner has all the legal paperwork in their possession before committing to taking a long drive to view. Do they have the V5, MOT? Also ask if the car is taxed and insured.

It is strongly advised that if there is no legal paperwork, walk away from any deal. Also no tax or insurance means no test drive unless you buy temporary cover.

If you are stopped by the police on a test drive without insurance it's 6-8 points on your licence plus a £300–£5000 fine. If you hit somebody and they are badly hurt you could be looking at possible prison. The endorsement points will stay on your licence for 4 years and the code is IN10. Insurance companies deem drivers with no insurance as extremely high-risk, so the price will be sky high for future cover.

Document Checks

- Is the V5 (logbook) it in the seller's name?

- Is the vehicle description correct?

- How many former keepers (owners)?

- Previous vehicle history if stated i.e. was it a private vehicle, a taxi, a police car et cetera.(Some vehicles have a very hard life and succumb to excessive wear and tear)

- Is it a category C or D vehicle?

MOT (Ministry of transport road work test)

- Date of expiry

- Mileage

- Advisories, if any (an advisory is a minor fault that at the date of the MOT wasn't deemed serious enough to cause a fail of the test). **Note:** If stopped by police with no MOT it's a fine of up to £1000.

- In the event of an accident a vehicle without MOT maybe deemed unroadworthy thus technically voiding any insurance. The insurer can claim the vehicle was not roadworthy and so they do not have the responsibility to pay out.

Service History

- Not all sellers keep this

- it is a very good indication of how well a vehicle has been looked after

- It is a written record of all services, garage reports, receipts of parts bought plus all previous MOT's

- It is a very useful account of a vehicles history

Note: Most modern vehicles engines are fitted with a cam belt, not chain. This needs replacing on average around every 60.000 miles or 6–8 years, whichever comes first. The consequences of a cam belt failure usually results in serious or terminal engine damage. If there is no service history to say when it was last changed it is important to get it replaced. It is costly. When changing the cam belt it is advisable to also change the water pump at the same time.

Test Drive

Prior Vehicle Checks

- Is the exhaust warm or cold? (if warm the car's been pre run)

- Check underneath for signs of leaking oil or water (leaks from pipes or seals)

- Check for accident damage. Is the vehicle straight? Are there the same continuous gaps found around all the panels?

- Check windscreen for cracks or chips

- Check tyres for cracks, splits, uneven tread wear

- Check exhaust for rust or if broken

- Check underneath for damage or rust

- Engine oil: check dipstick level. Is there cream on it? Also check the underside of the oil filler top for cream. (Creamlike substance can indicate head or head gasket problems).Note/If a vehicle has not been used much during the winter ,condensation can build up and cause a small amount of cream like substance on the underside of the oil filler top. This definitely will not show on dipstick ...

- Water (coolant) Check the level. Is there antifreeze? Also check underside of the filler top for cream or signs of oil (head gasket)

- Brake fluid: check the level. Check for leaks. DANGER-brake fluid is extremely corrosive. Do not get it on your skin

- Power steering: check fluid level and also check for leaks

- Dashboard lights: are they all working? Are there any intermittently flashing?

- Start the car. Check for excessive smoke and odd noises

- Rev up the engine, listen for any odd noises

- Pull out the dipstick, check for smoke. There should be little to no smoke

- Steering. Move steering wheel lock to lock. Check for noises and squealing. It should be smooth and quiet

During Test Drive

- Does the engine pull well in all gears?

- Check there are no strange engine noises, smells, misfiring or flat spots?

- Gearbox. All gears including reverse should engage cleanly. No gear should jump out

- Clutch: engages and disengages correct. Is the bite point correct? i.e. Not too low, not too high and no excessive noise. No slipping under acceleration

- Steering. Should be responsive, smooth, precise and quiet. There should be no free play. Vehicle should not pull to one side

- Brakes: there should be no spongeyness (indicates air in the system) and vehicle should brake in a straight line. Braking should be immediate, responsive and quiet

- Exhaust should be quiet. No rattling or blowing

- Dashboard Lights: should go out, none should intermittently flash

- Temperature gauge: observe the engine temperature. It should stay roughly between 70 and 90. It should stay steady and not vary too much

Return from Test Drive

Repeat prior to test drive checks. These include oil levels, cream on the dipstick, oil in the radiator water, coolant levels and leaks. Make sure all switches work: lights, wipers, heater etc.

Personal Dangers When Engines Running

Note: Be very careful not to get your hands or any clothes snagged into the moving parts of the engine, i.e fan, pulleys, belts. Also, once the engine's up to temperature the coolant system pressurises and becomes very hot. Stand well back and undo the top slowly to steadily release the pressure. Ideally use a cloth to cover your hands and keep your face well back.

The Deal

Most Private and trade sellers will be reluctant to spend too much time and effort on a long test drive in case there is no end deal to be done. They will not want to waste their time. The best way to get around this is to go for a short test drive. Then, if you have decided you want buy, make a provisional deal. Most sellers are more likely to go for an extended test drive if they are offered the asking price or close to it. A test drive of 20 to 40 minutes is recommended. Some faults such as engine overheating and automatic gearbox issues may not show up until the vehicle gets hot and has travelled a fair distance.

Recommended Professional Checks

Both the AA and RAC offer appointment based comprehensive mechanical vehicle checks at very reasonable costs. You do not need to be a member to use these services. Full details and prices can be found on line ...

Receipt

Always get a detailed receipt. Mark it clearly with the date and time of purchase and make sure it's signed by the seller. Examples and print off vehicle receipt templates can be found on line.

Warranty

Any due warranty should be gained in writing at the point of sale.

Road Tax

To avoid a large fine the car has to be taxed before being driving away. Tax can be bought either at the post office or on line. The V5, MOT and insurance will be needed to do so. The maximum fine for no tax is £1000.

V5 (logbook)

The seller and you have to fill in the appropriate sections and sign and date the declaration. The seller posts the new details section and you keep the new keepers section. Instructions for using the V5 are clearly written on the form.

Fraudsters: Scams to be Aware of

Financial Frauds

Cloning
Exchanging the number plates and log book from a similar car that has been scrapped or stolen.

Clocking

Winding back the mileometre (compare seat condition, gear knob, pedals and floor mat wear against stated mileage. Do they appear to be worn more than you would expect for a low mileage car?)

Cut and Shut
Welding two halves of different cars together to make one (fraudsters get two modern damaged cars cheap and weld the good parts together creating a death trap).

Stolen Cars
Sold tantalisingly cheap (seller impersonates the owner and often states they have bought the car recently hence they are waiting for the V5 to arrive. It's in the post and once it arrives they will forward it on).

Too Busy for Test Drive
Hiding mechanical faults that only show up on a run.

Slight of Hand
Whilst the buyer is distracted looking at paper work, they slip money away and then claim some is missing. The buyer must have miscounted and owe them.

Deposit Fraud
Usually attempted from a bogus address, the seller uses high pressure techniques, such as "I've got a definite buyer on the way who is happy to pay the full price. If you want it, you'll have to give me a strong cash deposit now for me to hold it". Buyer goes to get remainder of the balance and they've disappeared.

Sub Hiring
The seller reels in a buyer by offering a great car at a bargain knock down price. Due to PPI check they own up to still having outstanding finance on the car but promise to keep up the payments. This is illegal. They don't pay the balance and the finance company repossesses the car.

Car Swop
The fraudster offers a tantalisingly desirable car swop to a vehicle seller. However the car will often still be on finance or is stolen.

Mechanical Frauds

Cleaning out and refilling radiator header tank and wiping the top. In the short term this hides head gasket trouble.

Changing and refilling the oil plus wiping filler top. This hides head gasket trouble.

Hard wiring engine cooling fan to be constantly on. This hides over heating trouble.

Running car before buyer arrives. This hides valve seals and starting issues.

Bodywork: rust damage being hidden by filler and then over sprayed.

Note: Obsolescence
Most vehicles have a built level of obsolescence. Cheaper models tend to show this at lower mileage than more expensive models. More expensive makes tend to last longer if looked after and in the long run have less mechanical issues. Most obsolescence is written in and occurs after a vehicle is 10 years old or has done 75,000 miles or more. It is therefore ideal to buy a vehicle which is good quality and is 75,000 mileage or less.

Note: Buying in the Rain
It is not recommended to buy on a rainy day. The rainwater obscures any imperfections with the paintwork. It is only when the vehicle is dry that the hidden blemishes show up.

What is an HPI Check?

An HPI Check is a vehicle check that examines all of the history of any motorised vehicle registered in the UK. The HPI Check Report give clear detailed information held on the vehicle by the Police, the DVSA (Driver Vehicle Standards Agency) and finance and insurance companies.

What is Included in an HPI Check?

Record of Stolen Vehicles

Is the vehicle currently recorded on the Police National Computer as stolen?

If so the vehicle still belongs to the original owner. If found they are returned. If you were to buy a stolen vehicle you are likely to lose it alongside the money that you paid. No ifs no buts.

Outstanding Finance

Is there an outstanding loan or finance agreement secured on the car?

Most finance agreements/loans will grant the lender complete ownership of the vehicle until the debt has been paid. The debt stays with the vehicle not the borrower. If the finance hasn't been settled then the lender could repossess the vehicle, if you buy a vehicle with an outstanding loan/finance you could lose the car and the money you paid.

Number of Previous Owners

How many previous owner/keepers have been recorded on the logbook by DVLA?

Useful for checking that the number is the same that has been stated by the seller.

Been an Insurance Write-Off?

Has the vehicle ever sustained too much damage to have been viably repaired? Has the insurance company declared it a total loss, a write off?

When the damage to a vehicle is so substantial that it cannot be repaired it will be recorded as a Category A or B Write Off. These vehicles should never return to road use. They present a risk to life to anyone who drives them.

Vehicles recorded as written off after October 1st 2017 are categorised as A, B, S or N.

Current Cat C or D vehicles will remain as such. Cat C&D/S&N vehicles have been written off as the work necessary to return them to road worthiness is not considered to be worth the cost. These vehicles are known as damage repairables in the trade. It is possible to find fixed up road worthy vehicles previously rated as Cat C&D/S&N for sale. Note/Some insurers will not insure these vehicles. Always check before buying one.

Logbook Check

Checks that the logbook actually belongs to the car you're looking at and is the most recent issue.

Note: There are over 200,000 stolen V5C registration documents (logbooks) in circulation.

Recorded as Scrapped

Has the car been marked as scrapped on the DVLA data base?

If a vehicle has been marked as scrapped by the DVLA it should not be up for sale or be on the road.

Mileage Discrepancies

Is the car displaying the correct mileage?

A mileage discrepancy could indicate that the vehicle has had the clock messed with and the mileage has been altered. A vehicle that has been clocked could have hidden wear and tear. The mileage of a vehicle also directly affects what it's worth so you could be paying over the book price if the clock has been rolled back.

Number Plate Changes

How many plate changes has the vehicle had and is there anything outstanding on a previous plate?

This register indicates whether a vehicle has had a legitimate registration plate. Some plates are changed to personalise a vehicle, some to hide a vehicle's history ...

Imported/Exported

Has the car been imported or exported?

Insuring an import will be more expensive due to the fact that there is no way to check its history. Vehicles registered with the DVSA as exported are likely to be uninsurable in the UK. They should not be in the country.

Valuation

A guide valuation for a vehicle of the make and model with average mileage and condition for its age is provided.

Estimated Fuel Costs

The estimated fuel cost is based on 12,000 miles. This figure will help to ascertain the ongoing running costs of the vehicle you're looking to buy.

VIN/Chassis Check

As well as checking the vehicle's registration number this checks that there are no issues recorded against the car's VIN (Vehicle Identification Number).

The HPI check also ensures that the VIN/Chassis numbers on the car match the one on the V5C/Logbook. A mismatch could indicate that the vehicle was stolen, cut and shut, or cloned at some point.

MOT History Check

Lists all previous ministry of transport checks (MOT's). Where, when, mileages etc.

NOTE

Never trust someone else has done a thorough HPI check! Always do your own!

Driving Abroad

Licence Requirements

A UK driving licence can be used to drive within the EU / EEA, but if you drive outside these countries, you'll need an International Driving Permit (IDP).

It's cheap and can be bought from the Post Office. You have to be over 18 and have a full driving licence to be able to gain an IDP.

Although the minimum age for driving a car in the UK is 17, other countries have their own rules. Research the country / countries that you're heading to.

Travel Check List

Note: Different countries have their own rules regarding what papers a driver must carry on his/her person, and the equipment to be kept in the vehicle. Always do research. Failing to do so can result in the police issuing large on the spot fines.

- Full driving licence

- Insurance documents

- V5 (log book)

- Magnetic GB Great Britain stickers attached to rear of car

- Red warning triangle

- High vis vest

- Fire extinguisher

Tool Kit

- Torch

- Sat nav

- Maps

- LPG nozzle adapters (gas powered cars)

- Head light beam converters (depending on country)

Insurance

It is necessary to make sure that your insurance covers you for outside of the UK. Contact the insurer to check, policies can often be upgraded for foreign travel. Fully comprehensive cover is highly recommended. You may find the insurer offers free third party cover as a standard part of the policy. This is very basic and only pays for repairs to other drivers vehicles, not your own.

Always read the policy in case of any hidden clauses, such as a 30 day only European cover limit clause.

Carrying a Green Card

In the past green cards issued by the insurer were mandatory in most countries. This is no longer the case but they are still recognised and it is recommended to carry one. Ask the insurer to provide it. While it's no longer required in most countries, taking one with you will make it easier if you need to make a claim or exchange details with another driver or the police.

Green Cards are still compulsory in the following countries: Israel, Iran, Macedonia, Morocco, Moldova, Montenegro, Turkey, Herzegovina, Tunisia, Turkey, Ukraine and Russia.

Breakdown Cover

Breakdown cover is important! If you have bought it through your insurer get the cover in writing, read it and carry with you. If bought separately, get it in writing, read it and carry it with you.

Scams Targeted at Tourists

Criminals sometimes target foreign drivers by identifying them by the vehicle number plate or by following them from an airport or car hire company.

PROTECT YOUR CAR FROM THEFT

Examples

Impersonating the police.

If you are stopped and get a bad feeling, keep the engine running, wind down the window an inch and ask to see official badges.

Scams Using Open Windows/Open Vehicles

Car Hire

Someone walks up looking official wearing a high vis vest/jacket and carrying a clip board. They act as an employee and start to do vehicle checks. Then at an opportune moment they reach through an open window, grab a wallet or hand bag, and make a run for it then dive into an accomplice's car.

Problem With the Vehicle

Persons flags the driver down whilst they are driving by flashing their head lights etc. When stopped one distracts the driver by engaging them in conversation, claiming there is a vehicle problem, while the other grabs valuables, then they jump into their car/motorbike and speed off.

Cut Tyres

At a petrol station, junction etc someone cuts the tourists tyre, the ensuing slow puncture causes them to pull over further down the road. Whilst they are out of the vehicle a car or motorcycle stops, and at an opportune moment a grab is made through the open window.

Changing a Tyre

Procedure

Find solid level ground. Locate the jack and wheel brace. They are usually found in the boot or sometimes under the bonnet.

Locate the spare wheel – this is usually easily accessible, it is either found in the boot under the rubber mat or underslung beneath the boot. To release an underslung wheel, undo the mechanism anti-clockwise until the spare wheel descends then remove it from the carrier. Use a screw driver to prize off hub caps (if fitted).

Before raising the vehicle, pull handbrake on tight and put a wedge under a tyre on an axle that is not being jacked up. Before jacking up use the brace to loosen the wheel nuts so that they are hand tight. (**Do not remove wheel nuts**). Jack up the vehicle. It needs to be raised until the flat tyre has an inch of daylight showing beneath so as to accommodate the larger inflated tyre. Have the spare wheel ready at hand. Remove remaining wheel nuts. Remove the flat tyre and fit the new one. Make sure that the new wheel is fully aligned and slotted in the correct place. Tighten all the wheel nuts evenly until tight. The sequence for tightening is to tighten each wheel nut a bit at a time. Start with one and then the one diagonally opposite and repeat the procedure until the wheel is evenly fitted to the hub. Ensure that it is as tight as possible by hand. (There should be very little to no thread on any of the nuts showing). Lower car and tighten up with brace, a bit at a time. Tighten one nut, then its diagonal opposite. Keep going round until all are tight. Re-secure the wheel carrier.

Note: If you fit a space saver tyre, due to the odd size newer vehicles sensors may illuminate an A.B.S or Traction Control dashboard light.

Following On

At a garage, fix the spare tyre, check tyre pressure is correct and ensure the wheel nuts are torqued up to correct tightness.

Hazards/Safety

Once the car is jacked up: before removing the wheel, try to physically push the car off jack. If it feels safe, check jack position has not moved, then proceed.

To avoid damaging the car see handbook for correct jacking point. It is usually found under the sill.

Make sure that no part of your body is **ever** under the raised vehicle. A jack is never to be trusted!

Avoid changing a tyre on the hard shoulder or the side of a busy road. Wind off a passing large vehicle can blow the car off jack.

Be vigilant. Watch out for the danger of being hit by a passing vehicle or another one manoeuvring and knocking yours off the jack.

Avoid taking the old tyre off, finding the car has not been raised high enough to fit the new tyre, leading to having to jack up without a wheel on (this is unsafe!).

Avoid brace slipping off under applied pressure. Fit it correctly. If it slips off it may well take the skin off the back of your hands. If the nuts are really tight, the options are add an extension then pull it upwards or push it down with your feet.

Beware: Old cars jacking points can be rotted through. Jacking points can collapse.

On an incline wedge the wheels to stop the car from shifting and rolling off the jack (wedge axle that's not being raised).

Do not use inferior tools. Jacks can collapse and worn braces round off the wheel nuts.

Most standard issue wheel braces aren't long or strong enough. It is worth buying a strong half or three quarter inch T bar and socket.

Periodically check the spare tyre is inflated. They tend to go down over time if unused. Some cars are fitted with locking wheel nuts. Always check you know where the key is before travelling.

Towing Trailers

Hitching Up a Large Heavy Trailer

Reverse the car up to the trailer until the tow ball is close to the trailer hitch .

Apply hand brake.

Adjust the trailer height by winding down the jockey wheel on the trailer to raise it up (small wheel at front).

The tow hitch on the trailer needs to be slightly higher than the tow ball on your car.

Reverse under the tow hitch until the trailer's tow hitch is directly above the tow ball.

Wind the jockey wheel up until the tow hitch drops down onto the tow ball and locks into place with a firm 'click' .

Release handbrake (if any) on your trailer.

Wind the jockey wheel all the way up and lock it into stowed position.

Connect the breakaway cable between the caravan and towbar. This is a legal requirement. It applies the trailer brakes should the trailer become unhitched.

Connect the trailer electrics cable to the socket on towbar. Caravans often also have a 12V cable to connect for internal power.

Fit extension mirrors to the car if required (depends on overall size and especially width of trailer).

Fit number plate.

Take Time to do All Checks

Tow hitch condition: Securely fitted.

Trailer solid. No rusty weak points.

Trailer is fully locked correctly onto the tow bar.

Stabiliser legs and the jockey wheel have been fully wound up and stowed.

Electric cable connections secure.(no part of the cable in contact with the floor).

Trailer lights all working (tail, brake lights, indicators and number plate light).

Correct Number plate fitted and secure.

If loaded the trailer is fully secured. Heavy items on the bottom, lighter on top (a top heavy trailer is an accident waiting to happen!)

A loaded caravan should be placed over the axle and tied down or wedged in tight. You do not want it to slide whilst cornering.

Towing on the Road

- Allow plenty of extra room when cornering and also watch out for the trailer swinging during tight manoeuvres

- Be mindfull of extra weight and extra axles. Allow more stopping time for braking distances and brake gently

- Allow more space for extra width. Don't stray over the centre white lines

- Drive steadily. Smooth and gentle with the controls

- Slow down for sharp bends and roundabouts

- Keep to the towing rules of the road:

  - Single carriageways: 50 mph

  - Dual carriageways & motorways: 60 mph

  - Remember you're banned from the outside lane on three-lane motorways

Reversing

- Reversing is counter intuitive. Steer left, trailer will go right/steer right, it will go left.

- During tight manoeuvres the pivoting motion caused by the tow hitch will cause the trailer to be moved slightly sideways.

- Allow extra turning width room for the swing (over hang behind back wheels).

Safety Tips for Loading & Towing a Trailer or Caravan

Locate the main weight directly over the axle.

Keep the heavier items low down and close to the axle.

To prevent snaking make sure you have a well-matched car and caravan and possibly try using stabilisers.

Avoid exceeding speed limits.

Avoid carrying passengers.

Periodically stop and check all lights are working

Avoid sudden erratic movements

Avoid hard braking on a downhill incline

Weather

Check weather forecast.

Avoid travelling in windy conditions.

In strong winds; be aware when leaving sheltered areas and entering exposed areas or elevated sections, bridges etc.

Pay special attention to large vehicles overtaking you, especially on high ground or exposed areas. Added wind generated by the large vehicle plus it temporarily blocking prevailing side winds can mean once it passes, you get hit by a strong double gust.

The Law

The weight and size of trailer that you can tow depends on at least 7 key factors. Any maximum weight specified under any of these cannot be exceeded – even if other criteria seem to permit a higher weight.

The Capability of the Towing Vehicle

The chassis plate on the vehicle states the maximum weights allowed – the Gross Vehicle Weight (GVW) and the Gross Combination Weight (GCW).

The vehicle handbook will either repeat what is on the chassis plate, or for convenience, might directly specify the maximum weight of trailer (e.g. 750 kg) which is allowed to be towed. The V5C registration certificate often shows this too, under sections O1 and O2 (depending on whether trailer has brakes or not). Exceeding any of the above weights is likely to be construed as using a vehicle in a dangerous condition.

Where the sum of the maximum plated weights of the towing vehicle and of the trailer added together exceed the plated GCW of the towing vehicle, this is not a problem as long as the 'actual' weights of the vehicle and trailer (which may not be fully laden at the time) do not exceed the plated GCW.

The Weight Capacity of the Trailer

A trailer manufacturer must decide the maximum weight the trailer can be loaded to, the Gross Vehicle Weight (GVW) of the trailer, and mark it on the trailer chassis plate. This cannot be exceeded. Sometimes the maximum axle weights are quoted instead and these must not be exceeded.

The Brakes on the Trailer

This depends on the weight capacity of the trailer.

A trailer with a GVW of 750 k.g. or lower, is not required to have brakes, but if brakes are fitted they must be in full working order.

A trailer with a GVW from 751 k.g. up to 3,500 k.g. is required to have brakes, normally over-run (inertia) brakes that operate automatically are fitted.

Driving licence entitlement

You are not allowed to exceed the entitlement to tow trailers given on your driving licence, even if the vehicle you are driving has the capability. Your entitlement varies depending on when the licence was granted – if you passed a standard car test (category B) after 1 Jan 1997 your entitlement is more restricted than for persons who took a car test before that date.

Unlike the situation in section 1 above, driving licence entitlement is calculated on potential weight – Maximum Authorised Mass (MAM) – rather than actual weight. So if your entitlement allows you to tow a trailer with MAM 750 k.g., you cannot tow a trailer with GVW of 1,500kg that is unladen, and so only weighs 500 k.g. You can only tow a trailer with GVW 750 k.g.

Gross Weight of Towing Vehicle and size of Trailer

A towing vehicle with GVW of 3500 k.g. or lower is restricted as to the size of trailer it may tow. The trailer can be a maximum of 7m long by 2.55m wide. A heavier vehicle can tow a trailer of maximum 12m long by 2.55m wide. Exceptionally, where the trailer is specially designed to carry long loads (e.g. one or more boats, gliders), the 7m limit does not apply.

Drivers hours / tachograph and operators licence – GCW over 3,500 k.g.

The towing vehicle for combinations with a GCW above 3,500 k.g. may require a tachograph if used for commercial purposes and the driver must obey drivers hours regulations. Similarly operator licensing may apply.

Chassis Plate

Plate or sticker affixed by the manufacturer specifying the maximum weights allowed. It is often found on a front door sill. For HGVs, the maximum weights will be specified on the Ministry Plate (or Plating Certificate VTG) issued by VOSA/DVSA.

Information displayed on a typical chassis plate on a car, and what it means.

Ford	Manufacturer
e112001/1160045	Type approval number
WAE123DEFGH123456	VIN (vehicle identification number)
2235	Gross Vehicle Weight – GVW
4235	Gross Combination Weight – GCW
1050	Front axle – maximum load
1230	Rear axle – maximum load

GVW – Gross Vehicle Weight

This is specified by the manufacturer and it means the maximum weight the vehicle or trailer is allowed to be when fully loaded. It is the unladen weight of a vehicle plus the maximum permitted payload. Also known as Maximum Permissible Mass, item F1 on the V5C.

GCW – Gross Combination Weight

This is specified by the manufacturer of the towing vehicle and it means the maximum permitted weight of the combination (i.e. total of the towing vehicle and the trailer, including the loads on both). Also known as Gross Train Weight (GTW). To help find the maximum weight of trailer that can be towed, you could subtract the GVW of the towing vehicle from the GCW (in this example a 2000 k.g. trailer would be permitted). However if the towing vehicle is not fully laden, any spare weight capacity can be used by the trailer, so long as the GCW and trailer GVW are not exceeded.

Payload

The maximum weight of the load that can be carried on a vehicle. (Can be calculated: GVW minus the unladen weight of a vehicle).

Unladen or Kerb Weight

The weight of an empty vehicle, with no driver.

Maintenance, Servicing and Warranty

Part A

Keeping Your Car on the Road

Part A is about maintaining an older vehicle. This part assumes that the vehicles warranty will have expired by this point and so mechanical servicing will no longer be necessary to ensure a warranty. By carrying out all the recommended maintenance tasks here you should be able to keep your trusty vehicle on the road and  in good condition. Some tasks need to be completed every month and some maintenance is best done after a certain time period or mileage. This chapter contains recommended maintenance schedules.

Vehicle Maintenance Schedule

Monthly (or More Often)

- Check the tyre pressures

- Check for leaks

- Check windscreen washer fluid level

- Check the oil level

- Check the coolant level

- Check brake fluid level

- Check power steering fluid level

- Check all lights, including brake lights

Every 5,000 Miles

- Change the oil and replace the oil filter

- Change fuel filters

- Adjust the clutch(if necessary)

- Check the condition of the tyres

- Inspect window wipers for deterioration

- Wax the car to prevent rust and to extend the life of the paint

Every 10,000 Miles/Annually

- Check the belts

- Check tyre's condition

- Inspect the hoses and clamps

- Clean the battery connections

- Inspect the brakes

- Check the manual transmission fluid

- Check the brake fluid level

- Flush the radiator

- Change the coolant

- Rinse off the air conditioner condenser

- Check that the spare tyre is still inflated

- Replace air filter

Every 30,000 Miles/ Two years

- Replace the spark plugs (if a petrol vehicle).

- Inspect the spark plug wires (if applicable)

- Replace the distributor cap and rotor (if applicable)

- Change the transmission fluid

- Inspect the shocks for leaks and perform bounce test

- Check the throttle body

- Check the clutch cable

- Check CV joints

- Check prop shaft (rear wheel drive)

- Flush the coolant system

- Check the battery electrolyte level

Every 60,000 Miles

- Replace the fuel filter

- Change the automatic transmission fluid

- Inspect the brakes

- Replace the air filter

- Replace the timing belt (if your vehicle has a timing chain, it doesn't need to be replaced unless there's a problem with it)

- Inspect the ancillary drive belts

- Have the front-end alignment inspected and checked

- Inspect the U-joint

- Replace the rear axle lubricant

- Have the wheel alignments adjusted

Part B

New Vehicles: Servicing/Warranty

When a car is designed, the manufacturer produces a service schedule. In this it recommends the intervals at which all the main maintenance tasks should be carried out, along with recommendations for when many of the important parts should be examined and/or replaced.

Why is there a Service Schedule?

Its most important purpose is to make sure that the manufacturer's original warranty remains valid. All the checks, and their respective required intervals, are listed in every car's owner's manual. This means that, in theory, anyone servicing a vehicle can check with the schedule in order to know what checks

 276

and inspections will be required given the vehicle's approximate age and mileage. If you want to ensure that you keep your vehicle under warranty, you need to make sure that the service schedule is maintained and that your mechanic stamps the vehicle's warranty booklet to say that it's been done. This doesn't have to be completed by a franchised dealer.

What Are the Different Levels of Service Checks?

Oil & Filter Change

These are the most basic and crucial of tasks carried out, and should be included in every service. Having clean oil in your engine helps keep all moving parts lubricated and ensures the engine runs smoothly.

Basic or Interim Service

Car servicing schedules are based around yearly services, or sometimes require a service every so many miles. The most basic car service will include a handful of basic checks. These are mostly just inspections – but the person carrying out the work will note any problems or anomalies found, and report these to the person who's picking up the bill. These basic checks are legal requirements on a garage carrying out a service under their duty of care towards the customer. (It is worth noting that a check on your vehicles brakes is **not** a legal requirement).

On top of this, a **basic service** – usually carried out once a year, or at various mileage intervals if the car covers more than what is considered by the manufacturer to be average – will include a check and top-up if necessary of the levels of all the important fluids – washer, brake, steering and anti-freeze. A further checklist of up to 35 key parts will also be inspected. You may need to ask the manager if there are specific areas of your vehicle that you would like to have investigated, but are not part of the standard basic service.

Full Service

This will probably add 15 to 30 further checks on top of the basic service. Note that if the car is undergoing an MOT test at the same time, several of these additional operations are likely to be included as part of this.

The full service cost may not cover any additional remedial or repair work which comes to light as part of the inspections carried out, or the cost of any extra checks above that included in the garage's full service 'menu' but which are recommended by your car's manufacturer.

Major Service

This type of service is usually recommended every two or three years, and again the frequency may be reduced if you cover a higher than average mileage. Extra jobs undertaken could include changing the spark plugs and/or fuel filters, injectors and replacing any other items suggested in the manufacturer's schedule.

Jobs Included in a Full Service

Check and report any issues found with:

- Engine management system self-diagnosis fault codes

- Instrument/warning lamps

- Switches/controls

- Front wiper blades

- Front screen wash

- Rear wiper blade

- Rear screen wash

- Headlight wash/wipe

- Horn

- Interior lamps

- Instrument panel and switches illumination

- Lighting system

- Direction indicators and hazard warning lights

- Headlights and headlight levelling system

- Engine oil leaks

- Auto transmission oil

- Road springs

- Steering joints

- Steering rack

- Steering column couplings

- Suspension joints, seals and gaiters

- Shock absorbers and mountings

- Brake pipes – check for corrosion

- Fuel tank and fuel pipes

- Brake hydraulics

- Front brake pads and discs

- Rear brake pads and discs

- Rear brake drums and linings

- Brake flexible hoses

- Battery condition

- Brake fluid reservoir

- Clutch fluid reservoir

- Power steering system

- Engine coolant level and anti-freeze concentration

- Coolant heater hoses

- Radiator

- Auto transmission level

- Steering joints

- Steering rack/box

- Steering column couplings

- Suspension joints/seals/gaiters

- Air filter – check and clean if required

- Driveshaft joints/seals/gaiters

- Fuel tank and fuel system – check for leaks

- Auxiliary drive belts – check history and renew any if schedule recommends

- Air conditioning – check and report any issues found

- Engine cooling fan

- Central locking system

- Alarm/immobiliser

- Vehicle locks and hinges – lubricate if required

- Road wheel nuts and bolts – check and tighten if required

- Bonnet latch and lock

- Steering – check for free play

- Clutch operation

- Suspension operation

- Engine performance

- Transmission

- Brakes

- ABS system function

Trouble Shooting Vehicle Faults

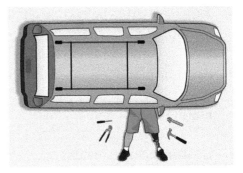

This table is designed to help diagnose mechanical problems and provide solutions.

Problem	Causes	Solution
Engine Won't Start but is Turning Over (Old Car)	**Petrol:** Out of Fuel / Coil / Carburettor / Points / Condenser / Fuel Pump / Spark Plugs / Electronic Ignition	Check Fuel Gauge Working and add Fuel. Check HT Leads For a Spark Check Fuel in Lines. Fit New Carburettor / Ignition
Diesel Engine Won't Start but is Turning Over (Old Car)	**Diesel:** Out of fuel / Fuel pump Air Lock / InjectorsBlocked Filter	Add Fuel and Bleed SystemFit New Injectors, and Change Filters
Engine Won't start and not turning over	Flat Battery / Loose Battery Leads / Broken Starter Motor /	Check Battery Voltage / Tighten Leads / Fit New Battery / Fit Starter Motor
Engine Issue: Blue Smoke Coming From Exhaust.	Very Low Oil Level / Burning Oil.	Add Oil / While Engine is Running Pull Out Dipstick :Is It Smoking? / Worn Engine-Replace
Engine Issue: White Smoke Coming From the Exhaust.	Water in the Oil / Head Gasket Cracked Head	Check Back of Oil Filler Top for Cream / Oil in Radiator / Replace Gasket and / or Head
Engine Noisy, Rattling	Cam / Big or Little Ends Worn	See a Mechanic / Replace Engine
Engine: Turbo Malfunction	Lack of Engine Power / Whining Noise / Smokey Exhaust	Fit New or Reconditioned Turbo and Check Supply Pipes for Blockages or Splits.

Problem	Causes	Solution
Engine Overheating	Low Water Level/Blocked Radiator/ Thermostat Not Opening/Blown Head Gasket/Faulty Fan/ Faulty Fan Switch	Add Water/Feel the Radiator for Cold Spots/ Check All the Water Pipes Get Hot With the Engine Running/Listen for Whether the Fan Kicks In Once Engine Is Hot/Fit New Parts
Engine Running Rough/ Miss Firing	**Petrol:** Spark Plugs/Coil/ Points/ Distributor/Electronic Ignition/Poor Fuel Supply	Do Diagnostic Work, Establish Faults, Fit New Parts **Note Danger-Extreme High Voltage. Do Not Handle Any Ancillary Electrics Feeding Off Electronic Ignition**
Diesel Engine Running Rough/ Miss Firing	**Diesel:** Blocked Filters / Injectors/Dirty Fuel/Split Fuel Pipe	Change Filters and Bleed the System/ Drain and Change Fuel/ Fit New Pipe/Take to Fuel Injector Specialists
Engine is Running: Making Squealing Noise	Loose Fan Belt/Loose Power Steering Belt	Tighten Belt/ If Belt is Cracked Then Change It
Battery Not Charging	Faulty Alternator/Faulty Battery **Note:** Dashboard Battery Light on Whilst Engine Running Indicates Alternator Problem	Check Voltage at Battery with a Meter Whilst Engine is Running-Fit New Alternator or Battery
Sulphur (Rotten Eggs Smell)	Faulty Alternator Overcharging Battery	Change Alternator
Battery in Good Condition but Constantly Keeps Going Flat	Electrical Wiring Bleed/ Something Left Switched On e.g. Interior Lights or Stereo **Note:** Heated Rear Window Element Uses a Lot of Volts to Power.	Charge Battery. Take Off Live Battery Lead (**Red**) Do not use for 48 Hours. Replace Lead If Engine Starts it Points to Electrical Problem/Bad Earth-See Car Electrician
Coolant Leak	Hole in the Radiator / Hole in Water Pipe/ Faulty Water Pump	Check Point of Leak: Fit New Radiator/Pipe or Pump
Steering Vague or Loose	Faulty Rack or Steering Box	Adjust or Fit New Part

Problem	Causes	Solution
Vehicle Tends to Pull to Left or Right/ Groaning Noise When Moving Steering Wheel from Lock to Lock.	Tracking Out/Faulty Steering Pump	Take to Garage to be Realigned/Fit New Steering Pump
Juddering in Steering Wheel-This Can be Intermittent i.e. Come On or Off at Various Speeds	Wheels Unbalanced/Bulge in Tyre(s)	See Tyre Fitters. Get Tyre(s) Checked or Changed/Get Wheel(s) Balanced
Brakes Spongey and Unresponsive	Air in the System/Leaking Part/ Faulty Master Cylinder/Servo	Change Leaking Part/ Fit New Master Cylinder/ Servo
Squealing Brakes	Low Brake Pads or Shoes/Stone Trapped In Between Brake Lining and Disk	Fit New Brake Pads or Shoes/To Release a Stone Drive Forward and Back Dabbing Brake Pedal
Clonking Noise Coming From Underneath Vehicle	Drive Shaft /Prop Shaft/ Loose Exhaust	See Mechanic/Do Not Drive/Fit New Part
Engine Tone Altered and Become Louder	Blowing Exhaust	Weld or Fit New Exhaust
Gearbox: Manual – Difficult to Use	Difficult to Select a Gear/Jumps out of Gear/Faulty Clutch or Gearbox	Change Gearbox or Clutch
Gearbox: Automatic – Problematic	Noisy/Slipping	Check Fluid Level-Top Up or Fit New Gearbox
Vehicle's Losing Momentum During Acceleration on Uphill Roads. Can be Accompanied by Burning Smell	Slipping Clutch/Oil on Clutch	Take to Clutch Specialist./Fit New Clutch/Change Oil Seals.
Limp Mode in New Vehicles. Loss of Power Leading to Warning Lights on Dashboard.	Either a Malfunctioning Part or a Sensor Fault.	Go to a Computer Diagnostics Garage
Ignition Key Faulty	Old Car: Key Wear/ New Car: Code Problem	Get Key Cut/Go to a Dealership
Brake Lights Not Working	Pedal Switch/ Wiring/Bulb/ Blown Fuse.	Check Fuses/Change Bulbs/See Electrician

Problem	Causes	Solution
Clutch Bite Point Too Low	Poorly Adjusted or Faulty Pressure Plate	Adjust/Change Clutch
Clutch Point is Too High	Poorly Adjusted or Worn Clutch Plate	Adjust/Change Clutch

Lightning Source UK Ltd.
Milton Keynes UK
UKHW020733231119
354081UK00002B/9/P

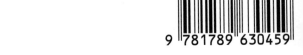